RADICAL *Review*
HISTORY

Issue | 131

The Global South: Histories, Politics, Maps
Issue Editors: Pamila Gupta, Christopher J. Lee, Marissa J. Moorman, and Sandhya Shukla

IN MEMORIAM

AFTERWORD

Editors' Introduction

*Pamila Gupta, Christopher J. Lee, Marissa J. Moorman,
and Sandhya Shukla*

At the recent meeting of BRICS—the global economic group consisting of Brazil, Russia, India, China, and South Africa—held in Beijing in September 2017, Chinese President Xi Jinping declared that a "historical opportunity" had presented itself as a result of adjustments in "the world economic structure." He urged enhanced "solidarity and cooperation among emerging market and developing countries" to work against the protectionism that had recently gained traction in Western countries, as evidenced in the ascendancy of Donald Trump in the United States and Great Britain's imminent departure from the European Union. Xi's promotion of South-South cooperation as an "irreversible trend" built upon the political positions of earlier periods. The 1955 Asian-African Conference in Bandung, Indonesia, the founding conference of the Non-Aligned Movement (NAM) in Belgrade, Yugoslavia, in 1961, and the establishment of the South Commission at the NAM summit in Harare, Zimbabwe, in September 1986 all exhibited a similar rhetoric of solidarity.[1] The Global South of our political present consequently has a long and complicated history, yet distinctions between the past and present must also be drawn. As Vijay Prashad has written in *The Darker Nations* (2007), the "Third World" captured not a geography as such, but rather a political project that sought to work against the neocolonial influences of the United States and its allies (the so-called "First World") and the Soviet Union and its Eastern Bloc partners (the "Second World").[2] The expression "Third World" drew from an earlier genealogy connected to the French Revolution and the notion of a "third estate" representing the common people.[3]

Radical History Review
Issue 131 (May 2018)   DOI 10.1215/01636545-4355069

The Global South, on the other hand, has been more politically inchoate, at once recalling this earlier political program while also mapping, literally and figuratively, a geography that at times betrays more affinities than differences with the Euro-American world. The economic aspirations of BRICS in particular—what Prashad has referred to as "neoliberalism with southern characteristics"—raise fundamental questions about the radical potential of the Global South, whether as a place or project.[4] The acronym BRICS was coined, after all, by a Goldman Sachs analyst in 2001.

The Global South has existed as a provisional category since at least the mid-1970s, though its increasing use and importance as a rubric for political alignments, economic developments, and cultural histories demand a renewed and focused critical engagement. This special issue of *Radical History Review* acknowledges that need by taking stock of the term's limits, meanings, and prospects for future analytic work. Indeed, the diverse invocations of the Global South, for both late capitalist projects, such as BRICS, and for a variety of insurgent and progressive grassroots alliances which have sought to challenge the continued power of North American and European hierarchies of state power and knowledge, suggest that it remains a highly contested marker for setting global agendas. Scholars in a number of academic fields have proposed that the Global South offers not only a new vantage point for readdressing imperial pasts and aspiring toward new futures, but, as such, presents the potential for new epistemologies to take hold. In this latter regard, it conforms to a range of existing critical paradigms, from the Black Atlantic as promoted by Paul Gilroy, to Dipesh Chakrabarty's call to "provincialize" Europe, each of which has outlined counter-modernities which unsettle the claims of European thought.[5] In the work of Jean and John Comaroff, Raewyn W. Connell and Boaventura de Sousa Santos, the Global South has provided theoretical reorientation, often through the redeployment of older terminology such as decolonization.[6] The decolonial turn, in the work of Enrique Dussel, Walter Mignolo, Arturo Escobar, and other Latin Americanists, has directed the recovery of local languages, indigenous practices, and regional worldviews as a means of "decolonizing" knowledge.[7] These critical efforts resemble—and at times directly connect to—research and political agendas such as Subaltern Studies, in both its South Asian and Latin American forms, as well an argument like Ngũgĩ wa Thiong'o's, for writing in African languages.[8] And yet so much of this work, which has urged different ways of looking at the world in the past and the present and enabled many important historical, anthropological, literary and other projects in recent years, still bears distinct traces of intellectual entanglement with Western epistemologies, whether through shared genealogies of Marxist and poststructuralist thought or by virtue of working against—and thus working through—such legacies.

This special issue of *Radical History Review* embraces this complexity and contradiction, suggesting that while present scholarship has provided compelling insights into the varied histories, diverse itineraries, and provisional maps of the

Global South, critical work still remains to be done on just how the Global South as a radical position can be more fully achieved. Though we do not profess to "newness" vis-à-vis the Global South concept, we do believe that our current historical conjuncture—one of uneven patterns of political-economic crisis, shaped by competing challenges of emergent authoritarian movements and global climate change, to offer two pressing cases—necessitates an especially focused inquiry into political and social formations that provide new critiques of power. The Global South as a political space, extending through formerly colonized regions of Asia, Africa, and Latin America, certainly challenges the geopolitical frameworks of the United States and Europe from a territorial standpoint, underscoring the role alternative regional and global geographies can play in remaking a new world order. By extension, as an analytic category that is different from preceding terms such as "postcolonial" or "Third World," the Global South asks us to reconsider the continuing significance of colonialism for understanding countries that have experienced sustained economic growth, such as India and China, while, by the same stroke, accounting for social and political movements—such as *Narmada Bachao Andolan* (India), *Abahlali baseMjondolo* (South Africa), and the World Social Forum—that are not determined by "the West" as traditionally understood. Put simply, the Global South presents a revised temporal framework, in addition to the promise of spatial and epistemological innovation, for thinking through the politics of the present, given that it has been over half a century since decolonization and political independence occurred in many parts of today's Global South.

In sum, to fully play out the possibilities of this concept's intervention, the contributions to this special issue suggest a wider and deeper reach—geographically, intellectually, and politically—into spaces that have been heretofore less examined, despite the sweep of the Global South. Indeed in contrast to previous approaches that have stressed (quite naturally) a global perspective on this geography, we have taken a counterintuitive approach, by foregrounding stories of the everyday and their intersectional components of race, class, and gender, thus departing from "grand narratives" of the Global South, as defined by occasions like Bandung, as well as "great men," whether Jawarhalal Nehru, Fidel Castro, or Frantz Fanon. We believe that the Global South and its possibilities might be better grasped through an emphasis on the texture of interpersonal exchanges and categories of analysis that might be seen, prima facie, as peripheral, but in practice retain value and meaning for local and regional communities, rather than global ones. We have aimed to put together a collection of materials that renders the Global South less abstract and more palpable—a space of ordinary concerns of work, politics, and livelihood, in addition to being a generative setting for critical theory. In short, the Global South, as we position it here, is less a monolithic geography, a diplomatic project, or a transnational historical space and paradigm, as argued elsewhere, but instead a crucible for sustaining popular agency, one that allows for old and new forms of cultural freedom to express themselves through a myriad of mediums against structures of power, national and international alike.

Hidden Histories and Generative Itineraries of the Global South

To begin, can we think of the Global South as offering up a "map, counter-map and modus operandi" all at the same time, as suggested by this issue's contributor Emily Callaci? Or can we shift the terms of debate and consider the Global South to be a "path," following contributor Aharon de Grassi, thus making it more of an innovative tool to be used in a diversity of settings? Similarly, what happens when we take "Global North" events and recast them from the vantage point of the Global South, as Michelle Moyd and Maurice Jr. M. Labelle do for World War I and Lebanon's decolonization, respectively? Or, what if we juxtapose and compare the divergent scales of South-South entanglements, such as the role of China in Africa (Ronald Po, Phineas Bbaala, and Mingwei Huang), Black and Asian solidarities in the United States (Roseann Liu and Savannah Shange), or a female country singer (Pahole Sookkasikon) based in Thailand? What happens if we take on peripheral places—the margins of the marginal—like Melanesia (Quito Swan) and Guyana (Sarah Vaughn) and attach them to more familiar circuits and flows of people, ideas, and things? Can we utilize such refigured landscapes to, in turn, refigure the Global South? What methodological possibilities emerge when we position such locations as a permanent starting point—not simply as sites for data collection to be mined, assessed, and extracted by the Global North, but rather as a source of interpretive theory? We raise these questions at the start to resituate ongoing inflections of North and South as being less in a state of opposition to one another and instead as already historically enmeshed. Put differently, we want to open up the category of "the North" to interrogation as we do "the South" by recognizing that Southern formations can also be located in the North, underscoring multidirectional flows of politics, culture, and history that require an attentive methodology.

The potential power of Global South thought is especially vivid in moments of political, cultural, and economic transition. As some of our contributors make clear, the Global South is often the theater for other liberatory dramas which draw attention to the ordinary and peripheral. The frictions of freedom whetted on difference become visible in such settings. One ongoing flashpoint can be seen in recent student movements all over the world. Student activists in South Africa, India, Chile, and Mexico have raised specific issues like tuition fees and housing as part of a broader inquiry about educational opportunity and economic futures, in some instances promoting the issue of workers' rights on college campuses; this student-worker alignment is part of a larger project to make and remake the laboring nation. Another vector of critique that connects and perhaps reformulates the "South" can be seen in efforts to confront the racialized memorialization of national history. The colonial-era statue of Cecil John Rhodes that had stood on the University of Cape

Town campus since 1934 was brought down in February 2015 by a student movement, which then fed into a nationwide campaign to decolonize curricula across South Africa. The white supremacist rally in Charlottesville, Virginia, in August 2017, which resulted in the death of activist Heather D. Heyer and the injury of nineteen others, laid bare deep fissures of racism based on revisionist histories of the Confederacy and inflamed by Trump's America. These episodes cannot be seen as autonomous from one another. Representations of brutal colonial pasts and institutionalized racism, seized upon in various ways by authoritarian political leaders and deeply anxious citizens of "new" economies, have quickly become instruments of divisive spectacle in our media-saturated, global age.

This special issue foregrounds the Global South vis-à-vis these emergent situations. In order to underwrite the potential of this expression, we approach the Global South as marking both a departure from the "postcolonial," "decolonization," and the "Third World" while not sacrificing the importance of readdressing the long-term legacies of colonialism and decolonization across Asia, Africa, and Latin America. Our contributors have looked for new archives that tell different stories and have read old archives in new ways, confirming the continued vitality of postcolonial critique. The work in this issue disrupts facile assumptions of uniform solidarity within the Global South. We see as much tension as cooperation. Race-making both divides and binds, creating a consistent fault line that troubles political affinities and exposes what author Labelle calls "the forgotten color line within the global color line." If Moyd pushes back our timeline for conceptualizing the Global South, calling troops from the colonies in World War I "Global South soldiers," Labelle exposes how Lebanese nationalists after World War II reiterated and fixed Western-generated ideas of race to mark distinctions between themselves and the West African troops that occupied Lebanon. Nation-making claims against the metropole mobilized European race-making practices that constrained the liberty of Africans subjected by the same empire. These dynamics strain and pucker the smooth surface of common cause associated with decolonizing countries, with shared oppression, and with solidarity across the Global South.

Swan similarly mines a contradiction at what is often considered the Global South's generative place and moment. He takes us on a tour of Melanesia, an area that is rich in the Western ethnographic imaginary through the influential work of Bronislaw Malinowski, but less so in the historical archival one. Swan introduces an analytic of blindness to show the ways in which the Indonesia-led Bandung Conference of 1955 overshadowed, or rather blinded, Black power movements to Indonesia's aggressive imperial role in the Pacific, discriminating against a Black Melanesian population in West Papua in the aftermath of Dutch colonialism. Blindness becomes an active component of archival amnesia—or, rather, political not-seeing (by historians and activists alike) to what happened to this marginalized group—that persists in the ongoing decolonizing moment. Swan unearths new archival materials and brings forth fresh dissenting voices. This minority Black Asian diaspora, despite having made alliances across multiple Black diasporas (with Senghor's Senegal and Black internationalism), continues to struggle for political self-determination, employing the political discourses of Blackness and Oceanic belonging against the Global South powerhouse that is Indonesia.

Interest in the sometimes unequal encounters within the Global South led us to develop a full section on China and Africa, which contends with the important economic and geopolitical dominance of China in the Global South. It is a nod to the contemporary, yes, but with serious ramifications for how we think about all kinds of national and nationalist histories. The China in Africa forum showcases a variety of contact zones between China and the Global South. Ronald Po revisits the ambitious idea of the "China dream" in the Global South from a twenty-first century perspective. He looks at its slow buildup and expanding role across Asia and Africa from three angles: historic, economic, and geostrategic (military). Historically, he showcases China's strong ties to Southeast Asia and South Asia via migration; economically, he takes on China's involvement in bankrolling infrastructural developments in the Global South; and finally, he focuses on the geostrategic by taking us on a tour of China's military build-up in three African nations—Sudan, Zimbabwe and Uganda. Phinneas Bbaala provides a more generalized overview of China's expanding ideological and infrastructural role in Africa (its *zouchuqu,* going out) policy that took root in 1971. That program has included membership in BRICS, support of liberation movements in Mozambique, Angola, Namibia and Zimbabwe, an anti-apartheid stance in South Africa, the building of the Tanzania-Zambia Rail line (TAZARA), and more recently, trade deals (of weapons and loans) with Zambia and the Congo. Bbaala reorients our thinking from looking at China's role as being of the Global South to now operating in the Global South. Shifting the scale, Mingwei Huang sets up two "China in Africa" ethnographic scenes from her recent fieldwork in Johannesburg. It is 2015, the self-declared "Year of China in South Africa," when she is working at China Mall in Johannesburg as a sales clerk in one of its many shops. South Africa and China's joint meetings, advertisements, and infrastructural investments fill in that cultural-economic landscape of the first scene, while the mysterious murder of a female Chinese trader, most likely by her Malawian workers, is the backdrop for the second. Both of these episodes capture the fraught, anxious, and intimate encounters between Africans employees and Chinese bosses that transform everyday lives and make us rethink China's increasingly "ungrounded" imperial role (following Aihwa Ong and Donald Nonini 1997) in postcolonial Africa, as well as through more vertically oriented South-South engagements.[9]

The frame of encounter helps us think about gender and racial formations differently in and across the Global South. Michelle Moyd, for example, argues for redefining Black and Brown soldiers from the empire fighting in World War I as "Global South soldiers." That analytic makes the work of these soldiers and role of empire in war visible. Global South thinking, she asserts, raises new questions about how violence brought subjects of different corners of empire together through war and enlarged the violence of conquest on African populations. Moyd's article productively challenges a Global South timeline that overlaps with decolonization while reiterating the entanglements we associate with the postcolonial: specifically, its imbrication with colonial epistemologies and violences. She suggests that there are Global South histories still to be written, but only if we are "willing to look." Moving into the field of biography, Muhammad Ali's recent death offers Sean Jacobs an opportunity to take up Moyd's cue and to revisit the politically complicated subject onto whom so much has been projected. Jacobs argues for seeing Ali's many and shifting perspectives on US imperialism and Third-World struggles as part of a necessary discussion on the vexed relationship between race and nationality. But he reminds us that contradictions, too, illuminate a particular historical moment and a life lived like many others: desirous, aspirational, and deeply aware. Unlike so much that has been written and said about Ali, Jacobs declines hero worship in favor of a fuller, though still appreciative, appraisal of the man.

Two other pieces in this collection stress the importance of seeing the imbrication of the local and the global a bit differently from the perspective of the Global South. Maurice Jr. M. Labelle takes up Lebanon's decolonization in the wake of World War II. Promised sovereignty at the end of the war, Lebanon instead found itself occupied by French colonial troops: *tirailleurs sénégalais*. The French did what Moyd describes in World War I: they used soldiers from one colony to secure another. Lebanese nationalists invoked European imperial racial thinking and hierarchies inherited from Lebanon's Ottoman past to protest the French presence. By the same token, Lebanese nationalists racialized French occupation, describing it as uncivilized and retrograde. At the very moment decolonization undid racialized imperial hierarchies across North-South lines, some nationalist movements reinforced them between South-South locations. In a contrasting example, Sarah Vaughn's essay considers how the work of engineers to manage water in the "small state" of Guyana was, and continues to be, articulated vis-à-vis pressing issues such as climate change. Her careful ethnographic and historical analyses of debates on damming practices show the complicated relationship between colonialism and science. But an awareness of the half-life of that project of control (of lands, of peoples, of resources) and the need to adapt to a changing environment were also mobilized in an insurgent regionalism tied to decolonization, in order to develop the area on terms not entirely of colonial administrators' making.

Mobile Artifacts

Contributors to this issue attend to various kinds of objects, highlighting the significance of interdisciplinary inquiry. Emily Callaci looks at Depo-Provera, a highly mobile form of biomedical contraception, or what she refers to as a "traveling technology of the Global South." Beginning in the 1970s, Depo-Provera use came to embody distinctions between the Global North and South: banned in the United States, it was promoted as a tool of population control in the developing world. Ignoring the legacies of colonialism, aid agencies and the population establishment naturalized poor health and reproductive conditions in the Global South. Callaci explores three sets of actors working at different scales—the "population establishment," transnationally organized anti-Depo-Provera activists, and "local gate-keepers." Tracing multiple iterations of this biomedical contraceptive, including its uses and the discourses and debates around it, Callaci argues that the Global South as an open concept enables connections of solidarity, vulnerability, and dispossession to be traced at once.

Three short pieces additionally focus on cultural products and their itineraries. Pahole Sookkasikon looks at Thai country singer Pumpuang Duangjan's transformative role in the genre. Her music—its sounds, theme, and "forlorn lyrics"—emphasized quotidian elements of gender, class, and location that pressed against the patriarchal, monarchical, and Bangkok-centric construction of Thai identity. Duangjan embodied the struggles of migrant rural women in the city who shored up this emerging Global South economy. Sarah Van Beurden explores how the modernism of the Zairoise avant-garde makes visible previously hidden Global South networks: not just links between artistic movements, but between news forms of authoritarianisms, like that of Mobutu and Communist China, where artists found enduring markets. Her work raises the intriguing possibility of studying connections between novel aesthetic practices and transnational authoritarian governance as also productive of the Global South. This approach might help us think recent interventions in the global art world by Global South players like Angola and China. Keith Wagner looks at the Hollywood film *Total Recall* (2012) as an imagination of an urban "divided Anthropocene" Global South and the resistant, maybe even revolutionary, potentials therein. He offers the expression "Aesthetic Cooperation among Developing and Developed Countries" to underscore the aesthetic hybridity in cinematic North and South megacity spaces.

How might the Global South change how we think about the work we do as scholars and researchers? In the section "Historians, Geographers, and Activists at Work," a group of contributors suggest the porous boundaries between academic disciplines. Jelmer Vos plumbs the forgotten archive of nineteenth-century Dutch-Angolan trading records to highlight Angolan coffee producers as consumers. This short piece underscores the temporary dominance of European traders in longer history of Angolan commerce, which today is focused on major manufacturers of the Global South. Aharon de Grassi produces a new artifact: a map of precolonial African paths. He urges us to reconsider the infrastructural significance of this fundamental human mode of social meaning making. Understanding old paths as dynamic processes can brighten the possibilities for new political alliances. The Afro-Asian Networks Research Collective presents a similar manifesto, albeit academic: they advocate for collaborative work by historians to open up dispersed archives and employ digital humanities to bring nonstate transnational actors of the Global South into the historical record. Likewise working at the interface of activism and the academy, anthropologists Roseann Liu and Savannah Shange propose "thick solidarity" as a research methodology with much potential for traversing the fraught territory of Black-Asian solidarity in US racial politics.

Finally, in his Afterword entitled "Between Two Clarities," Vijay Prashad charts the collision course between capitalism and the environment, in this instance how state-led Global South coalitions have promoted the interests of elites while small Pacific island states face the threat of complete territorial erasure. Prashad asks how we will answer the global challenge of putting the earth and human lives before capitalist growth and elite-centric development. This afterword presses on the crisis of the present where Global North and Global South are bound most tightly, yet where old political equations and new inequalities continue to fragment common cause. Giving visual force to Prashad's clarion call are the photographs of Kiluanji Kia Henda. His images and text explore the birth, life, and death of a city in the desert in *A City Called Mirage*. The framing of construction at a building's birth anticipates the void it contains at its death. Using Dubai as model, Angolan politicians have rebuilt Luanda, Kia Henda's hometown, as a Dubai on the Atlantic in a post-war oil boom. Kia Henda's work questions the value of this south-south exchange.

Global South Futures

The Global South intrigues partly because its power of diction lies in the contemplation of the universal and the particular. While certainly far-reaching, this category also elevates the importance of the directional, of a set of places with a specific temporality. As editors who are positioned in both the Global North and the Global South, we cannot help but underscore how profoundly the dense dynamics of late capitalism are shared across a North-South divide yet continue to be shaped by the inequalities that have been formed and experienced in terms of that very opposition. The challenge, then, is to confront and acknowledge a shared history that is not flattening or simplifying but that retains a political coherence that offers ideological direction and enables political mobilization. To put it most directly: the recent emergence of autocratic-minded figures in the Global North like Donald Trump is part of a global political landscape with counterparts in India, the Philippines, and South Africa. The growing power of the Global South in the new world economy does not mean that Narendra Modi, Rodrigo Duterte, or Jacob Zuma can wreak the sort of political, military, economic and ecological damage that Trump can. Nonetheless, this political pattern of populist nativism led by flagrant demagoguery that has quickly surfaced across the world over the past several years indicates that a common struggle must be forged. As many of the contributions in this issue show, such solidarities are possible, even if they have not always been fulfilled.

Considered together, the work of this volume exposes old and new linkages in the Global South and repositions what have been considered peripheral histories, which have often emerged in unexpected and sometimes hopeful moments, into the center of a constantly unfolding story of the world. To remap is to reveal and to take lessons from the South, and not only to rethink the North. It is to see the peoples of the Global South as living less in the shadow of the West, but rather as taking on innovative processes of place-making. Through this project there has been a commitment to make visible the possibilities that emerge even from bleak analyses of unequal power relations. Are we seeing the resurgence of a resilient state playing itself out in certain spaces of the Global South in new and insidious ways? Or are we witnessing a resurgence of grassroots social movements against the weakening apparatuses of the nation-state and against intensely globalized capital formations? Either way, we would like to think that both sets of conditions have been predicted in the exchanges and futures we offer here. The intervention of radical historians, we believe, should ultimately offer methods for negotiating complexity in moments of historical, political, and economic crisis, as so many of the works collected here do.

—Pamila Gupta, Christopher J. Lee, Marissa J. Moorman, and Sandhya Shukla

Pamila Gupta is associate professor at WiSER, University of the Witwatersrand in Johannesburg, South Africa. She is the author of *The Relic State: St. Francis Xavier and the Politics of Ritual in Portuguese India* (2014), and coeditor of *Eyes Across the Water: Navigating the Indian Ocean* (2010). Her book, entitled *Portuguese Decolonization in the Indian Ocean World: History and Ethnography,* is forthcoming in 2018.

Christopher J. Lee is an associate professor of history and Africana studies at Lafayette College. He has published five books, including *Making a World after Empire: The Bandung Moment and Its Political Afterlives* (2010); *Unreasonable Histories: Nativism, Multiracial Lives, and the Genealogical Imagination in British Africa* (2014); *Frantz Fanon: Toward a Revolutionary Humanism* (2015); *A Soviet Journey: A Critical Annotated Edition* (2017); and *Jet Lag* (2017). He has two forthcoming books: a reader on race and racial thought in Africa and an edited collection of essays by the South African writer Alex La Guma, entitled *Culture and Liberation: Exile Writings, 1966–1985.*

Marissa J. Moorman, associate professor of African History and of Cinema and Media Studies, Indiana University, is author of *Intonations: Music and Nation in Late Colonial Angola* (2008) and is writing the book "Powerful Frequencies: Radio, State Power, and the Cold War in Angola." She is a member of the *Radical History Review* editorial collective and blogs for Africa is a Country, the blog that is not about famine, Bono, or Barack Obama.

Sandhya Shukla is associate professor of English and American Studies at the University of Virginia and a longtime member of the editorial collective of *Radical History Review*. She is the author of *India Abroad: Diasporic Cultures of Postwar America and England* (2003), and a coeditor of *Imagining Our Americas: Toward a Transnational Frame* (2007). She is currently completing a book entitled *Harlem Stories: Space, Race and Time in the Modern World*.

Notes

1. On these events, see, for example, Acharya and Tan, eds., *Bandung Revisited*; and Prashad, *The Poorer Nations*.
2. Prashad, *The Darker Nations*.
3. Ibid., 11.
4. Prashad, *The Poorer Nations*, 10.
5. Gilroy, *The Black Atlantic*; Chakrabarty, *Provincializing Europe*.
6. Connell, *Southern Theory*; Comaroff and Comaroff, *Theory from the South*; de Sousa Santos, *Epistemologies of the South*.
7. Mignolo, *Local Histories/Global Designs*; Morana, Dussel, and Jauregui, eds., *Coloniality at Large*.
8. Ngũgĩ wa Thiong'o, *Decolonising the Mind*. On subaltern studies, see, for example, Guha and Spivak, eds., *Selected Subaltern Studies*; and Rodriguez and Lopez, eds., *The Latin American Subaltern Studies Reader*.
9. Ong and Nonini, eds., *Ungrounded Empires*.

References

Acharya, Amitav and See Seng Tan, eds., *Bandung Revisited: The Legacy of the 1955 Asian-African Conference for International Order*. Singapore: National University of Singapore, 2008.

Chakrabarty, Dipesh. *Provincializing Europe: Postcolonial Thought and Historical Difference*. Princeton, NJ: Princeton University Press, 2000.

Comaroff, Jean and John L. Comaroff. *Theory from the South: Or, How Euro-America is Evolving Toward Africa*. New York: Routledge, 2011.

Connell, Raewyn W. *Southern Theory: Social Science and the Global Dynamics of Knowledge*. London: Polity, 2007.

de Sousa Santos, Boaventura. *Epistemologies of the South: Justice Against Epistemicide*. New York: Routledge, 2014.

Gilroy, Paul. *The Black Atlantic: Modernity and Double-Consciousness*. Cambridge, MA: Harvard University Press, 1993.

Guha, Ranajit and Gayatri Chakravorty Spivak, eds., *Selected Subaltern Studies*. Oxford, UK: Oxford University Press, 1988.

Mignolo, Walter. *Local Histories/Global Designs: Coloniality, Subaltern Knowledges, and Border Thinking*. Princeton, NJ: Princeton University Press, 2000.

Morana, Mabel, Enrique Dussel, and Carlos A. Jauregui, eds. *Coloniality at Large: Latin America and the Postcolonial Debate*. Durham, NC: Duke University Press, 2008.

Ngũgĩ wa Thiong'o. *Decolonising the Mind: The Politics of Language in African Literature*. London: James Currey, 1986.

Ong, Aihwa and Donald M. Nonini, eds. *Ungrounded Empires: The Cultural Politics of Modern Chinese Transnationalism*. New York: Routledge, 1996.

Prashad, Vijay. *The Darker Nations: A People's History of the Third World*. New York: The New Press, 2008.
———— *The Poorer Nations: A Possible History of the Global South*. London: Verso, 2014.
Rodriguez, Ileana and Maria Milagros Lopez, eds. *The Latin American Subaltern Studies Reader*. Durham, NC: Duke University Press, 2001.

Color Lines, Front Lines

The First World War from the South

Michelle Moyd

Introduction: A South-South Invasion

In November 1914, the small port town of Tanga in German East Africa (today, mainland Tanzania) was the site of an improbable battle.[1] Soldiers from the India Expeditionary Force (IEF) 'B' and African soldiers (*askari*) of the German imperial army in East Africa (*Schutztruppe*) fought against each other in the first of many clashes in the East African theater of World War I. In a "shambolic state" of disorganization, the 8000 Indian troops of the IEF 'B' had sailed from Bombay on fourteen transport ships two weeks earlier, enduring miserable shipboard conditions that left most of them in poor health upon their arrival off the coast of Tanga.[2] On November 2–3, they commenced a seemingly unopposed amphibious assault. But a series of British missteps had given the *Schutztruppe askari* the opportunity to race into defensive positions in Tanga where they reinforced their numbers, eventually reaching a strength of 1000. Although the *Schutztruppe* also made a number of mistakes that could have cost it dearly, British commander General A. E. Aitken ordered a full retreat from Tanga, which occurred in such a disorderly and harried fashion that the IEF 'B' left behind most of its equipment and supplies, including everything from machine guns to boxes of condensed milk.[3]

Tanga was a demoralizing defeat for IEF 'B' and a "major tactical and operational victory" for the *Schutztruppe*.[4] In one of several memoirs published after

Radical History Review
Issue 131 (May 2018)   DOI 10.1215/01636545-4355109
© 2018 by MARHO: The Radical Historians' Organization, Inc.

the war, *Schutztruppe* commander General Paul von Lettow-Vorbeck captured the chaos and lethality of the scene for the Indian troops: "In wild disorder the enemy fled in dense masses, and our machine-guns, converging on them from front and flanks, mowed down whole companies to the last man." But the *Schutztruppe askari* celebrated the moment, and even displayed some magnanimity toward their defeated opponents: "Several askari came in beaming with delight with several captured English rifles on their backs and an Indian prisoner in each hand. The handcuffs, however, which we found in their possession for use with German prisoners, were not used on them by any of us."[5] The British forces sustained over 800 casualties, with some 300 Indian troops killed in action or mortally wounded. *Schutztruppe* casualties were far lower, with 55 *askari* killed.[6] Indeed, the British defeat at Tanga was labeled "one of the most notable failures in British military history."[7] Lettow-Vorbeck, on the other hand, pinpointed Tanga as "the birthday of the soldierly spirit in our troops."[8] Or as *Schutztruppe* doctor Ludwig Deppe put it, Tanga was of "decisive meaning" for their morale, as well as for their material well-being, given the wealth of supplies they had gained from IEF B's retreat.[9] The Battle of Tanga contributes to a larger narrative of German heroism in the East Africa campaign.[10] In this narrative, an outnumbered but scrappy army of *askari*, led by Lettow-Vorbeck, defeated the British invaders who were poorly led by Aitken. In addition, its tropical yet urban setting, the swarm of angry bees that attacked soldiers in the midst of battle, and the chaotic British retreat provided all the elements of a rousing battlefield story.[11]

The war between the Entente and the Central Powers was a war between empires, immersing colonized African lands in the conflict from its onset in August 1914.[12] For the next four years, different configurations of British imperial forces fought against the *Schtuztruppe* across eastern and southeastern Africa. Great Britain's Entente allies also took up the fight against the Germans across the continent, with troops drawn from French, British, Belgian, and Portuguese colonies all fighting against German colonial armies. The Battle of Tanga was the first of many such battlefield encounters between troops mobilized to fight for imperial causes in places that become visible mainly through the history of European colonialism and World War I, but almost never through the troops' eyes.

These men were not just colonial soldiers. They were part of a global labor force mobilized by Europeans to fight for empire. Their own motivations, struggles, and fears, and their destructive roles in theaters far from Europe are strangely absent from much World War I historiography. European platitudes about loyal and brave troops who fought for empire have impeded our ability to see the dimensions of this massive labor mobilization for a global war that sought to preserve certain empires while destroying others. Perhaps it is time to rethink these soldiers' roles through an "alternative geography," taking seriously the idea that "the South might have something to teach the North."[13] This alternative geography, the

Global South, trains our attention on the mechanisms by which longstanding colonial labor regimes generated armies of Black and Brown troops who fought to maintain and expand European empires. With few exceptions, they did so either because they were somehow coerced into this work, or they imagined that soldiering would secure better futures for themselves and their kin. Imperial formations structured these recruitment efforts, but men responded to these efforts in their own ways and using their own logics and priorities.

The Great War was waged as much by workers—including soldiers—from the South as the North. From across Africa, some 2,350,000 troops and laborers were mobilized. India supplied 1.4 million soldiers and workers.[14] Black and Brown soldiers recruited from across European empires experienced and perpetrated extreme violence in the African campaigns in which they took part. These men were deployed from one imperial space to another, sometimes multiple times, throughout the entire conflict.[15] They came from far-flung reaches of the colonized world to fight in German East Africa, the longest of the four African campaigns. The soldiers' battlefield experiences molded them, for a time, into a community of "violence workers" whose varied aspirations for the postwar period stemmed from the particular kinds of labor they had done during the war, especially wounding or killing others.[16] These soldiers of empire participated in lethal violence on battlefields that only existed because of European imperial priorities.

Their histories have remained largely submerged under the surface of a conflict with obvious global dimensions that nonetheless consistently centers Europe. This essay imagines colonial troops as Global South soldiers, and centers them instead, using the space of German East Africa as a site where they become visible as such. It acknowledges the European recruitment, training, and leadership that brought them together in ever-shifting imperial formations, but it foregrounds their battlefield histories to call attention to two new ways of thinking about their roles in the war.[17] First, it speculates on how experiences between 1914 and 1918 in one African theater of the war created shared meanings amongst soldiers, regardless of their origins. It analyzes these troops as part of a global "colonial political economy," organized around what W.E.B. DuBois famously termed "the color line," and mobilized to serve imperial needs.[18] Second, this article posits that the violent work soldiers performed in the name of empire was a formative experience for millions of men who fought.

Against the racist labor logics that attempted to limit soldiers' combat experiences to certain geographies, these soldiers came of age as men with the power to kill. Arrayed against each other in European-led colonial armies, they also waged war against African peoples who resisted the predatory actions of armies on the march through unfamiliar lands. In this way, World War I in Africa should also be interpreted as a continuation (and an exacerbation) of colonial warfare. Soldiers who survived the war's harrowing violence entered the postwar era as men whose relationships to the empires that still governed them had become more complicated, even as the racist structures and logics of the prewar era remained in place and constrained their future possibilities.

Finding the Global South in a Global War

The term "Global South" typically diagnoses a postcolonial condition. At first, it thus seems an anachronistic tool for analyzing events prior to the 1955 Bandung Conference, where Asian and African leaders from decolonizing countries met to create a wide-ranging political agenda that eventually led to the Non-Aligned Movement (NAM). References to the "Global South" often gesture towards the intellectual traditions of pan-African, pan-Asian, and anti-imperial thought of the early twentieth century.[19] "Global South" often stands in for "Third World" or "developing world," because it is presumed to be "a less hierarchical—or evolutionary—term than these two."[20] Yet scholars have criticized the term, arguing that it reinscribes alterity, so that "the other remains an externally imposed exotic caricature," leaving "Euro-American privilege . . . intact."[21] "Global South" does not solve the problem of how to describe vastly different conditions of political and economic inequality around the world. It does, however, provide an analytic framework for recognizing patterns in how these inequalities manifest across time and space. Here, I want to highlight intersections of patterns of thought on race, labor, and violence that manifested in the mass mobilization of colonial soldiers between 1914 and 1918. "Global South" thinking enables such analysis.

World War I's centenary has recast the conflict as global, occasioning newly inclusive commemorative events, scholarship, and public engagement. New research has shown how soldiers and workers recruited from Africa, Asia, the Middle East, and the Caribbean contributed to the war's prosecution, both within and outside Europe. Campaigns fought outside of Europe are no longer considered mere sideshows. These campaigns redefined imperial boundaries, established new colonial political regimes and economies, and laid the basis for postwar international relations that have continued to shape politics up to the present.[22] Increasingly, as historians of non-European parts of the world narrate histories of those who fought the Great War outside of western Europe, they look to each other for new insights into this consequential era. The textured histories of different colonial militaries that historians have painstakingly reconstructed over the last few decades now allow for writing entangled histories of soldiering in the Great War.[23] We can think about the sites where Black and Brown soldiers of empire crossed paths, undertaking what Mbembe calls "a thinking of circulation and crossings" to uncover different histories of the transnational and global war and the registers of violence it unleashed in disparate locations linked only through imperial geographies.[24]

Turning a Global South lens on the war renders visible otherwise invisible wartime labor, sacrifices, and struggles of peoples living in Europe's imperial spaces between 1914 and 1918. Adopting this perspective quickly reveals how much more there is to learn about the scope of the war's histories of violence, disruption, destruction, and recovery. Soldiers and laborers recruited in the colonies were part of a global mobilization that enmeshed millions in a conflict unleashed by Europeans that reverberated out into their empires and back again. Ordinary peoples living under colonial rule experienced the war not primarily as a conflict between empires, but as extension and exacerbation of the depredations of colonial conquest, labor exploitation, straitened economic opportunities, and state-making. Soldiers drawn from colonized lands during World War I were violence workers. Their distinctive forms of labor and the mass mobilizations that brought them to distant theaters became the bases for heroic military narratives. They should also inform new interpretations of World War I that recognize the centrality of violence they experienced and inflicted on others as part of their work.

Soldiering for Empire, Race, and the Meanings of Battlefield Violence

Colonial armies did most of the fighting in the First World War campaigns in Africa, as had been the case in the preceding decades' wars of imperial conquest. Soldiers in these armies were mainly African men drawn from a combination of the rank-and-file of existing colonial armies, new recruits mustered through conscription campaigns, and levies of auxiliaries called up to meet manpower needs caused by World War I.[25] In addition, the British called up thousands of troops from across its empire and Dominions, using its fleet to transport them across vast distances, from one imperial space to another.[26] The Battle of Tanga, described in the opening of this article, shows that this imperial mobilization shaped the war's conduct from its earliest stages.[27] The image of German-led African soldiers fighting against British-led South Asian soldiers does not jump to mind readily in thinking about World War I. Yet the makeup of the fighting forces at the Battle of Tanga became the norm over the next four years of in East Africa.[28] Beyond the striking use of troops drawn from such distant reaches of the British Empire, imperial armies incorporated troops from a vast array of linguistic, cultural, religious, and geographic backgrounds. To write of an "Indian army," "the King's African Rifles," or "the *Schutztruppe*" is to gloss over the tremendous differences between soldiers, and their recruitment histories. This shorthand aids in narrating the history of imperial warfare but fails to capture the textured composition of the forces that fought.[29] And indeed, the composition of the opposing forces would become even more complex as the campaign progressed, bringing in not just increasing numbers of troops from the British empire and Dominions, but also soldiers from allied Belgian and Portuguese colonial armies whose differentiated backgrounds dissolve underneath these labels.

This model of mobilizing troops worked because of the recruitment and training practices imperial armies used to build their ranks.[30] The armies that fought against each other in East Africa were, for the most part, small armies of professional troops experienced in colonial counterinsurgency operations.[31] Recruits from different backgrounds underwent European-style training in drill, marksmanship, and military comportment. They wore uniforms that conveyed their belonging to the army, their interchangeability, and their rank and status within units. Their rank hierarchies reflected individual soldiers' relative levels of experience and longevity within the organizations. Soldiers who stayed with their units for long periods of time were rewarded with promotions, salary increases, family allowances, and prestige within the colonial state (if not among colonized populations who viewed them, with good reason, as predators).[32] The haste with which new recruitment took place in 1914 to increase troop numbers for the war certainly affected the abilities of new recruits to hone their skills before being tested under fire. But the structural benefits of trained armies coupled with some advances (albeit uneven ones) in logistics could absorb some of these vagaries, making it possible to move soldiers across oceans and empires and to expect them to perform well upon arrival in distant theaters.

European officers' racist assumptions that colonial troops would better manage the physical and mental challenges of fighting in distant and unfamiliar climes than white soldiers (who were, in any case, otherwise busy fighting the war in Europe) underpinned the logic of deploying Global South soldiers to places like German East Africa. A British officer keen on boosting the "brilliant achievements" of white South African soldiers in defeating the Germans in East Africa argued this in the early 1920s: "Coloured troops were present in large numbers and showed magnificent fighting qualities, while they were able to withstand a climate in which white troops could not continue to campaign successfully."[33] By this logic, the military skills and endurance of the "coloured troops" who did the bulk of the fighting in East Africa was naturalized: their battlefield prowess sprang from their alleged biological capacity to withstand fighting in the tropics, making them a better choice than white soldiers. Still, white soldiers remained the ideal, even if their supposed biological frailty in tropical theaters undermined their abilities to persevere.[34] Racial thought fortified imperial labor paradigms to great effect during World War I.

But of course colonial soldiers who mobilized to fight in distant theaters faced many of the same perils as white troops in moving between different disease environments, in managing the disorientation inherent in long-distance travel, and assuming the risk of oceanic travel in an age of mines and unrestricted submarine warfare. Their long-distance oceanic transit times in many cases exceeded those experienced by white troops, with corresponding negative effects on health and readiness to go into combat upon arrival, as evidenced by the Indian troops' experience at Tanga described in the opening paragraph.[35] And as a British report noted on medical preparedness for conditions in East Africa in 1917, "No criticism on the work in German East Africa would be just unless the extraordinary difficulties of the campaign were indicated."[36] Nigerian troops who arrived in German East

Africa in 1916 maintained their health until late 1917 when they shifted from "high and comparatively healthy localities" in the northern part of the colony to the Rufiji Valley region. There, they faced much harsher environmental conditions, including an exceptional wet season that brought incessant rains, exacerbating hunger and illness.[37] Indian troops deployed to the southeastern region in 1917 experienced similar hardships, with many succumbing to malaria, dysentery, and pneumonia.[38] The problem of adequate and appropriate rations exacerbated the imposing challenges these armies faced in caring for their troops' and porters' health. Beyond the logistical obstacles to provisioning troops in the East African theater, a 1918 British report noted that these failures should be attributed to "the initial error in laying down [ration] scales physiologically faulty or deficient."[39] In painstaking detail, the report explains the differences between the ration scales set out at the beginning of British operations in German East Africa and the scales they should have used in provisioning the pan-imperial force they deployed to the theater.[40] Using a Global South lens to interpret the "sideshow" theaters of World War I exposes the racist fallacy that colonial troops could better withstand fighting in environments where white soldiers suffered. The notion that racist thought affected troop recruitment and deployments is hardly novel. But the scope of racialized labor practices imperial governments and militaries used to position soldiers and other workers in distant theaters across empires deserves more attention than it has received. Indeed, the mass mobilization of imperial troops from the Global South coincides with the rise of a "nonbiological, sociological racism"—a "racism of exploitation and subordination rather than a racism of conquest and annihilation"—that shaped the world after the war.[41]

Soldiering as Work, Work as Violence

The Battle of Mahiwa is the quintessential example of a specific "sideshow" theater becoming a site of violent contestation between empires that involved Black and Brown troops from around the world. This battle, fought in southeastern Tanzania from October 15–18 , 1917, was "the bloodiest battle of the East African campaign."[42] It marked a significant operational turning point for both sides.[43] This operational turning point also intensified the exploitative dimensions of the conflict, with the soldiers' aggressions turned on populations with no stake in the European war. Nonetheless, their abilities to determine their social, economic, and political futures were inextricably connected to how these armies of empire prosecuted the war. Colonized spaces became occupied zones.

This battle and the subsequent smaller ones that took place in the last months of 1917 turned the tide for the KAR and its allies not because they won a clear victory, but because it forced the *Schutztruppe* to fight differently for the remainder of the war. The British formation designated as Linforce (Lindi force), which had been operating near the southeastern coastal town of Lindi, began advancing towards Mahiwa with the goal of destroying the *Schutztruppe*'s remaining contingents entrenched there. By attacking the *Schutztruppe* at Mahiwa, Linforce's commander sought to prevent them from escaping across the border into Portuguese East Africa. Both sides imagined a decisive battlefield victory that would knock their opponent out of the campaign. A Reuters dispatch printed in a Rhodesian newspaper summed up the British objective in October 1917: "We press the enemy everywhere, and are endeavouring to envelop each separate position with the object of forcing the elusive [German] Askari to come to grips."[44]

But this was not to be. At Mahiwa, the "understrength" force of *Schutz-truppe askari* and German NCOs and officers held its ground against the substantially larger and better equipped advancing British force, composed of units drawn from across the British empire and Dominions.[45] These included Nigerians, West Indians, South Asian, and South African troops. The *Schutztruppe* inflicted massive casualties on their opponents but also lost many troops themselves, and unlike the KAR, the *Schutztruppe* could not easily replace those lost. Fighting between German and British armies continued in the region into late November, with Lettow-Vorbeck's column finally crossing the Rovuma into Portuguese East Africa on the 25th.

An astonishing array of colonial soldiers came from far and wide to face off on this obscure battlefield in German East Africa. How can a Global South frame illuminate shared experiences? While colonial armies had long recruited soldiers to fight their wars of conquest, secure conquered lands, and defend the colonizers against insurrection, decisions to deploy thousands of Black and Brown soldiers to fight in World War I typically unfolded under clouds of doubt on the part of racist colonial officials. While usually perfectly happy to conscript Black and Brown men for the purposes of menial labor, European officers often balked at putting them in combat roles. British West Indian volunteers who tried to join the British army when the war began were at first rebuffed by the Colonial and War Offices, who "drew upon racialized notions of martial fitness to disparage West Indians' soldiering abilities."[46] When the 2nd South African Cape Corps battalion passed through Buluwayo, Southern Rhodesia in August 1917, British observers were taken aback by the new corps's professionalism:

The dusky Tommies—very slightly dusky, some of them—were in town only about an hour, but in that period they exhibited themselves in a route march through some of the principal thoroughfares, headed by a quite passable drum and fife band. The spectacle was an 'eye-opener' to some of our citizens to whom the name of the Cape Corps conveyed nothing in the way of soldierly smartness. The battalion marched as steadily, almost, as any 'regiment of the line' and gave the impression that they could go on marching that way right to Timbuctoo or wherever was their destination.[47]

White observers' and officials' skepticism and disparagement of nonwhite soldiers as being inherently unfit for combat roles on the one hand, and the elevation of certain groups of men to martial race status on the other, illustrates the range of ways that race shaped both recruitment discourse and practice in this era.[48]

Nonetheless, the pressing need for manpower to fight in new theaters opened up by the war's dramatic expansion in 1915, especially in the Dardanelles, convinced skeptics to change their minds. The British Colonial Office and War Office had refused to permit men from the British West Indies to enlist. But in May 1915, the War Office created the British West Indies Regiment (BWIR) and began recruiting to fill the ranks that summer.[49] Following combat actions in Cameroon in 1915, Jamaican troops of the BWIR were deployed to German East Africa in 1917, where they won accolades for bravery in fighting near Mahiwa.[50]

Fighting in East Africa was notoriously difficult for all soldiers, regardless of where they had begun their journeys to war. Tropical illnesses like malaria and other communicable diseases exacted a high toll on troops' ability to function, as did poor nutrition.[51] Wildlife, including crocodiles, lions and poisonous snakes posed a relentless threat, whether troops were on the march, crossing rivers, or encamped.[52] Extreme heat and humidity, monsoon rains, and thick vegetation hampered the long columns' maneuverability. Battles were intense, bloody, and exhausting, as was the case in other theaters. Troops often had limited time to recover, as they had to resume marching after battles, whether to evade (*Schutztruppe*) or to pursue (British forces). A *Schutztruppe askari* named Ali Kalikilima recalled the march from Dodoma to Kisaki, which required them to cross the river Ruaha:

We were completely exhausted by the end of the fourth day [of trying to cross the river Ruaha], yet there was to be no rest. We were urgently needed on the battlefield [at Kisaki], regardless of the strain and fatigue that overwhelmed us, not to mention those battling with fever and the constant stomach troubles caused by our sole diet of meat. Many were also suffering from infected wounds—some so septic that those afflicted suffered severe bouts of delirium.[53]

Inadequate medical supplies, both in terms of quantity and suitability for treating serious wounds including those inflicted by bullets and shrapnel, as well as difficult terrain and animal bites posed additional problems for columns so constantly on the move. Ali described how his unit treated a soldier's cobra bite since there was no serum on hand to use: "The only thing we could do was cut away the flesh where the bite had occurred. The blood would pour out and hopefully the poison with it, but this was only successful in a few cases."[54] These features of the war in East Africa have been well-documented in the literature and provide some indication of the harsh work conditions these soldiers faced.

These troops' violent encounters took place within a campaign where spatial dislocation paired with the chaos of a highly mobile and fluid campaign. The unpredictability of these encounters, whether in formal battle contexts or outside of them,

compounded the stresses and fears that soldiers faced each day. In a mobile campaign like this, the condition of being "in battle" or not was often murky. *Schutztruppe* soldiers struck the KAR and allied troops without warning and then disappeared, to the endless frustration of British commanders. This was a hallmark
of Lettow-Vorbeck's campaign, though the common claim that his columns' mode
of operations deserves the label "guerrilla warfare" warrants skepticism.[55] Still, his
style of hit-and-run attacks on the British and their allies took a toll.

Schutztruppe veteran Mzee Ali Kalikilima recalled the vivid complex of fear,
stress, and confusion that he experienced in battle at Kisaki in September 1916, a
year before Mahiwa. It is difficult to reconcile Mzee Ali's memory of the events at
Kisaki with conventional military histories. Nonetheless, his recollection shows the
extreme violence these soldiers witnessed, endured, and committed in the name of
empire and in the name of proving their manhood.[56] Ali's unit was dug into a defensive position at Kisaki in September 1916 when, he recalled, a British field artillery
barrage landed close behind German lines. This attack, which threw his mind "into
a jumble of confusion," cut off their supply and communication lines and caused
"general chaos in the rear," destroying ammunition supplies, and killing or wounding support personnel working in the rear handling those supplies.[57] As the barrage
continued, Ali found himself "amidst . . . blood and severed limbs" and "wailing and
agony to which one never grows accustomed." Once the artillery barrage's horrors
subsided, Ali's unit still had to face the opponents' advancing troops. Close-in fighting with bayonets ensued as "they poured into [the *Schutztruppe*'s] trenches."[58] Ali
and others escaped to rejoin other German forces south of Kisaki. They lived to fight
another day. Indeed, Ali lived to witness the German surrender in November 1918.

Ali's memories of intense combat between German and British colonial soldiers, and enemy troops' use of bayonets, unsettles East African campaign historiography because it foregrounds not just his resolve under harrowing conditions, but
also the fear, stress, and pain characteristic of combat. Postwar military histories
provide rich descriptions of battle actions, noting soldiers' movements, accomplishments, and when they succumbed to the inevitable in battle—wounds and death.
Yet many of these accounts are also oddly bloodless, failing to reckon with colonial
soldiers' experiences in the war.

This bloodlessness becomes more difficult to sustain when soldiers are
counted as workers, whose work was to kill. This vantage point sheds light on their
work's meanings and, crudely stated, the tasks and tools involved in doing their
work.[59] New and old technologies like the bayonet and dumdum bullet feature in
soldiers' testimonies as characteristic of East African battlefield experiences.[60] In
the 1950s, a former Gold Coast Regiment soldier named Jacob Dosoo Amenyah
recalled fighting around Lukuledi in October 1917. There, he witnessed his fellow
soldiers "practically mowned down by German don don [that is, dumdum] bullet fir-
ings leaving very few" alive or unwounded. He continued, "The dead and wounded

were hitted over and over again with Enemy's don don bullets." Amenyeh also described German "hand to hand fightings i.e. 'Charge' with their brutal weapons, saw-bladed bayonets." Sergeant-Major Yessefu Mamprusi, who assumed command following the death of the unit's lieutenant in the "disastrous engagement," also received three bullet wounds in the battle.[61] Later, Amenyah was ordered to return to the battlefield to "take down [i.e., record] the battalion Casualties." He claimed to have observed German troops "plunging their bayonets into the bodies of the dead Gold Coast men" and cursing them in German. In order to save himself from being captured and suffering a similar fate, he hid himself under "dead soldiers of other British units" until the next morning. He did this because the Germans harbored "bitter feelings" toward the GCR soldiers, believing that they were cannibals, and were therefore to be dispatched on the spot rather than taken prisoner. After this gruesome experience, he returned to British lines to submit his casualty report and provide intelligence to his superiors on the Germans' departure from the area.[62] Amenyah's recollection shows the extreme brutality that characterized these soldiers' work.

In November 1917, Nigerian forces advanced on Chiwata, thirty miles south of Mahiwa, and took control of a German hospital situated there. African and Indian prisoners of war interned at Chiwata by the Germans reported horrible treatment, especially by a guard named Tsetse, "a brute of the worst kind," and presumably an *askari*. Tsetse had habitually abused a Hausa POW by forcing him to work despite a horrible injury[63]:

One of the prisoner's ankles was damaged by [a] leg-iron, and a sore developed that at first only lamed him. Instead of being handed over to the medical authorities he was forced by Tsetse to continue working till the ankle became so bad that he became a drag upon other prisoners on the same chain. He was therefore taken out of the chain and forced to go on working by himself.[64]

When the Hausa POW rested or faltered because of his injury, Tsetse beat him and forced him back to work. The POW eventually died from the infection caused by his gangrenous leg. Tsetse later fell into British hands, and some of his "own ex-prisoners" escorted him to the coast to eventually be tried in a court martial for "acts of cruelty."[65] South Asian troops of the 57th Wilde's Rifles (Frontier Force) captured at Kisaki reported similar levels of cruelty in testimonies collected in 1919, following their demobilization to India.[66] Germans also reported cruel treatment perpetrated by the British and their allies against *Schutztruppe* members, though only abuses against German officers or NCOs, and not against *askari*, registered in postwar memoirs.[67]

Ali's and Amenyah's narratives convey battlefield chaos, offering glimpses into how these two soldiers made sense of their experiences as men. Richard Smith has argued that the bayonet featured centrally in shaping BWIR veterans' masculine self-identities. Although the bayonet "provided a sign of autonomy and action in the face of industrialised warfare and discipline" for British infantry troops generally, he argues, "for the black West Indian volunteer, it symbolized a demand to participate on equal terms within the realm of imperial masculinity and to claim the rewards for such participation once hostilities were over."[68] The bayonet continued to convey powerful messages about West Indian soldierly masculinity and the role of veterans in postwar quests for recognition from the empire that their work, sacrifices, and suffering had meant something. Immersion in violent acts, or witnessing them, surely played a part in veterans' postwar sensibilities, rhetoric, and activism around self-determination, but it is an area in need of further research.[69]

Indeed, following the war, a common feature of narratives about its prosecution in different theaters included the elaboration of colonial soldiers' heroism, bravery, and dedication. Postwar military histories provided lists of soldiers' accomplishments under fire, often with accompanying narratives of actions that garnered them recognition worthy of military decorations. These narratives, like many sources, must be interpreted carefully since they served the colonizers' needs in perpetuating ideals of heroic militarism. Yet they offer glimpses into the nature of soldierly work, the hierarchies that ordered it, and the risks involved. Private Lowani Ede of the 4th Nigerian Regiment received a medal for gallantry at Mahiwa on 15th Oct. 1917:

When little more than a recruit himself, and in his first action, collected
magazines for a Lewis gun under very heavy fire, which magazines had
been dropped in the bush by runaway and frightened carriers in action,
thus enabling the gun to remain in action, covering the retirement of the
Company.[70]

Two other privates, Tanko Katsena and Osuman Lakai, "both little more than recruits at the time," received the Distinguished Conduct Medal (DCM) from the West African Frontier Force (WAFF): "At Mahiwa on 16th Oct. 1917 they twice carried water to the firing line under intense fire from machine guns, previous attempts having failed."[71] In both of these cases, the troops' status as "recruits" conveyed that they did not have extensive experience in combat.[72] Indeed, the feats that garnered them military decorations had more to do with support to soldiers in the firing line—roles that suited their inexperience as combatants. Their actions are also contrasted with those who failed. In the first case, they outperformed the porters, whose cowardice resulted in Lewis gun ammunition being dropped. In the second case, previous attempts by unnamed soldiers to bring water to the firing line stood in contrast to the two recruits who got through under these difficult conditions.[73] New recruits' trial by fire transformed them into seasoned soldiers who would benefit their units in the future.

Courage under fire while maintaining the presence of mind to fire back with accuracy and lethality was another hallmark of an effective soldier, which British officers recognized with military decorations. Thus the Nigerian Gunner Modi received a DCM for

Gallantry and devotion to duty at MAHIWA on 16th Oct. 1917, when he continued to work his gun under heavy fire until the rest of the gun team were either killed or wounded. Though wounded, he then assisted his officer in attempting to remove the breech block under very heavy flanking fire at close range. When he found this was impossible he damaged the breech block as much as possible, and only abandoned the gun to the enemy when ordered to do so by his officer, when the enemy were within 25 yards.[74]

Modi's cool demeanor enabled him to continue fighting even under the worst stresses of battle. His award narrative illustrates the steadiness that came along with higher rank, usually also indicative of years of experience.[75] Modi's actions were recognized because they stood out as a model for others to emulate, and his recognition reinforced this standard as a goal for younger recruits. Thus these decorations might have incentivized successive generations of recruits to join militaries since they validated masculine bravery as a worthy ideal.

For many of these soldiers, pride in their battlefield endurance, skill, and individual acts of gallantry that had won them military awards and decorations stamped their postwar political sensibilities. BWIR veterans, for example, "were not concerned with the glorification of war, but the enthusiasm for heroic narratives tended to conflate war with front-line service and to marginalize the service of those volunteers engaged in auxiliary and laboring duties."[76] World War I veterans across the Global South used their wartime service to position themselves as part of burgeoning Pan-African cosmopolitanisms in the postwar period, most notably Garveyism.[77] For example, Jamaican soldiers returning home from overseas theaters were involved in protest actions in British Honduras and Trinidad in 1919 and 1920.[78] Others wanted the colonizers to honor their service with rewards in the form of pensions, promotions, jobs, land, citizenship or other benefits once they returned home. But imperial racisms often yielded only limited rewards for most colonial troops. Evidence suggests that ex-soldiers who returned home from war played significant roles in decolonization movements and actions in South Asia, but this was not the case for most of Africa.[79] Postwar "crises of empire" manifested in uneven ways around the world. Rising calls for self-determination took hold in some places in Africa, but not others, in the 1920s. The relationships between war veterans and the wave of self-determination causes in the Global South is not at all straightforward but seems valuable for understanding the making of the postwar world order. In particular, such work could help illuminate how the war affected how race, labor, and imperial violence influenced each other through the 1930s, World War II, and beyond.

After Mahiwa. Occupied Zones, Mobility, and Resistance

Following the bloody military confrontations in and around Mahiwa in October 1917, General von Lettow-Vorbeck moved his remaining able-bodied troops south into Portuguese East Africa (Mozambique). There, they and the column's contingent of porters lived off the land, requisitioning supplies from Portuguese military forts and local communities. From the British perspective, Mahiwa was the moment of the *Schutztruppe*'s "expulsion" from German East Africa and the moment that consolidated their imperial dominance in the region, even though the campaign continued for another year.[80] From this point on, the *Schutztruppe*'s strategy was to evade the British and their allies. The King's African Rifles and their beleaguered Portuguese allies attempted to round up the *Schutztruppe*, to no avail. Lettow-Vorbeck finally surrendered in Abercorn, Northern Rhodesia on November 25, 1917 upon receiving word of the armistice in Europe. Postwar mythologies made much of Lettow-Vorbeck as a wily, heroic, and undefeated military leader, and the *askari* play supporting roles in this depiction of colonial warfare. But this perspective elides the armies' brutal conscription and requisitioning practices that enabled their troops to keep fighting the highly mobile style of warfare that became the campaign's hallmark. It also largely ignores the devastating effects these practices had on communities that lay in or near the paths of successive armies marching through their lands.

Military occupation relies on abuses and extraction that severely interfere with people's abilities to subsist and thrive. But everyday colonialism for many Tanzanians had always meant these sorts of abuses. The East Africa campaign exacerbated these conditions and compounded civilian suffering.[81] In the last phase of the East Africa campaign, the columns were engaged in near-constant searches for provisions. Columns split up into smaller units in order to lessen the provisioning burden on particular areas, though it increased their military vulnerabilities to the KAR columns who were in pursuit.[82] German officers described the regions they passed through as "provisioning areas" which could be "good" or "bad depending on how much they had to offer the columns.[83] In the best cases, columns compensated local inhabitants for supplies.[84] In July 1918, Ludwig Deppe, a *Schutztruppe* doctor, traded a 1.5-meter piece of "simple cotton cloth" for 30 kilograms of rice. He was willing to exchange another piece of cloth for a chicken, but, as he wrote, his trading partner "disappeared" before he could do so. Supplemented with the "heaps of peanuts available" in the area (Chalaua), Deppe noted with pride that his men now had provisions for two weeks through his trading efforts.[85] But just as often, columns used violence to take what they wanted. Raids on Portuguese military forts also yielded considerable quantities of food, medicine, ammunition, and other supplies.[86] In the worst cases, *askari* patrols went out into "surrounding villages" to order people to bring the columns food, and to gather intelligence.[87] As Deppe noted, "We could not count on support from the natives, because the troops . . . requisitioned the bulk of their provisions from their villages by force." Unsurprisingly, the "sub-jects" fled into hiding "with everything they could carry" or "put themselves under the protection of the enemy" to avoid losing everything.[88] This range of encounters between the invading German and British armies and the Portuguese East African communities in their way reveals the everyday complexities of the campaign. Deppe's observations indicate the value in viewing soldiers and civilians in the same frame as part of a dynamic, but coercive, colonial political economy.[89]

Between 1914 and 1918, African peoples living through the dire circum-stances caused by insatiable military columns and their extractive requisitioning practices resisted in different ways. Fears of being pressed into labor by the colo-nial armies, outrage over stolen food stores, livestock, and other goods, and concern over disruptions to planting and harvesting schedules led to acts of resistance on large and small scales. But the situation in Portuguese East Africa in 1917–18 was made even more complex by two rebellions against the Portuguese that overlapped with the *Schutztruppe*'s invasion and the KAR's pursuit. "The year 1917," a histo-rian writes, "was a long and drawn-out nightmare for the Portuguese in Africa," and it surely was for those living under Portuguese colonial rule.[90] At a time when the British needed their Portuguese allies to stop the *Schutztruppe*, from March to September 1917 they were instead fighting the Barue in Zambezia. The Barue had suffered under Portuguese taxation as well as ruthless labor and military con-scription drives in 1916. By early 1917, they had decided to fight back, initiating a coordinated and extensive rebellion. The Portuguese were forced to direct their military resources to defeating the Barue. In the north, the Makonde, who had long resisted Portuguese control, also took up arms against them in 1917. The Portuguese used scorched-earth methods to finally defeat them in July 1917.[91] And in neighbor-ing Northern Rhodesia (Zambia), where labor recruitment abuses similar to those occurring in Portuguese East Africa upset everyday life, the Watchtower religious revival movement that began in late 1917 unnerved colonial authorities, leading to a violent colonial response in early 1919.[92] Colonial logics of military necessity that prioritized troops' needs over those of local populations posed grave challenges to community values and priorities. Resistance to imperial war mobilization efforts in 1917–18 returns us to the value of thinking about the war as an expression of Global South identities. It is the outcome of the violence perpetrated by the thousands of colonial troops who descended on East Africa between 1914 and 1918 to fight Europe's Great War.

Concluding Thoughts

Soldiers deployed to fight in East Africa from as far away as the British West Indies, West Africa, and India had little choice but to depend on their units for survival dur-ing the war. In 1917–18, they were thus active participants in the violent exploitative practices that occupying armies undertook in all theaters of the war.[93] In the East

African theater, the violence of occupation exacerbated already harsh conditions of everyday life for colonized peoples. In this, the soldiers continued longstanding practices of colonial warfare, in which mobile columns and their accompanying logistics trains provisioned themselves by taking supplies from local populations, using scorched-earth methods to punish communities perceived as uncooperative. Colonial troops' actions in German East Africa, Portuguese East Africa, and Northern Rhodesia created conditions that led to massive suffering and upheaval for local populations in ways that barely feature in the wider World War I historiography.[94] Soldiers' battlefield experiences and the often self-affirming meanings that soldiers took with them into the postwar period must be considered in conjunction with their roles in inflicting pain on populations unfortunate enough to live in proximity to the colonial armies' paths. We need to rethink colonized spaces during the war as zones of occupation. A Global South lens sharpens our ability to see how empires manipulated the intersections between soldiering, race, and labor in building armies to fight the war, which also made them key agents in violence that only deepened European colonial entrenchment when the war ended.

Without these local histories, Africa and other parts of the Global South appear as spaces where battles happened but also as spaces devoid of populations faced with often devastating violence in colonized, occupied zones. World War I historiography has thus produced multiple erasures. It erases the vexed histories of soldiers who fought for empires, as represented by the hundreds of thousands of colonial troops and laborers mobilized for war within Europe and outside of it. It also erases the histories of the thousands of people outside of western Europe who experienced the war's violence firsthand. This article argues that we might "apply the microhistorical cultural methods that we have developed over the past decades to the macrohistorical political-economic questions" that dominate our understanding of World War I.[95] This exercise will reveal patterns in how empires have gone to war over the last century—patterns that emerge most vividly through a Global South lens. The momentous events of 1917—the October Revolution in Russia, the United States' and China's declarations of war against Germany, the carnage on battlefields at Ypres and Paaschendaele, and the United States' entry into the war—also have Global South histories waiting to be revealed, if we are willing to look.

Michelle Moyd is associate professor of history at Indiana University in Bloomington. She is the author of *Violent Intermediaries: African Soldiers, Conquest, and Everyday Colonialism in German East Africa* (2014) and she is currently at work on the book "Africa, Africans, and the First World War."

Notes

I would like to thank the editors of this special issue for their encouragement and the two anonymous reviewers for their incisive, constructive comments on the first draft of this piece.

1. Tanga was the coastal terminus of the Usambara railway, which connected the port to Moshi, a colonial economic hub in the Mt. Kilimanjaro region.

2. "Shambolic": Strachan, *The First World in Africa*, 108; Anderson, "The Battle of Tanga," 320, 321.

3. Deppe, *Mit Lettow-Vorbeck*, 45.

4. Anderson, "The Battle of Tanga," 319.

5. Lettow-Vorbeck, *My Reminiscences*, 42–3.

6. Hordern, *Military Operations*, 107. For British casualties, see p. 96. See also Boell, *Die Operationen in Ost-Afrika*, 82, which offers slightly different figures.

7. Hordern, *Military Operations*, 101. See also Anderson, *The Battle of Tanga*; Paice, *Tip and Run*, 40-58; and Pradhan, *Indian Army in East Africa*, 56–67.

8. Hordern, *Military Operations*, 107; Moyse-Bartlett, *The King's African Rifle*, 278. See also Paice, *Tip and Run*, 59–66.

9. Deppe, *Mit Lettow-Vorbeck*, 46.

10. See, for example, Mass, *Weisse Helden;* and Michels, Schwarze *deutsche Kolonialsoldaten*.

11. For more on the different kinds of battlefields—beaches, urban streets, rubber and sisal plantations—British and Indian forces encountered at Tanga, see Hordern, *Military Operations East Africa*, 83–90.

12. In 1914, Germany had four African colonies—Togo, Cameroon, German Southwest Africa and German East Africa. The Allies defeated German forces in Togo in 1914, German Southwest Africa in 1915, and Cameroon in 1916. The East Africa campaign continued until Lettow-Vorbeck's surrender to the British on November 25, 1918. For overviews of these campaigns, see Strachan, *The First World War in Africa*.

13. Jonathan Rigg, *An Everyday Geography*, 2, 4; Comaroff and Comaroff, *Theory from the South*, 12, 15.

14. Africa: Lunn, "War Losses (Africa);" India: Singha, "Labour (India)." China provided another 140,000 laborers as part of an effort to secure its interests in postwar negotiations with Japan, which had seized territories formerly colonized by the Germans.

15. See, for example, Indian soldiers' narratives in FO 383/497, pp. 539, 541, 543, National Archives, Kew, London.

16. Huggins, Haritos-Fatouros, and Zimbardo, *Violence Workers*, 1. On soldiers in labor history, see Van der Linden, " Promises and Challenges," 63–65; and Zürcher, *Fighting for a Living*, 11–14.

17. "Imperial formations are not steady states, but states of becoming, macropolities in states of solution and constant formation." Stoler and McGranahan, "Refiguring Imperial Terrains," 8–9.

18. For Zimmerman, the Global South is a "colonial political economy" that is "separated from core capitalist countries by what W. E. B. DuBois called the 'color line' and the African American novelist Richard Wright later called the 'color curtain,' at least as important as the better known 'iron curtain' that once separated East and West." Zimmerman, *Alabama in Africa*, 1.

19. See Lee, "Between a Moment," 5–19; Prashad, *The Darker Nations*, 31–50.

20. Wolvers et al., Introduction, "Concepts of the Global South."

21. Figueira, "'The Global South,'" 144–145.

22.   Gerwarth and Manela, *Empires at War*; Pederson, *The Guardians*.

23.   Werner and Zimmermann, "Beyond Comparison," 31–33; Seigel, "Beyond Compare," 62–65.

24.   Mbembe, *Critique of Black Reason*, 8.

25.   For an overview, see Koller, "The Recruitment of Colonial Troops," 111–133. For specific cases, see Echenberg, *Colonial Conscripts*, 7–19, 25–69; Moyd, *Violent Intermediaries*, 36–87. See also Moyd, "Soldiering On," 11–16.

26.   The Dominions included South Africa, Canada, Australia, and New Zealand.

27.   The French also mobilized thousands of African soldiers from western and northern Africa to fight in Europe. Planning for the recruitment and deployment of francophone West African troops had begun several years before the war started.

28.   Moyse-Bartlett, *The Kings African Rifles*, 276. On the composition and performance of the Indian troops at Tanga, see Pradhan, *Indian Army in East Africa*, 56–67; and Pradhan, "Indians in the East African Campaign," 69–74.

29.   Omissi, *The Sepoy and the Raj*; Stapleton, "The Composition of the Rhodesia Native Regiment," 283–95.

30.   Moyd, *Violent Intermediaries*, 88–114.

31.   For more on German colonial warfare before 1914, see Kuss, *German Colonial Wars*; Moyd, *Violent Intermediaries*; and Porch, *Counterinsurgency*.

32.   Ibid.

33.   Colvile, "The South Africans," 459. See also Nasson, "British Imperial Africa," 144–47.

34.   Colvile, "The South Africans, 467.

35.   Osuntokun, *Nigeria in the First World War*, 248; Lunn, *Memoirs of the Maelstrom*, 98–103.

36.   *Report on Medical and Sanitary Matter*, 6; found in CO 691/19, National Archives-Kew (NA-Kew).

37.   "high and comparatively healthy": Osuntokun, *Nigeria and the First World War*, 255. See also Downes, *With the Nigerians in German East Africa*, 90–91; and CO 691/19, NA-Kew, pp. 274–75.

38.   Thatcher, *The Fourth Battalion*, 161, 166, 167.

39.   *Report on Medical and Sanitary Matters*, 56

40.   Ibid., 55–64. The report is fascinating in the level of detail used to document the foodways of different British imperial soldiering and laboring contingents deployed to German East Africa. It also reveals that some troops received smaller rations by design, seemingly tied to racialized assumptions about what constituted suitable rations for different imperial troops.

41.   Zimmerman, *Alabama in Africa*, 205, 206.

42.   Gregg Adams, *King's African Rifles Soldier*, 45. According to Paice, "Casualties among the 5,000-strong British force – including three battalions from the Nigerian Brigade, three from the King's African Rifles, and the Bharatpur Infantry and 30th Punjabis from India—were estimated at between one third and a half. The 16 companies of German Schutztruppen opposing them—about 2,000 men—sustained 25% casualties." See Paice, "How the Great War Razed East Africa."

43.   See for example Adams, *King's African Rifles Soldier*, 43–58.

44.   "Round-Up in East Africa: Chasing the Elusive Askari," *Bulawayo Chronicle*, October 19, 1917.

45.   "understrength": Adams, *King's African Rifles Soldier*, 43.

46.   Goldthree, "'A Greater Enterprise,'" 63–5. See also Smith, *Jamaican Volunteers*, 33–51; and Smith, "Propaganda, Imperial Subjecthood and National Identity," 107–110.

47.   "Coloured Battalion Pays a Visit to Bulawayo," *Bulawayo Chronicle*, August 3, 1917, 8; and

"Dar es Salaam. A Huge Camp. Farewell Parades," *Bulawayo Chronicle*, December 28, 1917, 6. On the First Cape Corps, see Difford, *1st Battalion Cape Corps*.

48. See Omissi, *The Sepoy and the Raj*; Parsons, "'Wakamba warriors,'" 671–701.

49. Goldthree, "'A Greater Enterprise,'" 65–66.

50. Smith, *Jamaican Volunteers*, 90.

51. MacDonnell, *Mzee Ali*, 197. For a useful overview of the disease environment and its effects on troops in the East African campaign, see Taute, "A German Account of the Medical Side of the War," 2–20.

52. MacDonnell, *Mzee Ali*, 194, 195–97, 198; Christensen, ed., *Blockade and Jungle*, 180–81.

53. MacDonnell, *Mzee Ali*, 197.

54. Ibid., 198–99.

55. Strachan, *The First World War in Africa*, 94-5, 177-78.

56. MacDonnell, 201–04. For other accounts of what happened at Kisaki in September 1916, see Lettow-Vorbeck, *My Reminiscences*, 152–56; Anderson, *The Forgotten Front*, 142–48; Christensen, ed., *Blockade and Jungle*, 154–70; orig. 1940; transl. Eleanor Arkwright. For comparison, see Joe Lunn, *Memoirs of the Maelstrom*, 128–35.

57. MacDonnell, *Mzee Ali*, 202. I have been unable to confirm the presence of British field artillery at Kisaki.

58. Ibid., 203.

59. Moyd, "Soldiering On," 10–11; Luedtke, "Appeal of Exterminating Others," S63, S66. I am grateful to George Njung for this insight into the historiography of World War I in Africa.

60. Dumdum bullets expand and fragment upon contact, causing devastating wounds. The 1899 Hague Convention outlawed them, but international law norms were ignored in the colonies.

61. His gallantry at Lukuledi was rewarded with a DCM. Lawler and Wilks, "Jacob Dosoo Amenyah," 16, 18. See also Clifford, *The Gold Coast Regiment*, 173–79.

62. Lawler and Wilks, "Jacob Dosoo Amenyah," 19.

63. The Hausa, from northern Nigeria, was one group heavily recruited into the WAFF. See Njung, "West Africa."

64. Downes, *With the Nigerians*, 248–49.

65. Ibid., 249.

66. National Archives, Kew, FO 383/497, pp. 539, 541, 543.

67. Lettow-Vorbeck, *My Reminiscences*, 220–21; Lettow-Vorbeck, *Heia Safari*, 95.

68. Smith, "The Permanent West Indian Soldier," 312. On the continued importance of bayonet training in the British imperial army in this period, see Bourke, *Intimate History of Killing*, 77–80.

69. Adas, "Colonial Hegemony: The Great War and the Afro-Asian Assault on the Civilizing Mission Ideology," 59–60.

70. Downes, *With the Nigerians*, 337.

71. Ibid., 330.

72. Fendall, *The East African Force 1915–1919*, 106.

73. Soldiers deployed with the express purpose of working as laborers are another interesting case open to analysis of imperial labor hierarchies and their intersections with racial and gender paradigms. For example, BWIR troops launched a six-day riot in Taranto, Italy in December 1918 in protest of "humiliating work assignments and disparaging treatment by commanding officers." Goldthree, "'Greater than the Panama Canal,'" 78. Smith describes the British use of Jamaican soldiers as laborers as "the application of the plantation labor regime to military service." Smith, "The Permanent West Indian Soldier," 312–14. See also

Smith, *Jamaican Volunteers*, 82, 130–31. On differential military justice between white and Black troops, see Saltman, "'The Full and Just Penalty?,'" 170–74.

74. Ibid., 325–326. Emphasis in original.

75. For similar narratives of the 129th Baluchi Regiment, which fought in a number of battles before Mahiwa, see Thatcher, *The Fourth Battalion*, 234–41, 253–90.

76. Smith, "Permanent West Indian Soldier," 310.

77. Ibid., 317-322; Adas, "Contested Hegemony," 31–63.

78. Baptiste, *The United States and West Indian Unrest*, 8–9. See also Goldthree, "'Greater than the Panama Canal,'" 78–9; and Smith, "World War I and the Permanent West Indian Soldier," 317–23.

79. Egypt is an important exception. Egyptian Labour Corps conscripts rioted in 1918 against poor conditions while deployed in the Sinai and Palestine campaigns. In 1919, widespread "revolutionary unrest" upset Britain's political hold on Egypt, leading ultimately to the 1922 constitutional settlement that reduced British power there. Kitchen, "Colonial Empires." See also Adas, "Contested Hegemony," 56–63.

80. Clifford, *The Gold Coast Regiment*, 180.

81. Stapleton, "The Impact of the First World War," 113–37.

82. Deppe, *Mit Lettow-Vorbeck durch Afrika*, 330.

83. Ibid., 330–31.

84. Ibid., 363.

85. Ibid., 363.

86. Ibid., 344.

87. Ibid., 344–45.

88. Ibid., 345–46.

89. For the KAR, see Moyse-Bartlett, *King's African Rifles*, 398, 403, 404–05.

90. Ribeiro de Meneses, "The Portuguese Empire," 188.

91. Barue: Isaacman with Isaacman, *The Tradition of Resistance*, 156–85. Makonde: Ribeiro de Meneses, "The Portuguese Empire," 189. See also Moyd, "Resistance and Rebellion."

92. Yorke, "Second Chilembwe," 373–9; Fields, *Revival and Rebellion*, 128–62.

93. Moyd, "Gender and Violence," 187–191.

94. Moyd, "Centring a Sideshow," 111–130.

95. Zimmerman, *Alabama in Africa*, 3.

References

Adams, Gregg. 2016. *King's African Rifles Soldier Versus Schutztruppe Soldier: East Africa 1917-18*. Oxford, UK: Osprey Publishing.

Adas, Michael. 2004. "Contested Hegemony: The Great War and the Afro-Asian Assault on the Civilizing Mission Ideology." *Journal of World History* 15, 1: 31–63.

Anderson, Ross. 2001. "The Battle of Tanga, 2-5 November 1914." *War in History* 8, 3: 294–322.

Anderson, Ross. 2002. *The Battle of Tanga 1914.* Stroud, UK: Tempus.

Anderson, Ross. 2004. *The Forgotten Front: The East African Campaign 1914–1918*. Stroud, UK: Tempus.

Boell, Ludwig. 1951. *Die Operationen in Ost-Afrika: Weltkrieg 1914–1918*. Hamburg: Dachert.

Bulawayo Chronicle

Christensen, Christen P. ed., 2003. *Blockade and Jungle*. Translated by Eleanor Arkwright. Nashville: Battery Press. Orig. 1940.

Clifford, Hugh. 1995. *The Gold Coast Regiment in the East African Campaign*. Nashville: The Battery Press. Original publication London: The Imperial War Museum, 1920.

Colvile, Major K. N. 1921 -1926. "The South Africans in East Africa." In *The Empire at War*, Vol. IV, edited by Sir Charles Lucas. London: Oxford University Press.

Deppe, Ludwig. 1919. *Mit Lettow-Vorbeck durch Afrika.* Berlin: August Scherl.

Difford, Ivor D. No date. *The Story of the 1st Battalion Cape Corps.* Cape Town: Hortors Limited.

Dirlik, Arif. 2007. "Global South: Predicament and Promise." *The Global South* 1, 1: 12–23.

Downes, W. D. 1919. *With the Nigerians in German East Africa.* London: Methuen & Co.

DuBois, W. E. B. 1918. "Close Ranks." In *W. E. B. DuBois: A Reader,* edited by David Levering Lewis, 637. New York: Henry Holt and Company.

Fendall, C. P. 1921. *The East African Force 1915–1919.* London: H.F. & G. Witherby.

Fields, Karen. 1985. *Revival and Rebellion in Colonial Central Africa.* Princeton, NJ: Princeton University Press.

Figueira, Dorothy. 2007. "'The Global South': Yet Another Attempt to Engage the Other." *The Global South* 1, 1: 144–152.

Fogarty, Richard. 2014. *Race and War in France: Colonial Subjects in the French Army 1914–1918.* Baltimore: Johns Hopkins University Press, 2009.

Fogarty, Richard and Andrew Jarboe., eds. *Empires in World War I: Shifting Frontiers and Imperial Dynamics in a Global Context.* London: I. B. Tauris.

Gerwarth, Robert, and Erez Manela. 2014. *Empires at War.* Oxford, UK: Oxford University Press.

Ghosh, Durba. 2012. "Another Set of Imperial Turns." *American Historical Review* 117, no. 3: 772–93.

Goldthree, Reena. 2016. "'A Greater Enterprise than the Panama Canal': Migrant Labor and Military Recruitment in the World War I–Era Circum-Caribbean." *Labor: Studies in Working-Class History of the Americas* 13, no. 3–4: 57–82.

Hordern, Charles. 1990. *Military Operations East Africa, Volume 1 August 1914–September 1916.* Nashville, TN: The Battery Press. Orig. pub. London: HMSO 1941.

Isaacman, Charles with Barbara Isaacman. 1976. *The Tradition of Resistance in Mozambique: Anti-Colonial Activity in the Zambesi Valley 1850–1921.* London: Heinemann.

Kitchen, James E. 2014. "Colonial Empires after the War/Decolonization." In *1914–1918 Online. International Encyclopedia of the First World War*, edited by Ute Daniel, Peter Gatrell, Oliver Janz, Heather Jones, Jennifer Keene, Alan Kramer, and Bill Nasson. Freie Universität Berlin. DOI: 10.15463/ie1418.10370

Koller, Christian. 2008. "The Recruitment of Colonial Troops in Africa and Asia and their Deployment in Europe during the First World War." *Immigrants and Minorities* 26, 1/2: 111–33.

Kuss, Susanne. 2017. *German Colonial Wars and the Context of Military Violence.* Cambridge, MA: Harvard University Press.

Lawler, Nancy and Ivor Wilks. 2009–2010. "The World War One Service of Jacob Dosoo Amenyah of Ada." *Transactions of the Historical Society of Ghana*, New Series, no. 12: 1–34.

Lettow-Vorbeck, Paul von. 1920. *Heia Safari.* Leipzig: K.F. Koehler.

Lettow-Vorbeck, Paul von. No date. *My Reminiscences of East Africa.* Nashville: Battery Classics. Orig. German publication *Meine Erinnerugen aus Ostafrika.* Leipzig: Koehler, 1920.

Lunn, Joe. 1999. *Memoirs of the Maelstrom: A Senegalese Oral History of the First World War.* Portsmouth, NH: Heinemann.

Lunn, Joe. 2015. "War Losses (Africa)." In *1914–1918 Online. International Encyclopedia of the First World War*, ed. by Ute Daniel, Peter Gatrell, Oliver Janz, Heather Jones, Jennifer Keene, Alan Kramer, and Bill Nasson, issued by Freie Universität Berlin, Berlin 2015-06-22. DOI: 10.15463/ie1418.10668.

MacDonnell, Bror. 2006. *Mzee Ali: The Biography of an African Slave-Trader turned Askari and Scout*. Johannesburg: 30 Degrees South Publishers.

Manela, Erez. 2007. *The Wilsonian Moment: Self-Determination and the International Origins of Anticolonial Nationalism*. Oxford, UK: Oxford University Press.

Mass, Sandra. 2006. *Weisse Helden, schwarze Krieger: Zur Geschichte kolonialer Männlichkeit in Deutschland, 1918–1964*. Cologne: Böhlau.

Mbembe, Achille. 2017. *Critique of Black Reason*. Translated by Laurent Dubois. Durham, NC: Duke University Press.

Michels, Stefanie. 2009. Schwarze *deutsche Kolonialsoldaten: Mehrdeutige Repräsentationsräume und früher Kosmopolitismus in Afrika*. Bielefeld, Germany: transcript.

Moyd, Michelle. 2014. *Violent Intermediaries: African Soldiers, Conquest, and Everyday Colonialism*. Athens, OH: Ohio University Press.

Moyd, Michelle. 2017. "Gender and Violence." In *Gendering the First World War*, edited by Tammy Proctor and Susan Grayzel. Oxford, UK: Oxford University Press.

Moyd, Michelle. 2016. "Centring a Sideshow: local experiences of the First World War in Africa," *First World War Studies* 7, no. 2: 111–30.

Moyd, Michelle. "Resistance and Rebellions (Africa)," in *1914–1918 Online. International Encyclopedia of the First World War*, ed. by Ute Daniel, Peter Gatrell, Oliver Janz, Heather Jones, Jennifer Keene, Alan Kramer, and Bill Nasson, issued by Freie Universität Berlin, Berlin 2017-06-20. DOI: 10.15463/ie1418.11112.

Moyse-Bartlett, H. 1956. *The King's African Rifles: A Study in the Military History of East and Central Africa, 1890–1945*. Aldershot: Gale and Polden, Ltd.

Nasson, Bill. 2014. "British Imperial Africa," in *Empires at War: 1911–1923*. In *Empires at War*, edited by Robert Gerwarth and Erez Manela. Oxford, UK: Oxford University Press.

Njung, George. 2014. "West Africa." In *1914–1918 Online. International Encyclopedia of the First World War*, edited by Ute Daniel, Peter Gatrell, Oliver Janz, Heather Jones, Jennifer Keene, Alan Kramer, and Bill Nasson. Freie Universität Berlin. DOI: 10.15463/ie1418.10462.

Omissi, David. 1994. *The Sepoy and the Raj*. London: Macmillan.

Osuntokun, Akinjide. 1979. *Nigeria in the First World War*. Atlantic Highlands, NJ: Humanities Press.

Paice, Edward. 2014. "How the Great War Razed East Africa." Africa Research Institute.

Paice, Edward. 2007. *Tip and Run: The Untold Tragedy of the Great War in Africa*. London: Phoenix.

Parsons, Timothy. 1999. "'Wakamba warriors are soldiers of the Queen': The Evolution of the Kamba as a Martial Race, 1890-1970," *Ethnohistory* 46, no. 4: 671–701.

Pedersen, Susan. 2015. *The Guardians: The League of Nations and the Crisis of Empire*. Oxford: Oxford University Press.

Porch, Douglas. 2013. *Counterinsurgency: Exposing the Myths of the New Way of War*. Cambridge: Cambridge University Press,

Pradhan, S. D. 1991. *Indian Army in East Africa*. New Delhi: National Book Organization.

Pradhan, S. D. 1978. "Indians in the East African Campaign—A Case Study of Indian Experiences in the First World War." In *India and the First World War*, edited by DeWitt C. Ellinwood and S. D. Pradhan, 69–74. New Delhi: South Asia Books.

Pike, W. W. 1918. *Report on Medical and Sanitary Matters in German East Africa 1917*. Nairobi: Swift Press.

Ribeiro de Meneses, Filipe. 2014. "The Portuguese Empire." In Gerwarth and Manela, eds., *Empires at War*, 179–96. Oxford, UK: Oxford University Press.

Rigg, Jonathan. 2007. *An Everyday Geography of the Global South*. Abingdon, UK: Routledge.

Saltman, Julian. 2014. "'The Full and Just Penalty? British Military Justice and the Empire's War in Egypt and Palestine." In *Empires in World War I: Shifting Frontiers and Imperial Dynamics in a Global Context*, edited by Richard Fogarty and Andrew Jarboe. London: I. B. Tauris.

Seigel, Micol. 2005. "Beyond Compare: Comparative Method after the Transnational Turn." *Radical History Review*. Issue 91: 62–90.

Singha, Radhika. "Labour (India)." In *1914–1918 Online. International Encyclopedia of the First World War*, ed. by Ute Daniel, Peter Gatrell, Oliver Janz, Heather Jones, Jennifer Keene, Alan Kramer, and Bill Nasson, issued by Freie Universität Berlin, Berlin 2016-02-19. DOI: 10.15463/ie1418.10836.

Smith, Richard. 2004. *Jamaican Volunteers in the First World War: Race, Masculinity and the Development of National Consciousness*. Manchester, UK: Manchester University Press.

Smith, Richard. 2014. "Propaganda, Imperial Subjecthood and National Identity in Jamaica during the First World War." In *World War I and Propaganda*, edited by Troy R.E. Paddock, ed., 107–110. Leiden: Brill.

Smith, Richard. 2014. "World War I and the Permanent West Indian Soldier." In *Empires in World War I: Shifting Frontiers and Imperial Dynamics in a Global Context*. London: I.B. Tauris, 309–10

Stapleton, Timothy. 2003. "The Composition of the Rhodesia Native Regiment during the First World War: A Look at the Evidence." *History in Africa* 30: 283–95

Stapleton, Tim. 2007. "The Impact of the First World War on African People." In *Daily Lives of Civilians in Wartime Africa*, edited by John Laband. Westport, CT: Greenwood Press.

Stoler, Ann Laura and Carole McGranahan. 2007. "Introduction: Refiguring Imperial Terrains." In *Imperial Formations*, edited by Ann Laura Stoler, Carole McGranahan, and Peter C. Perdue, 3–42. Santa Fe: School for Advanced Research Press.

Strachan, Hew. 2004. *The First World War in Africa*. Oxford, UK: Oxford University Press.

Taute, M. 1939. "A German Account of the Medical Side of the War in East Africa, 1914–1918." *Tanganyika Notes and Records* 8

Thatcher, W.S. 2007. *The Fourth Battalion Duke of Connaught's Own Tenth Baluch Regiment in the Great War*. Uckfield, East Sussex, UK: The Naval and Military Press Ltd.

Werner, Michael and Bénédicte Zimmermann. "Beyond Comparison: Histoire Croisée and the Challenge of Reflexivity." 45, 1: 30–50.

Wolvers, Andrea, Oliver Tappe, Tijo Salverda, and Tobias Schwarz. 2015. "Introduction," *Concepts of the Global South: Voices from around the World*, Global South Studies Center, University of Cologne, Germany; http://gssc.uni-koeln.de/node/451, accessed 26 February 2017

Yorke, Edmund. 1990. "The Spectre of a Second Chilembwe: Government, Missions, and Social Control in Wartime Northern Rhodesia, 1914–18." *Journal of African History* 31, no. 3: 373–91.

Zimmerman, Andrew. 2010. *Alabama in Africa: Booker T. Washington, the German Empire, and the Globalization of the New South*. Princeton, NJ: Princeton University Press.

Tensions of Decolonization

Lebanon, West Africans, and a Color Line within the Global Color Line, May 1945

Maurice Jr. M. Labelle

Beirut was in a festive spirit, so much so that folks danced in the streets. Jubilation spread as news of Nazi Germany's surrender hit Lebanese airwaves. Victory in Europe, many nationalists felt, was first and foremost a victory for Lebanon and decolonization more broadly. Complete Lebanese sovereignty was finally in sight, as in late 1941 Free French authorities promised full constitutional independence once the guns fell silent in Europe. Lebanese people gathered on balconies, rooftops, as well as in public squares to celebrate the end of World War II in the imperial métropole, France. Fireworks lit Lebanon's dark skies. Lebanese president Bechara el-Khoury went as far as declaring May 8, 1945—Victory in Europe Day—a national holiday.[1]

Much apprehension rested beneath Lebanon's euphoria, however. A few days earlier, Charles de Gaulle's Provisional French Government (PFG) landed roughly 900 *tirailleurs sénégalais* without the consent of Lebanese authorities.[2] Paris appeared to be challenging Beirut's newfound sovereignty. Roughly one week after Victory in Europe, France deployed two more battalions of colonial infantrymen—or "Black" troops, as Lebanese nationalists and Western diplomats wrongfully referred to them—and, once again, failed to consult Lebanon. There was no rejoicing the second time around. Lebanese reactions were unanimous: Paris openly disregarded the decolonizing Lebanese nation-state by attempting to regain

Radical History Review
Issue 131 (May 2018)   DOI 10.1215/01636545-4355121
© 2018 by MARHO: The Radical Historians' Organization, Inc.

control of the transitioning mandate territory. Imperial France, it seemed, refused to consider postcolonial Lebanon as its equal. Worse yet, it sought to recolonize the Lebanese through the bodies of so-called inferior West Africans.

This article explores how a part of Lebanese society applied perceived racial differences with West Africans to process, cope with, and respond to France's volte-face during the fateful month of May 1945. Within the vast domain of Lebanese public opinion, a loose collection of nationalists dehumanized West Africans and critiqued French imperialism at the same time, publicly distancing their nation from empire, while simultaneously fomenting a social Darwinian rapprochement of sorts with the emerging United Nations–led liberal international system. These Lebanese invoked the politics and grammar of cultural difference to further engender a political process of decolonization. The presence of "Senegalese" in Lebanon rapidly became a space in which decolonial Lebanese (re)produced racial prejudices, projected Blackness and whiteness, and contested their own national differences with France and French West Africa—that is, the vast colony that spanned from Mauritania and Senegal to Niger. This group of Lebanese nationalists hybridized shades of Western and Ottoman-Arab imperial racial categorizations—which justified superiority over dark-skinned, sub-Saharan African peoples—with a mandate-bred "style of reasoning" to distinguish themselves from fellow colonized, non-Westerners and highlight the uncivilized barbarity of empire.[3] This politico-cultural intervention and its racial formations not only critiqued the duplicity of modern imperialism, empowering the Lebanese nation-state in the process, but it also unearthed the tensions embedded within decolonization itself.

The very tensions of empire that Lebanese nationalists criticized so heavily in May 1945 and well before—that is, the fact that "the otherness of colonized persons was neither inherent or stable; his or her difference had to be defined and maintained"—now rest at the core of both imperial and international historiographies.[4] Ideas of racial superiority undergirded the modern exercise of imperialism at home, abroad, and everywhere in between. It is also common historical knowledge that, for their part, non-Western peoples in disparate parts of the world forged a transnational consciousness in response to shared experiences of racial domination. Both collectively and separately, Africans, Asians, Latin Americans, Middle Easterners, as well as Indigenous North Americans and Oceanians followed in the footsteps of African American intellectual W. E. B. Du Bois, who famously asserted in 1900: "The problem of the twentieth century is the problem of the color line."[5] Eventually, more and more peoples of European descent in the world followed suit and continue to do so.

Yet ensuing narratives of racial confraternities, especially within the Global South, have resulted in an overpowering historical and historiographical "will to a color-blind account of solidarities" in the current era of decolonization. This article, therefore, contributes to nascent efforts that demystify the utopian racelessness within the ranks of anti-imperial internationalisms.[6] By exploring a frictional fault line within South-South relations, it complicates an essentialized global color line in the world, just like Du Bois did so eloquently in his less-recalled 1928 novel *Dark Princess*. Shortly following his inclusion amid the ranks of the Council of Darker Peoples, the novel's main protagonist Matthews Towns notes the exclusionary racial underpinnings *within* the non-Western, anti-imperial solidarity organization. The leading African American character experiences and unearths "plain and clear the shadow of a color line within a color line."[7] As Towns via Du Bois determined, the romance of anti-imperial solidarity amid "the colored world" overshadowed the tensions of decolonization and its many shades.[8] The Arab world and decolonial Lebanon, in particular, were no exception to this global tragedy, as the very color lines within the global color line have largely remained on the periphery of the globalization of decolonization.[9]

World War II and Lebanese Decolonization

The start of the process of formal, political decolonization in Lebanon dates to the French-Lebanese Treaty of 1936, which codified Lebanese national independence and League of Nations membership within three years, though it was never ratified by France. The Allied reoccupation of the Levant in the latter half of 1941 reopened the prospect of Lebanese decolonization. Upon regaining control of Lebanese territory from Vichy France, Free French leaders repeated the promise of independence to obtain popular allegiance for a struggling Allied war effort. Roughly a year later, in response to mounting Lebanese nationalist demands and expectations, the French National Committee reinstated the Lebanese constitution—devised during the interwar mandate period—and announced the holding of a national parliamentary election. The first in Lebanese history, this groundbreaking event produced a genuinely Lebanese-run government in late August 1943, led by President Bechara el-Khoury and Prime Minister Riad el-Solh. Beirut immediately announced its intention to legislate constitutional reform. Despite France's ongoing control of key national institutions, most notably the army, the Lebanese perceived that an apparently inevitable transfer of power was well under way. Lebanon, within its own teleology of national decolonization, no longer perceived itself as a colony.[10]

As Lebanese society soon found out, the French saw things differently. The French National Committee wholly opposed such constitutional amendments and opted, instead, to controversially turn back the clock on Lebanese decolonization. In the early hours of November 11, 1943, Free French authorities confronted Lebanese political leaders in the confines of their own bedrooms. The Lebanese president, prime minister, numerous cabinet ministers, as well as leading deputies and citizens were illegally taken from their homes, arrested, and imprisoned. Subsequently, the Lebanese constitution was once again suspended. As the sun rose and the news circulated around Lebanon, a national crisis ensued that ultimately spanned eleven days. Overwhelming protest from both Lebanese society and the Allied powers, most notably Britain and the United States, obliged the French National Committee to release the political prisoners and reinstate the recently elected Lebanese government in toto.[11]

As World War II continued, Franco-Lebanese relations were hereafter reoriented to proceed down the tenuous path of formal decolonization. Through ongoing vigorous negotiations, France hesitantly consented to the gradual transfer of administrative responsibilities to the Grand Sérail, or the Lebanese government headquarters. Ceremonial "flag independence" aside, the French National Committee maintained authority over the Land of Cedars.[12] Despite Lebanon baptizing November 22—that is, the last day of 1943 crisis— as national Independence Day, political decolonization was incomplete. French officials, once again, maintained that full independence would come only at the war's end. Lebanon, they deemed, was too strategically crucial to the contemporary Allied war effort.

This situation generated much tension between Lebanon and France. Whereas Lebanese nationalists perceived themselves as now being both politically and culturally equal to their former mandatory power, France simply did not. Negotiations concerning the transfer of the *troupes spéciales*, or Lebanese military forces directly under French command, became a central point of contention over hierarchy in Franco-Lebanese relations. Major Allied states, like the United States and the Soviet Union, as well as fellow Arab states, formally recognized Lebanon's status a sovereign nation-state. Lebanese society "regarded the possession of an Army as a formal attribute of independence." Franco-Lebanese discussions, however, "rapidly reached a deadlock."[13]

Lebanese state and society rejected the "imperialism of decolonization."[14] The French insistence that Lebanon separately grant them special privileges through a formal bilateral treaty—which would allow France to maintain some form of authority over Lebanon— engendered the diplomatic impasse. Paris demanded that such a treaty, which in many ways enforced French "informal empire" after complete Lebanese independence, preclude the transfer of the army. In the Lebanese Chamber of Deputies, Khoury declared that Lebanese independence "was a fait accompli." Solh followed suit, reassuring that "there was no question of reimposing [empire] through the form of a treaty." According to *Sawt al-Sha'b*, an influential Lebanese morning newspaper, the imperial rights outlined in a so-called special treaty with France "were incompatible with the national rights of Lebanon" and contradicted "its true sovereignty."[15]

The end of hostilities in Europe, many Lebanese concluded, would force France to relent its demand of special privilege. The Allied commitment to the declaration of the Atlantic Charter, which promoted the right of colonized peoples to self-determination, guaranteed it, as did the very language of the mandate system. Yet as war appeared to be ending in Europe, France refused to budge. Lebanon, in turn, formally declared war on the Axis powers and officially became a member of the United Nations. This action, many Lebanese concluded, protected Beirut from being coerced into a neoimperial contract with Paris. On the international level at least, the French and Lebanese nation-states stood side by side.[16]

Back in Paris, General Charles de Gaulle's regime conferred over the fate of its imperial place in Lebanon and privately discussed its postwar plan. De Gaulle insisted that the army in Lebanon stay under French command, at the very least until the departure of British troops stationed there since the Allied reoccupation of mid-1941. Above all, he considered it crucial that Lebanese territory remain at the disposal of France. Lebanon served as a strategic military site and, in de Gaulle's opinion, should eventually host French bases. This could not happen if Paris relented on its special privilege demand, transferred control of the army to the Lebanese government, and withdrew imperial troops. More troops, therefore, were needed to defend France's position in Lebanon and restore the French republic. He then ordered three additional battalions to Lebanon. French evidence unearths no trace of any serious, upper-level discussions of potential repercussions.[17]

A first battalion of French imperial troops departed immediately. Such a "provocative act" would not sit well with Lebanese society and the United Nations, whose contemporaneous conference in San Francisco publicly sought to establish a new international organization devoid of longstanding imperial machinations. London, unable to stymie the French initiative, demanded that Paris at the very least inform Beirut of the pending arrival of roughly 900 West African *tirailleurs*. Without soliciting Lebanese consent, French officials delivered the news on May 3. The Grand Sérail was incensed. The gesture contradicted the French promises of independence of 1941 *and* 1943. That very evening, Lebanese foreign minister Henri Pharaon failed "to disguise his feelings" in a meeting with British officials. The likelihood of popular demonstrations and town strikes was high, he confided, especially considering that the deployed French imperial troops were "Senegalese."[18]

Intracolonial relations between French-ruled Lebanese and West African peoples were fraught by cultural, and thus socio-political, tensions. From a Lebanese nationalist perspective during World War II, this shared inferior standing in the world held back Lebanon's decolonization. During the 400 or so years of Ottoman rule, Arabs politically, socially, and culturally often saw themselves as standing above West Africans in the incumbent order of things. The changing institution of slavery in the Mediterranean, which predated Ottoman times, alongside essentialist cultures of self-reinvention and empire-building in the face of Western imperialism in the late nineteenth century left a lasting imprint on the ways in which Ottoman Lebanese prejudicially perceived West Africans. Lebanese in the world commonly referred to the latter by the derogatory, dehumanizing monikers *zanuj/zanji* ("nigger") and *'abd/'abid* ("slave"), thus forging linkages between past bondages of slavery and the Western imperial present in the process.[19]

By the early twentieth century and the interwar establishment of French rule in the Levant, Lebanese society internalized a "superiority complex" of sort vis-à-vis West Africans by means of intercontinental migrations, Mediterranean economies, the globalization of Western imperial culture, the myriad unequal relationships it sanctioned, and the formation of a class "A" League of Nations mandate in post-Ottoman Lebanon.[20] Slightly elevated within the liberal international system and the powerful Darwinian pyramid of scientific racism, Lebanese perceived themselves as being situated higher than dark-skinned Africans. Global, modern ideas of race and racial differences between Arabs and sub-Saharan Africans, together with perceived different political standings between colonies and mandates within empires, informed the racialization of Lebanese nationalisms. Much like France, Lebanese society saw darker-skinned colonized peoples from sub-Saharan Africa through an imperial lens. Lebanese imperial ways of seeing commonly represented both "Senegalese" persons and the so-called Dark Continent as being barbarous, backward, savage, and uncivilized. Despite the formal political parameters established by the modern imperial politics of difference, Arabs saw themselves as being culturally better situated to climb the ladders of international race and state hierarchies, as well as overcome the global color line. As far as a group of Lebanese nationalists were concerned, this perceived superiority in relation to West Africans was supported by France's independence promises throughout World War II.[21]

West Africans *Tirailleurs* and the Lebanese Crisis of November 1943

The role and behavior of the *tirailleurs sénégalais* during the not-so-distant Lebanese crisis of November 1943 "left bitter memories" in decolonial Lebanese imaginations.[22] West Africans, as they had many times prior within the French empire and beyond, served as France's brazen foot soldiers during the imperial coup. In the early hours of November 11, 1943, they did most of the dirty work while French officers watched. The "Senegalese" reportedly "behaved with brutality" in the Lebanese president's home as they "broke doors, awoke and frightened [his] daughter," and physically "dragged [Khoury] out of bed where he had been sleeping with his wife." Laure el-Khoury reportedly stood outside her bedroom, "trembling, with one protecting arm flung around her daughter Huguette, as the Senegalese gaily plundered the house. Other soldiers were cheerfully slapping" her eldest seventeen-year-old son Khalil, "who had tried to reach his father's side." Elsewhere, West African troops stormed into the Lebanese prime minister's house and invaded his bedroom. Fayza el-Solh, "a strictly orthodox Moslem woman who never shows herself without a veil," watched as her husband was illegally detained. She was also forced to walk "about in her bare feet and in her nightdress" and nervously explained to British officers that "black troops invaded every room in the house including the maid's bedroom."[23] Other Lebanese cabinet ministers, political leaders, and their families suffered the same fate.

Such "Senegalese" conduct and imperialism's gendered intervention of pri
vate quarters, directed by French commanders, roused Lebanese society. Lebanese
nationalists responded by vociferously denouncing French recolonization. Beirut
was in "an uproar." At dawn, two Lebanese ministers who had escaped the rude
awakening rushed to the British embassy to deliver eyewitness testimonies of atrocities. A "terrified" Laure el-Khoury complained to the British that West African
troops surrounded her house: "Black troops were posted on all neighboring house-
tops and had been firing through windows," killing many innocent bystanders. Her
very doorstep, she lamented, "was running with blood."[24]

In step with French orders, West African troops reportedly established a
terrorizing presence throughout Beirut and the rest of Lebanon. Armed with guns,
they ousted a Lebanese speaker and six deputies who sought refuge in the Chamber of Deputies and symbolically cordoned off its doors to Lebanese society. Demonstrators were fired upon outside the Lebanese parliament, killing one child and
wounding many. The British embassy reported that "black troops," using tanks and
armed cars, "calmed" the Lebanese public. By the following day, they controlled
the streets. British reports revealed that, in the *Basta*, a populous Muslim quarter of
Beirut, West African *tirailleurs* lobbed "grenades into unarmed crowds" and "fired
on children going to school."[25]

Whereas many Lebanese demonstrated in public, a large group of Muslim
and Christian women opted to do so privately with British and US officers. Astonished, these women wondered how and why Free French officers unleashed the
"Senegalese" upon Lebanese society. Their presence offended the women delegation in more ways than one, as in transit to the British embassy, "they had been
grossly insulted by Senegalese who called them the foulest names in French." From
there, the group went to visit the US legation. "While they were waiting outside" to
speak directly with US minister to Lebanon George Wadsworth, two trucks of West
African *tirailleurs* "came up, got out . . . and trained machine guns, pistols and bayonets on the women." The US diplomatic representative, witnessing events unfold
from his office window, immediately stepped in and told them that "they could not
behave like that there." Pointing their pistols at him, the imperial troops "replied
that they did not care what building it was [since] their orders were to disperse any
crowd they saw." Bewildered, Wadsworth insisted that "many of the women t[ake]
refuge" in the US legation.[26]

Despite ongoing intimidation campaigns, Lebanese protests continued.
Unfortunately, so did French and West African reprisals. On the morning of November 13, 1943, "an orderly and unarmed" crowd of approximately fifty students from
the American University of Beirut quietly gathered across the street from the US
legation's main gate. They were met by a detachment of imperial troops "of all
colours from white to black," which "advanced down the street with fixed bayonets

and opened fire at five yards [from] the crowd who had, on seeing them, begun to sing the Lebanese National Anthem." The incident produced ten casualties.[27]

The public West African presence grew as the November 1943 crisis unfolded. Imperial troops regularly patrolled the streets of Beirut, as well as other major cities like Saida and Tripoli. Lebanese casualties, in turn, mounted. "Feelings [were] running high. . . . The shooting down of innocent crowds was producing an ugly temper," explained Mgr. Ignace Moubarak, the Maronite Archbishop of Beirut, to British officers. Incidents continued unabated. On November 15, "an orderly procession of schoolboys [walked through] the town [of Tripoli] when it was suddenly met by . . . Senegalese who charged the crowd[,] opening fire with their machine-guns at point blank range." Eight Lebanese children died and twenty-four were injured. In its report, the British embassy explained that "eyewitness accounts state[d] that Senegalese troops were quite out of hand and that there was not the slightest provocation from the crowd."[28]

West African aggressions only ended once Free French officials reinstated the Lebanese government and Khoury, Solh, and others returned to their homes. Despite this victory in the ongoing struggle for Lebanese decolonization and the raising of a new national flag, French-commanded "Senegalese" actions during the November 1943 crisis imprinted Lebanese public memory. Per a British official in Beirut, "one lesson emerged clearl[y]" from this bloody episode: "French colonial troops are completely unsuitable for us in contact with a civil population." Any future deployment of West African forces by the French to Lebanon would surely provoke another crisis.[29]

The Lebanese Crisis of May 1945

Many in Beirut begrudged De Gaulle's decision to send more West Africans to Lebanon at World War II's end. The "Senegalese" landing, a local French officer warned Paris, "would provoke a grave crisis."[30] On May 6, 1945, a first battalion set foot on the docks of the Lebanese capital. Henri Pharaon, the Lebanese foreign minister, immediately extended his protest in a private meeting with French officials. The war in Europe was almost over, he insisted. No internal security threats existed in Lebanon. More French imperial troops were unnecessary. "The political situation had completely changed [and] a sovereign state could not accept to abandon its sovereignty for military matters," he contended. The initiative, a French officer coldly responded, "was not up for debate." Thereafter, it was clear to everyone in Beirut that Lebanon lost all faith in the "good intentions" of France. The Lebanese government "now firmly believed that [the] French are seeking to spin matters out until they can build upon enough forces . . . to cow them into accepting . . . the re-establishment of French hegemony there."[31]

Word of a fresh arrival of "Senegalese" *tirailleurs* slowly found its way into the Lebanese public sphere. Despite the press's initial silence, due in large part to French censorship, numerous handbills circulated throughout Beirut, announcing the pending return of West African soldiers, surely exhuming traumatic nationalist memories of November 1943.[32] One Arabic pamphlet read: "Why are the French doing this?" The increased presence of West African *tirailleurs* exacerbated nationalist fears that "many others were on the way." Many Lebanese complained that France "did not win the war anyway," saying that they did not win it over us." Paris, they believed, "had no intention of releasing their hold on" Lebanon. The Lebanese press, once it engaged with this issue, expressed its utter objection regarding French recolonization, albeit couching it in rather gentle ways to avoid censorship. *Beirut*, Lebanon's most popular Arabic daily, openly asked: "Hasn't France already acknowledged our independence and hasn't it already set limits to this hateful mandate?"[33]

Once again, the political tensions of decolonization were high; the cultural ones between Lebanon, the French mandate, and West African troops boiled below the surface, at least for the time being. Lebanon's conflict with West Africans was predominantly justified in political terms rather than cultural ones. The Lebanese Chamber of Deputies met as Victory in Europe celebrations dissipated. The president of the Lebanese foreign affairs committee immediately tabled a matter that greatly preoccupied Lebanese state and society: the arrival of "Senegalese" *tirailleurs*. A bombardment of questions for the Lebanese government ensued. What exactly "was the purpose of their arrival in Lebanon?" Would others follow suit in the near future? Had Beirut "asked all the Allies that no soldiers hereafter be brought to Lebanon except with the approval of the Lebanese government?" And given that the war in Europe was now over, had it "taken the necessary measures for the departure of Allied armies from Lebanese territory?" The deployment of West African troops, one member asserted, "came at a time when, with the end of the war, everyone was hoping to see the independence of small nations augmented."[34]

Henri Pharaon replied that the Lebanese government officially opposed the French "re-enforcement" and insisted that the movement of Allied troops to Lebanese territory required and solely depended upon its approval. "Lebanon is an independent and sovereign state," Pharaon proclaimed, "and in its firm will, [it] takes the only attitude which is taken by every independent country. . . . Lebanon's sovereignty will be respected on all occasions and circumstances. . . . We have made the strengthening of Lebanon's independence our supreme objective," added the Lebanese foreign minister, "that we may live free and dignified in the shelter of sovereignty and honor." After further discussion, the Lebanese Chamber of Deputies unanimously supported the government's position.[35]

The following morning, the Lebanese press did not hold back commentaries. Imperial France's latest military intervention, embodied mainly by West Africans, disrespected Lebanese human dignity and territorial sovereignty. Lebanon's public sphere, for the time being, politically targeted France. The recent arrival of "Senegalese" *tirailleurs* filled the pages of Beirut's leading newspapers, such as the liberal *An-Nahar* and *Al-Hadaf*, the party organ of *An-Najjada*, a popular Muslim youth movement in Lebanon. And this time around, many Lebanese newspapers either circumvented or bluntly disregarded censorship. According to *Ad-Diyar*, "Lebanese owe it to themselves to prevent [French recolonization] from taking place" and should "adopt a more energetic attitude." "Imperialism" and its guardians, the West Africans, its editor Hanna Ghosn elaborated the following day, "would not strangle" the liberty out of Lebanon. It was time for France to drastically change its imperial *mentalité*. Its *mission civilisatrice*, many concluded, no longer applied to Lebanon. Lebanon, asserted *Beirut*'s Muhieddine Nsouli a few days later, "will not accept colonialism anymore."[36]

Meanwhile, French Commander-in-Chief in the Levant General Étienne-Paul-Émile-Marie Beynet returned to Beirut following a lengthy sojourn in Paris. His extensive leave generated much suspicion, as many feared that the PFG was plotting to recolonize Lebanon. Beynet's reappearance meant that Franco-Lebanese negotiations concerning "the liquidation of the mandate" would resume. A special privilege treaty, Lebanese nationalists firmly believed, was out of the question. Yet they could not help but wonder, given the increase in West Africans troops in Lebanon, whether "the French may attempt a coup d'état to reestablish their formal position, if they cannot get what they want through negotiations." One thing was for certain: "National feeling" ran high in Lebanon.[37]

It was within this atmosphere that news spread concerning the upcoming landing in Beirut of a second wave of French imperial troops.[38] On the morning of May 17, *Beirut* ignored censorship restrictions and falsely racialized the pending arrivals. Its headline Blackened French imperialism as it read: "More Senegalese troops will arrive shortly in Lebanon and install themselves." The Lebanese nation-state, it alluded, was once again at risk of imperial and racial savagery.[39] Shortly before noon, the *Jeanne d'Arc*, carrying six hundred French imperial troops, landed at the port of Beirut. These forces, contrary to Lebanese press reports, were not dark-skinned, sub-Saharan "Senegalese" *tirailleurs*; rather, they were "white" *zouaves* from France.[40]

The Lebanese public sphere racialized the French military presence. Dark-skinned West Africans epitomized the Blackness of French imperialism in decolonial Lebanese imaginations. The Lebanese Chamber of Deputies, which held an emergency session in light of the landing, unanimously agreed that the arrival of more "black" imperial troops was nothing but "a strike against the independence of Lebanon."[41] In a speech, Khalil Abou Jawdeh, a deputy from Mount Lebanon, denounced the increasing "Senegalese" presence in Lebanon, which the French claimed was merely replacing outgoing troops. Jawdeh insisted that more imperial troops set foot off the *Jeanne d'Arc* than its predecessor. Jawdeh's suspicion proved true, according to a US investigation, which claimed that although incoming troops were not "black," they were secretly scheduled to exceed reinforcement by four hundred troops.[42] In light of the new arrivals, Lebanese society undertook a nationwide general strike. On May 18, all shops were closed in protest. Myriad forms of demonstrations arose with the sun and Lebanese rapidly made their opposition heard.[43]

The public sphere further sowed seeds that racialized the political process of Lebanese decolonization. A group of Lebanese nationalists, in the name of liberal anti-imperialism, insistently invoked the politics and grammar of difference between themselves, West Africans, and imperial France. These decolonial Lebanese struck back at imperialism with race-thinking and, once again, critiqued imperial France's hierarchical perception of self in the world; this time, however, it was to the direct detriment of West African dignity.

In a sarcastic nod to racial solidarity against imperialism, *Ad-Diyar*'s Ghosn welcomed the "Senegalese brothers." This "humanitarian mission" enlisted West Africans to carry out Paris's infamous *mission civilisatrice*. "Our black friends," the newspaper read, "will impose upon us a 'special' friendship with France." These "brothers are welcomed among us because they represent the symbol of liberty and consist of the interpreters of the sentiments of our traditional friends," the French. This West African affront baffled Ghosn, as the "Senegalese" chose empire over racial anti-imperial solidarity. He openly asked: "Are we not part of the Eastern people that are backward and is it not a shame for people like us to stay uncivilized in today's world?" Do Lebanese want to open "their eyes to the sun of a new era, the era of civilization and freedom, the era of peace, the era of equality between the strong and the weak, the era of the abolishment of racism?" What about France? Had it not fought a global war against fascism to eradicate racism? According to *Ad-Diyar*'s leading editorialist, the French deployment of West Africans empowered the infamous global color line.[44]

It was at this moment in May 1945—a watershed political moment in world history, embodied by the creation of the United Nations—that a color line *within* the global color line briefly took center stage in the Lebanese public sphere. The "Senegalese" *tirailleurs*, many Lebanese nationalists contended, represented the very barbarism and liberal backwardness of French imperialism. Pamphlets propagating this message rapidly appeared in vast numbers throughout Beirut. One of these, addressed to Lebanese students, read: "Today the French are threatening our form of Government and hurting the feelings of your people by bringing in Senegalese soldiers without our Government knowing it and without their permission." France's objective was "by force to strengthen their mandate and steal the freedom which is the right of the Lebanese by the blood of their martyrs."[45] Lebanese demonstrations subsequently rose to unprecedented levels. Popular antipathy vis-à-vis the so-called barbarous Black presence worsened.

The *Ligue d'action nationale*, an influential Lebanese political organization, distributed pamphlets that reified historical prejudices toward West African
tirailleurs, the front-line, imagined representatives of French imperial savagery and
empire's Blackness, historically associated in the Eastern Mediterranean with sub-
Saharan servitude.[46] The Lebanese "nation," it read, in its glorious past "had taught
men the principles of civilization, while the lords of the Senegalese were still at
the same stage of evolution as the Senegalese of today." Lebanon, the pamphlet
asserted, "should not be afraid of Senegalese troops."[47]

Elsewhere, the Lebanese Arabian Women's Union, encompassing thirty
women's associations, submitted a petition to both the British embassy and the US
legation. The themes of fear and violence, embedded in tropes of Blackness, ran
through the text and were best captured by its opening sentence: "Yesterday the
peoples of the world have laid their hopes upon a newly born freedom, today they
are being choked by France," or more specifically, its "Senegalese force." The petition would go on to declare that World War II, unlike World War I, "must not end
by the oblivion of promise and the use of sheer power for the purporting of obsolete
imperialistic designs." The organization insisted that the French withdraw all forces
immediately, especially the apparently barbarous West Africans, and that Lebanese
decolonization be fulfilled.[48]

On May 21, as the *Jeanne d'Arc* sailed off with fewer troops than it had
brought, Lebanon unilaterally abrogated treaty negotiations with the PFG. Lebanese students displayed solidarity with the Grand Sérail and organized more protests against French imperialism, notably targeting the West African presence. Some
opted to do so via the silent and symbolic expression of mandated school shutdowns.
Others, however, took part in a large peaceful demonstration in the streets of Beirut.

Students from the American University of Beirut, *Al-Makassed*, and other
schools sang the Lebanese anthem as they made their way to the Lebanese parliament.[49] Along the way, pamphlets were distributed to onlookers. The march's
peaceful nature was not reflected in student handouts, which directly dehumanized
West African *tirailleurs* and racialized French imperialism. Lebanese violence took
cultural forms by stressing the "Senegalese" presence, even though French *zouaves*
matched the latter in Lebanon. While contending that it was their own dignity that
was under attack by imperialism, a group of Lebanese nationalists reciprocated in
race-thinking toward the so-called dark, Black presence in their midst. These various messages, while indirectly mocking France's *mission civilisatrice*, mimicked a
longstanding imperial way of seeing that hybridized the legacy of the Ottoman-Arab
slave trade, scientific racism in the world, and the French "imperialist superiority
complex."[50]

More specifically, Lebanese nationalists enforced the historically demeaning
epithet "slave," juxtaposed it with contemporary ideas based on social Darwinian
racial hierarchy to describe the "Black" West African presence in their midst, and

further racialized French imperialism. Empire, a pamphlet read, "wanted to beat down Lebanon, alongside those weak peoples that we sell and buy and" and that are "govern[ed] by negroes." Like West Africans, "it believed that [Lebanon] had the character of a slave that did not revolt for its dignity and was not irritated by provocations." Imperial France attempted to provoke Lebanon on multiple occasions, but failed. The latest wave of "Senegalese" would suffer the same fate. In a statement delivered before the Chamber of Deputies, Adel Osseiran, a deputy for southern Lebanon, echoed the students' core message. The French, he declared, "pretend to be the liberators of peoples, yet they send Senegalese soldiers to enslave us." Lebanon, he insisted, refused to be enslaved like colonized West Africans; rather, it deserved to sit at the table of fully independent nation-states alongside France. Lebanon already earned its freedom, unlike the obedient "Senegalese."[51]

At this juncture in May 1945, Lebanon sat at the historical crossroads of imperialism and decolonization. The politico-cultural tensions inherent in Lebanese decolonization failed to dissipate. As the Franco-Syrian situation worsened in neighboring Damascus, many Lebanese feared the worst: more "Senegalese."[52] Lebanese students, in turn, distributed posters that depicted a monstrous, near-naked, and "backward" West African soldier. Armed with a bayonet, the "savage," bare-footed giant sported an oversized loop earing on one ear and a mere diaper-looking garment on the remainder his body. His facial features showcased historical stereotypes of dark-skinned Africans: "corkscrew hair, broad noses, and wide lips."[53] The towering "Black" West African presence clouded Lebanon, threatening helpless, "white" Lebanese youth at his feet. Meanwhile, bourgeois, Western-dressed, and politically composed Lebanese adult onlookers frowned and raised their noses at the West Africans.

This telling representation invoked gender and class to buttress racial and national differences between decolonial Lebanese and colonized West Africans, as well as similarities with France. It projected a skewed, "progressive" image of Lebanese in the world. With her hands firmly placed on her hips, a defiant, fearless, modern-looking, light-skinned woman stands in disgust beneath the primitive-looking West African soldier and his bayonet. Two other matronly women with similar demeanors appear by her side along the front lines. Behind them, a man calmly smokes a cigarette with his hands in pocket. Farther in the background, another man symbolically wearing an Ottoman fez looks on calmly in disfavor—all the while the threatening West African soldier appears to be barking orders. The bottom caption of the pamphlet began in Arabic: "You have witnessed . . . the messenger of progress, or the [user] of the famous expression." Underneath the Arabic script, a bigger and bolder French text read the beastly, defaming statement: "Me civilize you!" The nationalist weekly *As-Sayyad* later reprinted the dehumanizing representation in its pages.[54]

The global politics of difference were on full display. Other Lebanese nationalist newspapers adopted similar a line, further exacerbating the tensions of decolonization through its cultural critique of empire. In an op-ed, *Sawt al-Sha'b* declared that "it was time for the elements of tyranny and imperialism . . . to understand that it was impossible to colonize" Lebanon and "enslave it." This, decolonial Lebanese imaginations thought, was anticivilizational. In the pages of *Ad-Diyar*, Lebanese lawyer Ibrahim Shoukayn expressed contradictory amazement toward France. Lebanese peoples approached it "with the language of international relations and the natural right to fix their own fate and enjoy their own sovereignty," he stated, yet "it responds with the language of black animals and bayonets of despots. We wished their liberation but it wishes humiliation and enslavement." France, through colonized West Africans, betrayed the anti-imperial promise that inspired the creation of a new international system around the recently victorious United Nations: freedom over slavery.[55] According to this racialized way of seeing, Beirut was on one side of the liberal binary and Paris was on the other, alongside West Africans.

On May 27, civil order fell apart in neighboring Syria. As bloody clashes between Syrian and French imperial troops unfolded, Lebanon watched on with "some popular excitement" and pondered its own political fortune. In protest, Lebanon and Syria collectively presented a statement opposing French actions to the founding United Nations conference in San Francisco, which stressed the racialized savagery and Blackness of empire. The joint declaration presented to the international arena explained how the current crisis in the Levant came to be and claimed that it was instigated by the French deployment of "Senegalese troops . . . immediately upon their arrival." Lebanese and Syrian representatives declared to the world community, "The Senegalese proved a constant source of provocation to both the people and the national forces of the two countries." Lebanese and Syrian peoples could not stand idly by, as the "Senegalese fired on the unarmed public, killing and wounding scores in Beirut . . . and many other towns."[56] Lebanon's globalizing anticivilizational critique of French imperialism, which ironically invoked an imperial way of seeing in order to dehumanize West Africans, now exceeded its geographical borders and those of the Middle East, crisscrossing both the national and the international as well as the racial politics of inclusion and exclusion in the process.

In spite of this, France held its ground and opted to drop "bombs on and machine-gun" Damascus. Lebanese society, in turn, called for a new, five-day general strike.[57] Political commentator Abdallah Machnoul published a discriminatory article in *As-Sayyad*, entitled "Deliver us from the Negroes." Lebanon, Machnoul contended, "went on strike to protest the arrival of the methods of black civilization" and its backwardness. From there, invoking the prejudiced idea of Black peril, he outlined a conversation with his daughter. "My darling," his piece read, "the French disembarked some Negroes with white teeth and they have asked us" through force "to love them . . . and if we do not love them, they will release the Negroes against us and eat us."[58] Lebanon here represented white virtue in the face of the peril of a racialized French imperialism. This politico-cultural claim, according to Machnoul, further evidenced the righteousness of a fully independent Lebanese nation-state in both popular imaginations and the world and identified paradoxical borders between empire and decolonization.

Such currents rapidly caught the attention of Allied powers and engulfed the attention of the globe. "Apart from their direct effect on the situation throughout the Near East," complained US secretary of state Edward Stettinius, Jr., "the events in Lebanon are seriously disturbing the atmosphere of the San Francisco Conference." The Levant crisis served as the first test of the postwar so-called antiracial liberal international system; it could not spoil this momentous event. In a "very strong" note addressed to the United Nations conference, which caught France's attention, Washington publicly denounced French actions and insisted that Paris withdraw its imperial troops from both Lebanon and Syria. "The situation was so serious," the US secretary of state reported, "that some of the Arabs were coming to the point where they were considering rejecting" the United Nations Charter itself.[59]

Britain, for its part, did not fail to waste any time and undertook a military intervention of its own in Syria, landing troops at the shores of Beirut in the morning of June 1. This move ended the Levant crisis of May 1945 and successfully returned the tensions of Lebanese decolonization to behind the scenes for the time being, while resolving an international crisis at the United Nations. By the end of June, United Nations member-states imprinted their signatures on the organization's charter. The UN Charter's preamble, alongside Chapter One, clearly outlined the body's commitment to the principles of self-determination, human rights, and universal equality. Meanwhile, West Africans gradually disappeared from the Lebanese public sphere as France's total imperial withdrawal wrapped up in late December 1946.

Conclusion

As Lebanon's five-day general strike ended, Khoury hosted US Minister Wadsworth. The Lebanese president reiterated his country's desire to witness a complete French evacuation as well as full national independence. Laure el-Khoury echoed her husband and directed Wadsworth's gaze toward "a tranquil residential district adjoining the [presidential] garden." The area symbolically hosted "a Senegalese barrack." The burgeoning flower that was Lebanon, she intimated, was under the constant watchful eye of French imperialism and its supposedly barbarous guardians. In more ways than one, the West African presence was "a continuing public nuisance" and threatened Lebanese nationhood. Lebanon, Khoury explained to Wadsworth, perceived the imperial troops "today as 'little less than a national humiliation,'" a black stain. Lebanese peoples, she insisted, deserved better.[60] They were different than West Africans.

In May 1945, a strain of Lebanese public opinion clearly drew a color line within the global color line. Tensions of decolonization served as an anti-imperial strategy. Lebanese nationalists chose to racialize decolonization both in language and visual representation by dehumanizing colonized West Africans to critique French imperialism, empowering themselves and their nation in the process. Modern ideas of race, politico-cultural hierarchy in the world, and historical prejudices vis-à-vis West Africans informed and fueled the final stage in the political process of Lebanese decolonization. Lebanese racism went hand in hand with anti-imperialism and the birth of a self-governing nation-state, at the expense of another colonized peoples during a pivotal moment in both global affairs and the decolonization of the world. Skin pigmentation and the myth of race aside, decolonial Lebanon racialized both French imperialism and its subaltern foot soldiers at the same time and in the same place.[61] Transracial solidarity and considerations of its consequences for colonized West Africans fell beyond the purview of this group of Lebanese nationalists, much like tensions of empire and the May 1945 military intervention had with French imperialists.

Shades of imperial culture, therefore, broke down the imagined walls between colonized and colonizer, while simultaneously parting the nascent "color curtain" of anti-imperial internationalisms, overshadowing confraternities in South-South relations, and darkening a romanticized teleology of decolonization.[62] Five years or so after the formal advent of Lebanese decolonization, imperial scholar George Balandier rightly asserted that, "for what amounts to an essentially racist reason, the colored man is rejected both by the colonial power and by the colonial peoples themselves."[63] Lebanese decolonization, in this instance, rejected empire's political structure but not its ways of thinking, seeing, and being. Ambiguous national identities, whether they were in imperial métropoles, its colonies, or transitioning pseudocolonized/decolonizing nation-states, were anchored in the politics of difference.[64]

Transnational racisms and their superiority complexes, differences aside, thus connected decolonial Lebanon to fellow Western member-states of the United Nations, serving as further evidence that the newly established international body ultimately sanctioned imperialism and its prejudicial cultures at its creation in May 1945.[65] A collection of decolonial Lebanese, at the same time as imperial France, invoked notions of inclusion and exclusion in an attempt to better situate themselves within the upper class of nations in the world. The (re)production of bigoted knowledge thus flowed not only between imperial métropoles; it also traveled between colonizers, colonized, and decolonizers, to the detriment of humanity. Consequent areas and moments of friction—whether in the global color line, or a color line within the global color line—evidenced the blurry borders between decolonization and empire in the postcolonial era.

Maurice Jr. M. Labelle is an assistant professor of history at the University of Saskatchewan in Canada. Articles of his have been published in *Diplomatic History*, the *Journal of Global History*, and *International History Review*. Labelle's current book project explores how postcolonial Lebanon came to identify the United States as an imperial power in the Middle East.

Notes

This essay originated in the 2012 International Seminar on Decolonization, hosted at the Library of Congress. I am forever indebted to the seminar leaders and my fellow seminarians for their constructive criticisms and moral support, most notably Roger Louis, Philippa Levine, Dane Kennedy, Jason Parker, Michael Collins, Elisabeth Leake, Daniel Haines, and Brian McNeil. I would also like to thank my University of Saskatchewan colleague Lesley Biggs for her sharp insights and editorial eye. All mistakes are solely my own.

1. 1945. *Sawt al-Sha'b*, May 9, 5; and Déclaration, 7 juin 1945; Carton 4H373; Dossier 2; Service historique de la Défense, Château de Vincennes [Henceforth, SHD].

2. The *Tirailleurs sénégalais* were not strictly from the French colony of Senegal. This label generally referred to all French colonial troops stemming from the federation of French West Africa. Fogarty, *Race and War in France*, ix.

3. Wheatley, "Mandatory Interpretation," 223.

4. Cooper and Stoler, eds. *Tensions of Empire*, 7.

5. Du Bois, *The Souls of Black Folk*, 9.

6. Burton, *Brown over* Black, 14; Lee, *Making a World After* Empire; McHale, "Understanding the Fanatical Mind?"; Troutt Powell, *A Different Shade of Colonialism*; and Vitalis, "The Midnight Ride." For more examples of non-Western populations using ideas of race to denigrate a different non-Western population during processes of political and cultural decolonization, see Brennan, *Taifa*; Desai and Vahed, *The South African* Gandhi; Uchida, *Brokers of Empire*; and Weinstein, *The Color of Modernity*.

7. Du Bois, *Dark Princess*, 22. For an analysis, see Bhabha, "The Black Servant and the Dark Princess."

8. Scott, *Conscripts of* Modernity, 7–8. The idea of "the colored world" was outlined in Stoddard's *The Rising Tide of Color*.

9. For transnational histories of Arab solidarity with nonwhite peoples, see Byrne, *Mecca of Revolution*; Chamberlin, *The Global Offensive*; Feldman, *A Shadow over Palestine*; Lubin, *Geographies of Liberation*; Nassar, "'My Struggle Embraces Every Struggle'"; and Takriti, *Monsoon Revolution*.

10. PIC Paper No. 28 (Revised), September 4, 1944. FO 226/253, National Archives of the United Kingdom, Kew [Henceforth, NA].

11. Zisser, *Lebanon*.

12. Hopkins, "Rethinking Decolonization."

13. PIC Paper No. 28 (Revised), September 4, 1944. FO 226/253, NA; and "Political Review of Syria and Lebanon for 1945," September 4, 1944. FO 371/52909/8746, NA.

14. Louis and Robinson, "The Imperialism of Decolonization."

15. "Revue de la presse libanaise," 15 Novembre 1944. Beyrouth, Ambassade, Série B, Carton 2054, Nantes, Ministère des affaires étrangères [Henceforth, MAE]; "Revue de la presse libanaise," 17 Novembre 1944. Beyrouth, Ambassade, Série B, Carton 2054, Nantes, MAE; "Newspapers in the Lebanon and Syria," March 6, 1943. RG 226, Intelligence Reports, 1941–45. Box 297, National Archive and Records Administration of the United States,

College Park [Henceforth, NARA], 1944; *Sawt al-Sha'b*, November 17, 1; and "Newspapers in the Lebanon and Syria," March 6, 1943. RG 226, Intelligence Reports, 1941–45, Box 297, NARA.

16. "Monthly Political Review—February 1945," March 31, 1945, RG 59, Central Decimal File, 1945–49, Box 7202, NARA; and "Political Summary, Lebanon, 25 February to 15 March 1945," March 24, 1945, RG 208, Informational File on the Near East 1941–46, Box 426, NARA.

17. Réunion, 5 Avril 1945. Syrie-Liban, Carton 6, Dossier 7, La Courneuve, MAE.

18. Foreign Office to Beirut, May 1, 1945. FO 226/298/249, NA; and Note, 5 Mai 1945. Syrie-Liban, Carton 6, Dossier 7, La Courneuve, MAE.

19. Arsan, *Interlopers of Empire*; Minawi, *The Ottoman Scramble for Africa*; Troutt-Powell, *A Different Shade of Colonialism*; and Weiss, "'Don't Throw Yourself Away to the Dark Continent.'"

20. Balibar and Wallerstein, *Race, Nation*, Class, 43.

21. Arsan, *Interlopers of Empire*; Elshakry, *Reading Darwin*; El Shakry, *The Great Social Laboratory*; Gualtieri, *Between Arab and White*; Schayegh and Arsan, *The Routledge Handbook of the History of Middle East Mandates*; and Wheatley, "Mandatory Interpretation."

22. Communiqué, May 5, 1945. RG 84, Beirut, Classified General Records, 1936–1961, Box 13, NARA.

23. Souki, *Middle Eastern Memories*, 1; Spears, *Fulfilment of a Mission*, 232; and Beirut to Foreign Office, November 11, 1943. FO 226/245/94, NA.

24. Beirut to Foreign Office, November 11, 1943. FO 226/245/94, NA.

25. Beirut to Foreign Office, November 12, 1943. FO 226/245/94, NA; and Beirut to Foreign Office, 11 November 1943. FO 226/245/94, NA.

26. Beirut to Foreign Office, November 12, 1943. FO 226/245/94, NA

27. Tueni, *Le livre de l'indépendance*, 64, 76; Beirut to Foreign Office, November 13, 1943. FO 226/245/94, NA; and Beirut to Foreign Office, November 14 1943. FO 226/245/94, NA.

28. Spears, *Fulfilment of a Mission*, 239; Beirut to Foreign Office, November 14, 1943. FO 226/245/94, NA; and Beirut to Foreign Office, November 15, 1943. FO 226/245/94, NA.

29. Beirut to Foreign Office, November 23, 1943. FO 226/245/94, NA; and Beirut to Foreign Office, November 24, 1943. FO 226/245/94, NA.

30. Note, 5 Mai 1945. Syrie-Liban, Carton 6, Dossier 7, La Courneuve, MAE.

31. Beirut to Foreign Office, May 7, 1945. FO 226/298, NA.

32. After regaining control of Lebanon in late 1941, French and British military authorities imposed strict censorship on the Lebanese press. After the November 1943 crisis, this censorship was loosened and partially handed over to Lebanese authorities. In January 1945, the Lebanese government increasingly weakened the French and British powers concerning press censorship, yet the latter retained some powers. For more on the Lebanese press during the 1940s, see Mellow, *The Making of Arab News*, 31; and Rugh, *The Arab Press*, 94–96. "Monthly Political Review—December 1944," January 24, 1945. RG 59, Central Decimal File, 1945–49, Box 7202, NARA; and "Monthly Political Review—January 1945," February 17,1945. RG 59, Central Decimal File, 1945–49, Box 7202, NARA.

33. Appel, 6 Mai 1945. Carton 4H373, Dossier 2, SHD; "The Incidents of May 10th, 1945," May 10, 1945. RG 84, Beirut, Supplemental General Records, 1944–45, Box 1, NARA; "The V-E Day Incident," June 7, 1945. RG 84, Beirut, Classified General Records, 1936–1961, Box 15, NARA; and 1945. *Beirut*, May 8, 2.

34.   Dower, *War Without Mercy*, 17.

35.   "Sitting of the Chamber, May 8, 1945," May 18, 1945. RG 84, Beirut, Classified General Records, 1936–1961, Box 13, NARA.

36.   1945. *Beirut*, May 9, 1; "Revue de la presse libanaise," 9 Mai 1945. Beyrouth, Ambassade, Série B, Carton 2094, Nantes, MAE; 1945. *An-Nahar*, May 11, 1; "Revue de la presse libanaise," 11 Mai 1945. Beyrouth, Ambassade, Inventaire 14, Carton 2094, Nantes, MAE; "Revue de la presse libanaise," 12 Mai 1945. Beyrouth, Ambassade, Série B, Carton 2094, Nantes, MAE; and 1945. *Beirut*, May 16, 1.

37.   1945. *The Eastern Times*, May 13, 2; "Revue de la presse libanaise," 15 Mai 1945. Beyrouth, Consulat, Fonds B, Carton 28, Nantes, MAE; and Henderson to Grew, May 16, 1945. RG 59, Subject Files, 1920–1954; Box 12, NARA.

38.   Beirut to Aleppo, May 15, 1945. FO 226/298/249, NA.

39.   1945. *Beirut*, May 17, 1.

40.   The *Zouaves* were a French infantry regiment formed by "white" French men. Prior to the Crimean War, colonized North Africans composed the regiment. Hopkins, "Sons and Lovers"; Note, May 17, 1945. RG 84, Beirut, Classified General Records, 1936–1961, Box 13, NARA; and D. W. Lockard to State, "The Crisis in Syria and Lebanon, May 1945," June 10, 1945. RG 84, Beirut, Classified General Records, 1936–1961, Box 13, NARA.

41.   17 Mai 1945, Syrie-Liban, Carton 6, Dossier 3, La Courneuve, MAE.

42.   Wadsworth to Secretary of State, May 17, 1945. RG 59, Central Decimal File, 1945–1949, Box 7203, NARA.

43.   D. W. Lockard to State, "The Crisis in Syria and Lebanon, May 1945," June 10, 1945. RG 84, Beirut, Classified General Records, 1936–1961, Box 13, NARA.

44.   "Revue de la presse libanaise," 18 Mai 1945. Beyrouth, Ambassade, Série B, Carton 2094, Nantes, MAE; "Analysis of Press Summary, week ending 21 May 45," May 29, 1945. RG 208, Informational File on the Near East, 1941–1946, Box 426, NARA; 1945. *Beirut*, May 18, 1; and 1945. *Ad-Diyar*, May 19, 1–2.

45.   "Monthly Political Review—May 1945," July 6, 1945. RG 59. Central Decimal File, 1945–49, Box 7202, NARA; and Pamphlet, May 18, 1945, FO 226/298/249, NA.

46.   Walz and Cuto, *Race and Slavery*, 8.

47.   "Revue de la presse libanaise," 19 Mai 1945. Beyrouth, Ambassade, Série B, Carton 2094, Nantes, MAE; and Beynet à Bidault, 28 Mai 1945. Syrie-Liban, Série L, Carton 6, Dossier 7, La Courneuve, MAE.

48.   Wadsworth to Secretary of State, May 19, 1945, RG 84, Beirut, Classified General Records, 1936–1961, Box 15, NARA; and Petition, May 19, 1945. FO 226/287/92, NA.

49.   Wadsworth to Secretary of State, May 21, 1945. RG 84. Beirut, Supplemental General Records, 1944–1945, Box 1, NARA; and 1945. *Beirut*, May 23, 1.

50.   Bhabha, *The Location of Culture*, 86.

51.   Rapport, 23 Mai 1945. Beyrouth, Consulat, Fonds B, Carton 28, Nantes, MAE; and Beynet à Bidault, 1 Juin 1945. Syrie-Liban, Carton 6, Dossier 9, La Courneuve, MAE.

52.   "Revue de la presse libanaise," 25 Mai 1945. Beyrouth, Ambassade, Série B, Carton 2094, Nantes, MAE; and Wadsworth to Secretary of State, May 26, 1945, RG 84, Beirut, Classified General Records, 1936–1961, Box 15, NARA.

53.   El Shakry, *The Great Social Laboratory*, 60.

54.   1945. *As-Sayyad*, June 7, 9; "Attaques de la presse contre les troupes sénégalaises," 4 Juin 1945. Syrie-Liban, Série L, Carton 6, Dossier 9D et H, La Courneuve, MAE; and Wadsworth to Secretary of State, May 25, 1945. RG 84, Beirut, Classified General Records, 1936–1961, Box 15, NARA.

55. 1945. *Sawt al-Sha'b*, May 26, 1; "Revue de la presse libanaise," 26 Mai 1945. Beyrouth, Ambassade, Série B, Carton 2094, Nantes, MAE; and Dower, *War Without Mercy*, 17.

56. Beirut to Foreign Office, May 27, 1945. FO 226/287/92, NA; and "Syrian and Lebanese Statement to San Francisco Issue Statement Protesting French Actions," May 27, 1945. FO 226/287/92, NA.

57. Wadsworth to Secretary of State, May 29, 1945; *Foreign Relations of the United States* [FRUS], 1945. vol. 8: 1114–15; and "Revue de la presse libanaise," 31 Mai 1945. Beyrouth, Ambassade, Série B, Carton 2094, Nantes, MAE.

58. Beynet à Bidault, 1 Juin 1945. Syrie-Liban, Carton 6, Dossier 9, La Courneuve, MAE.

59. Minutes, May 31, 1945; *FRUS*, 1945, vol. 1: 989–1011.

60. Wadsworth to Secretary of State, June 4, 1945. RG 84, Beirut, Classified General Records, 1936–1961, Box 15, NARA.

61. Sussman, *The Myth of Race*.

62. Wright, *The Color Curtain*.

63. Balandier, "The Colonial Situation," 33.

64. Balibar and Wallerstein, *Race, Nation, Class*, 37–68.

65. Mazower, *No Enchanted Palace*, 17.

References

Arsan, Andrew. 2014. *Interlopers of Empire: The Lebanese Diaspora in Colonial West Africa*. New York: Oxford University Press.

Aydin, Cemil. 2007. *The Politics of Anti-Westernism in Asia: Visions of World Order in Pan-Islamic and Pan-Asian Thought*. New York: Columbia University Press.

Balandier, George. 2010. "The Colonial Situation: A Theoretical Approach." In *the New Imperial History Reader*, edited by Stephen Howe, 33. New York: Routledge.

Balibar, Étienne and Immanuel Wallerstein. 1991. *Race, Nation, Class: Ambiguous Identities*. New York: Verso.

Bhabha, Homi. 2004. "The Black Servant and the Dark Princess." *ESQ: A Journal of American Renaissance* 50, no. 1–2: 137–55.

Bhabha, Homi. 1994. *The Location of Culture*. New York: Routledge.

Burton, Antoinette. 2012. *Brown over Black: Race and the Politics of Postcolonial Citation*. New Delhi: Three Essays Collective.

Brennan, James. 2012. *Taifa: Making Nation and Race in Urban Tanzania*. Athens: Ohio University Press.

Byrne, Jeffrey. 2016. *Mecca of Revolution: Algeria, Decolonization, and the Third World Order*. New York: Oxford University Press.

Chamberlin, Paul. 2012. *The Global Offensive: The United States, Palestine Liberation Organization, and the Making of the Post-Cold War Order*. New York: Oxford University Press.

Conklin, Alice. 1997. *A Mission to Civilize: The Republican Idea of Empire in France and West Africa, 1895–1930*. Stanford: Stanford University Press.

Cooper, Frederick and Ann Laura Stoler. 1997. *Tensions of Empire: Colonial Cultures in a Bourgeois World*. Berkeley: University of California Press.

Desai, Ashwin and Goolah Vahed. 2016. *The South African Gandhi: Stretcher-Bearer of Empire*. Stanford: Stanford University Press.

Dower, John. 1986. *War Without Mercy: Race and Power in the Pacific War*. New York: Pantheon Books.

Drescher, Seymour. 2009. *Abolition: A History of Slavery and Anti-Slavery*. New York: Cambridge University Press.

Du Bois, W. E. B. 2014. *Dark Princess*. New York: Oxford University Press.

Du Bois, W. E. B. 1994. *The Souls of Black Folk*. New York: Dover Publications.

Echengerg, Myron. 2009. *Les Tirailleurs sénégalais en Afrique occidentale française (1857–1960)*. Paris: Crepo-Karthala.

Elshakry, Marwa. 2013. *Reading Darwin in Arabic, 1860–1950*. Chicago: University of Chicago Press.

El Shakry, Omnia. 2007. *The Great Social Laboratory: Subjects of Knowledge in Colonial and Postcolonial Egypt*. Stanford: Stanford University Press.

Fargettas, Julie. 2012. *Les Tirailleurs sénégalais*. Paris: Tallandier.

Featherstone, David. 2012. *Solidarity: Hidden Histories and Geographies of Internationalism*. New York: Zed Books.

Feldman, Keith. 2015. *A Shadow Over Palestine: The Imperial Life of Race in America*. Minneapolis: University of Minnesota Press.

Fogarty, Richard. 2008. *Race and War in France: Colonial Subjects in the French Army, 1914–1918*. Baltimore: Johns Hopkins Press.

Geobel, Michael. 2015. *Anti-Imperial Metropolis: Interwar Paris and the Seeds of Third World Nationalism*. New York: Cambridge University Press.

Gualtieri, Sarah. 2009. *Between Arab and White: Race and Ethnicity in the Early Syrian American Diaspora*. Berkeley: University of California Press.

Hopkins, A. G. 2008. "Rethinking Decolonization." *Past & Present*, no. 200: 211–247.

Hopkins, David. 2001. "Sons and Lovers: Popular Images of the Conscript, 1798–1870." *Modern & Contemporary France* 91, no. 1: 19–36.

Hopper, Matthew. 2015. *Slavery of One Master: Globalization and Slavery in Arabia in the Age of Empire*. New Haven, CT: Yale University Press.

Khoury, Philip. 1989. *Syria and the French Mandate: The Politics of Arab Nationalism, 1920–1945*. Princeton, NJ: Princeton University Press.

Lake, Marilyn and Henry Reynolds. 2008. *Drawing the Global Colour Line: White Men's Countries and the Question of Racial Equality*. Carlton, Australia: Melbourne University Publishing.

Lee, Christopher. 2010. *Making a World After Empire: The Bandung Moment and Its Political Afterlives*. Athens: Ohio University Press.

Louis, Wm. Roger and Ronald Robinson. 1994. "The Imperialism of Decolonization." *Journal of Imperial and Commonwealth History* 22, no. 3: 462–511.

Lubin, Alex. 2014. *Geographies of Liberation: The Making of an Afro-Arab Political Imaginary*. Chapel Hill: University of North Carolina Press.

Mann, Gregory. 2006. *Native Sons: West African Veterans and France in the Twentieth Century*. Durham, NC: Duke University Press.

Mazower, Mark. 2009. *No Enchanted Palace: The End of Empire and the Ideological Origins of the United Nations*. Princeton, NJ: Princeton University Press.

McCulloch, John. 2000. *Black Peril, White Virtue: Sexual Crime in Southern Rhodesia, 1902–1935*. Bloomington: Indiana University Press.

McHale, Shawn. 2009. "Understanding the Fanatical Mind? The Viet Minh and Race Hatred in the First Indochina War." *Journal of Vietnamese Studies* 4, no. 3: 98–138.

Mellow, Noha. 2005. *The Making of Arab News*. New York: Rowman & Littlefield.

Minawi, Mostafa. 2016. *The Ottoman Scramble for Africa: Empire and Diplomacy in the Sahara and the Hejaz*. Stanford: Stanford University Press.

Nassar, Maha. 2014. "'My Struggle Embraces Evert Struggle': Palestinians in Israel and Solidarity with Afro-Asian Liberation Movements." *Arab Studies Journal* 22, no. 1: 74–101.

Prashad, Vijay. 2007. *The Darker Nations: A People's History of the Third World*. New York: The New Press.

Rugh, William. 1979. *The Arab Press: News Media and Political Process in the Arab World*. Syracuse: Syracuse University Press.

Schayegh, Cyrus and Andrew Arsan. 2015. *The Routledge Handbook of the History of the Middle East Mandates*. London: Routledge.

Scott, David. 2004. *Conscripts of Modernity: The Tragedy of Colonial Enlightenment*. Durham, NC: Duke University Press.

Souki, Samyr. 1993. *Middle Eastern Memories*. New York: Vintage Press.

Spears, Edward. 1977. *Fulfilment of a Mission: The Spears Mission to Syria and Lebanon*. London: Archon Books.

Stoddard, Lothrop. 1923. *The Rising Tide of Color Against White World-Supremacy*. New York: Charles Scribner's Sons.

Suleiman, Michael. 1966. *Political Parties in Lebanon: The Challenge of a Fragmented Political Culture*. Ithaca, NY: Cornell University Press.

Sussman, Robert Wald. 2014. *The Myth of Race: The Troubling Persistence of an Unscientific Idea*. Cambridge, MA: Harvard University Press.

Takriti, Abdel Razzaq. 2013. *Monsoon Revolution: Republicans, Sultans, and Empires in Oman, 1965–1976*. New York: Oxford University Press.

Toledano, Ehud. 1998. *Slavery and Abolition in the Ottoman Middle East*. Seattle: University of Washington Press.

Toledano, Ehud. 2007. *As If Silent and Absent: Bonds of Enslavement in the Islamic Middle East*. New Haven, CT: Yale University Press.

Troutt Powell, Eve. 2003. *A Different Shade of Colonialism: Egypt, Great Britain, and the Mastery of the Sudan*. Berkeley: University of California Press.

Troutt Powell, Eve. 2012. *Tell This in My Memory: Stories of Enslavement from Egypt, Sudan, and the Ottoman Empire*. Stanford: Stanford University Press.

Tueni, Ghassan, 2002. *Le livre de l'indépendance*. Beirut: Dar An-Nahar.

Uchida, Jun. 2011. *Brokers of Empire: Japanese Settler Colonialism in Korea, 1876–1945*. Cambridge, MA: Harvard University Press.

Vitalis, Robert. 2013. "The Midnight Ride of Kwame Nkrumah and Other Fables of Bandung (Ban-doong)." *Humanity* 4, no. 2: 261–288.

Walz, Terrence and Kenneth Cuto. 2010. *Race and Slavery in the Middle East: Histories of Trans-Saharan Africans in Nineteenth-Century Egypt, Sudan, and the Ottoman Mediterranean*. New York: American University of Cairo Press.

Weinbaum, Alys Eve. 2004. *Wayward Reproductions: Genealogies of Race and Nation in Transatlantic Modern Thought*. Durham: Duke University Press.

Weinstein, Barbara. 2015. *The Color of Modernity: Sao Paolo and the Making of Race and Nation in Brazil*. Durham, NC, NC: Duke University Press.

Weiss, Max. 2007. "'Don't Throw Away Yourself to the Dark Continent': Shi'i Migration to West Africa and the Hierarchies of Exclusion in Lebanese Culture." *Studies in Ethnicity and Nationalism* 7, no. 1: 46–63.

Wheatley, Natasha. 2015. "Mandatory Interpretation: Legal Hermeneutics and the New International Order in Arab and Jewish Petitions to the League of Nations." *Past & Present*, no. 227: 205–48.

Wright, Richard. 1956. *The Color Curtain: A Report on the Bandung Conference*. Cleveland: World Publishers.

Zisser, Eyal. 2000. *Lebanon: The Challenge of Independence*. London: I. B. Tauris.

Blinded by Bandung?

Illumining West Papua, Senegal, and the Black Pacific

Quito Swan

It was 1976, and Ben Tanggahma was in Dakar. Hailing from the former Dutch colony of West Papua, the Melanesian activist could easily pass for West African on the streets of Senegal. Tanggahma was the Foreign Minister of the Revolutionary Provisional Government of West Papua New Guinea (RPG), which was embroiled in a bitter armed conflict against Indonesian colonialism. With blood, iron, and fire, the Indonesian government claimed that it was historically and ethnically entitled to West Papua (Irian Jaya). In contrast, the RPG adamantly defended its sovereignty as an Oceanic (Pacific) people of African descent.[1] From Hollandia, Amsterdam, Dakar, and New York, West Papuan activists garnered support throughout the Black Diaspora. With the political and financial backing of Senegalese President Léopold Senghor, Tanggahma established a RPG coordinating office in Dakar in 1975. Senghor's reasoning for assistance was straightforward—Papuans were Black and *Negritude* defended their right to political self-determination and civilization.[2]

Dakar proved to be a fruitful space for fostering relations with the African Diaspora. In 1976, Tangghama attended Wole Soyinka's Seminar for African World Alternatives in Dakar. Black artists, activists, scholars, scientists and journalists from across Africa and the Americas participated in the Seminar. While there, journalists Carlos Moore and Shawna Maglanbayan asked Tangghama about the relationship between Oceania and Africa. He responded:

Radical History Review
Issue 131 (May 2018)   DOI 10.1215/01636545-4355133
© 2018 by MARHO: The Radical Historians' Organization, Inc.

Africa is our motherland. All of the Black populations which settled in Asia . . .
came undoubtedly from the African continent. . . . Hence, we the Blacks in
Asia and the Pacific today descend from proto-African peoples. We were linked
to Africa in the past. We are linked to Africa in the future. We are what you
might call the Black Asian Diaspora.[3]

By asserting West Papuans as a Black Asian Diaspora, Tanggahma was intentionally forging Diaspora with the broader Black world. Similarly, in the 1960s his
West Papuan counterparts internationally asserted themselves as "Negroids of the
Pacific." This was not simply a matter of political expediency, or a new appropriation
of Blackness triggered by Indonesian imperialism. This was part of a longstanding
conversation within the Black world about how its global dynamics stretched across
the Atlantic, Pacific, and Indian Ocean worlds. A binding factor of this Diaspora was
European colonial violence that had defined Oceanic peoples as being Black and
Brown since the sixteenth century.[4] It makes perfect sense, then, that West Papuans
would identify with other communities who had historically experienced the world
as Black people.

    Conceptually shadowed by scholarship focused on meetings such Tanzania's
Sixth Pan-African Congress (6PAC, 1974) and Nigeria's Festival of Arts and Culture
(FESTAC, 1977), Dakar's Seminar was a critical occasion of Black internationalism and rediscovery between the Black Pacific and broader Black world. Its participants included Senegal's Cheikh Anta Diop, Kine' Kirama Fall, and Annette Mbaye
d'Erneville; Trinidad's CLR James; Madagascar's Jacques Rabemananjara; Brazil's
Abdias do Nascimento; Guinea's Camara Laye; Mauritius's Edouard Maunick; Panama's Edilia Camargo; Ethiopia's Tsegaye Gabre-Medhin; and Harold Cruse of the
United States. These political stalwarts signed a *Declaration of Black Intellectuals*,
which called for the sovereignty of West Papua and East Timor from Indonesian
imperialism. The document asserted that Melanesia's racial, cultural and political
affinities with the African world were indisputable. Linking the struggles of Oceania
to those of Africa, Asia, and the Americas, this global roll call captured an incandes-
cent yet largely invisible nexus of Black internationalism. Still, Tanggahma argued
that the African Diaspora's *sympathy* for West Papua did not always develop into
solidarity—that is, tangible material aid. This was also because Black movements
were often hesitant to criticize Indonesia because they were blinded by its role in the
historic 1955 Afro-Asian Conference at Bandung, Indonesia.

    Bandung remains a figurative and literal symbol for the Global South. In
1963, Malcolm X famously cited the meeting as a model for Black and Brown unity
against white power: "At Bandung all the nations came together from Africa and
Asia. It was at Bandung where Black and Brown communities discovered who the
real enemy was—blonde hair, blue eyed and white skinned Europeans."[5]

    This article complicates and perhaps disorders this mainstream narrative by exploring Bandung from the perspective and voice of Oceania.[6] Indonesia used Bandung as a platform to solidify support from its African and Asian allies for its claims to West Papua. It framed these efforts within the context of resistance to Dutch colonialism. Indonesia publically lambasted West Papuan nationalists as being reactionary puppets of the Dutch, Stone Age peoples unready for self-determination or rebel traitors who needed to be violently suppressed. From this perspective, Bandung represented a consolidation of Indonesian imperialism in the region, as Indonesia functioned as a racialized colonial power. This critique does not invalidate the broader project of Afro-Asian solidarity, and it recognizes that there were Indonesian voices that disagreed with their government's claims to West Papua.

"Blinded by Bandung" uses the case of West Papua to illumine the relationships between Black internationalism, Melanesia, and decolonization in Oceania. Melanesia today refers to some 12 million persons, 2,000 islands, 1,300 languages and 386,000 square miles of land across the waters of Vanuatu, Papua New Guinea, the Solomon Islands, West Papua, Fiji, and New Caledonia. Lying north and north east of Australia, this chain of archipelagos witnessed the pandemonium of colonialism. Since the sixteenth century, European, American, Asian, and Pacific powers have played geopolitical musical chairs in the region. The ideas, memories and legacies of stolen generations, blackbirding—a nineteenth century system of kidnapping and enslavement in which European traders forcibly took Melanesians to work primarily on sugar and cotton plantations in Australia, Fiji, and New Caledonia—and nuclear testing became household terms as common as breadfruit, sandalwood, and kava. Still, Melanesia is not a sea of victims and possesses a longstanding tradition of resistance to colonial violence.[7]

This article highlights the South-South relations that spread the ideas of Black Power, *Negritude*, Pan-Africanism, and African/Caribbean liberation across Oceania. It challenges a conceptual cartography of Africana scholarship that has oriented Pan-Africanism as an Atlantic world experience. It further suggests that notions of the Black world have been blinded by a framework of the African Diaspora largely linked to a narrative of involuntary migration stemming from the Atlantic slave trade. But if we centralize the Pacific in the Diaspora framework, is it possible to speak of a Black Pacific—or Black Oceania?

Indeed, there is inherent hegemony implied in the notion of the "Pacific." It is a construct that reflects Europe's violent assault on indigenous Oceania through genocide, forced labor, sexual abuse, displacement, ecological destruction, and imperialism. In response, Tongan scholar Epeli Hau'ofa convincingly pushed scholars to use *Oceania* instead of the *Pacific* when referring to the region. For Hau'ofa, Oceania speaks to the region's precolonial worldviews, diversity, politics, economics, migration, kinship networks, and ecosystems.[8]

Yet, this article is informed by scholarship that engages the concept of a

Black Pacific. Etsuko Taketani's *Black Pacific Narrative* shows how interwar African Americans imagined China and Japan through culture and literature. Robbie Shilliam's *Black Pacific* is focused on the Polynesian Panthers and Black Power in New Zealand. Gabriel Solis's "Black Pacific" discusses racial identity in Papua New Guinea and Australia through ethnomusicology. Gerald Horne's *White Pacific* documents blackbirding, US imperialism, and African Americans in Oceania in the nineteenth century.[9]

"Blinded by Bandung" uses Black Pacific to refer to the intentional and complicated ways in which Oceanic communities forged Diaspora with the broader Black world politically and culturally by self-identifying as Black or by embracing Black movements. It also describes how Oceanic movements at times rallied around modern concepts of Blackness created by European colonialism. Furthermore, it explores the Global South and world disorder, particularly in the ways in which we think about interoceanic African Diasporas. In doing so, it critically adds to scholarship on Black internationalism, the Global South, and the African Diaspora, which have largely marginalized Melanesia. It also draws from Tracey Banivanua Mar's *Decolonization and the Pacific*, which details how decolonization in the Oceania was both an indigenous and an international phenomenon that transcended colonial and national borders.[10]

From Oceania to the Black Pacific

Recent DNA studies argue that "Aboriginal" Australians are direct descendants of Africa's first Diaspora from some 72,000 years ago. These communities traversed into Papua New Guinea, Australia and the Solomon Islands. Archeological unearthing of Lapita pottery marks a second major migratory wave throughout the region via Southeast Asia some 3,000 years ago.[11] Oceania has been brutally impacted by European imperial violence since the sixteenth century. The European racial imaginary defined Oceania in reference to Africa and the indigenous Americas. In 1545, Spanish explorer Yñigo Ortiz de Retez reached Papua and called it *Nueva Guinea*, as he felt that the people resembled those of Africa's Guinea coast.[12] By the 1830s France's Jules Dumont d'Urville divided Oceania by phenotype into Polynesia, Micronesia, Malaysia, and Melanesia. He defined Melanesia as being "the home of the Black race of Oceania" and, predictably, racially inferior to Polynesia.[13]

The turn of the twentieth century was an intense era of (re)discovery among the Black world. In a moment of Europe's scramble for Africa and the Pacific, Pan-African writers of the Americas framed their views on Oceania in the context of European colonial thought. Their questions about race in Oceania reflected their challenge—not without contradiction—to scientific racism. For them, the shared phenotypical similarities *and* histories of racial oppression across the Pacific and Atlantic Ocean worlds legitimized global political framings of Blackness that included Oceania.

In 1879, Martin Delaney asserted that indigenous persons in Australia, Tasmania, New Zealand, and Papua New Guinea were descendants of a mixed Malay race. "Who can doubt," asked the father of Black Nationalism, "that the African once preponderated and was the resolvent race among them?" Ana Julia Cooper's 1925 "Equality of Race and the Democratic Movement" decried Australia's "White only policy." In 1942, W. E. B. Dubois remarked that one could "trace the African black from the Great Lakes of Africa to the islands of Melanesia."[14]

In 1920, a branch of the Universal Negro Improvement Association (UNIA) was formed in Sydney, Australia. Its communications with Amy Jacques Garvey were published in the *Negro World*. Marcus Garvey referenced genocide in the Pacific as a political imperative for African unity. He once told New York's Liberty Hall, "Do they think that they are going to exterminate 400 million Blacks as they have exterminated . . . the North American Indians . . . and the Aborigines of [New Zealand] and Australia?" The UNIA's 1922 petition to the League of Nations charged, "If Black men have no right in America, Australia, Canada [or Europe] then White men should have no right in Africa."[15]

The *Negro World* continued a distinctly gendered focus on its coverage of Oceania. In September 1924, the paper reported that Blacks in Australia and New Guinea were being "enslaved, exploited and raped by white Europeans." It reprinted reports by Sydney's *Worker's Weekly*, which claimed that there was a slave trade in New Guinea.[16] It found these "vile horrors" to be worse than those of South Africa.[17]

World War II brought increased visibility to Melanesia in the African American press. Cleveland's *Call and Post* reported that African American soldiers stationed in Papua New Guinea "found colored men there already."[18] In 1943, Howard University's Merz Tate argued that the "darker" persons of the world lived in the Netherlands East Indies, India, Asia, the Malay Peninsula, Polynesia, Oceania, and Melanesia, which was populated by "Negroid inhabitants." For Tate, these darker peoples were no longer "filled with terror at the white man's power." They now questioned the reality of white superiority and contemplated their own "possibilities of attack."[19]

Back to Bandung

World War II brought significant change to West Papua as well, which, along with Indonesia, had been colonized by the Netherlands through the Dutch East Indies Company. An 1824 Treaty of London divided New Guinea between Holland, Germany, and Britain "without the knowledge or consent of its Black population." Germany's first overseas colony was German New Guinea, which it claimed by flag weeks before the 1884 Berlin Conference. Both Britain and Germany administered New Guinea with machine guns and punitive expeditions. In 1906, Britain transferred Papua to Australia. East New Guinea was passed on to Australia after World War II. In the 1920s, the Dutch exiled leftist Indonesians to West Papua.[20]

Papuans resisted Dutch colonialism. From 1938 to 1942, an indigenous priestess named Angganeta Menufandu led the *Koreri* anticolonial movement in Biak. She encouraged mass noncooperation against Dutch forced labor gangs, taxation, laws, and missionary bans on traditional dancing and singing. The *Koreri* inverted the Dutch tricolor flag (red, blue, and white) and added a morning star, a Biak cosmological symbol. Uprisings occurred when the Dutch arrested Angganeta and burned the homes of her community. She remained captive during Japan's occupation in World War II. Stephen Simopjaref freed her and transformed the *Koreri* into an armed resistance force. Both Simopjaref and Angganeta were recaptured and beheaded by the Japanese, who killed between 600 and 2000 persons on Biak.[21]

Led by President Surkarno, Indonesia secured political independence from the Netherlands in 1949. A deal with Holland granted Indonesia its former Pacific colonies, including the "Black" nations of West Timor and the South Moluccas. Sukarno immediately claimed that West Papua was ethnically and historically Indonesian. Intent on holding onto West Papua, the Dutch denied this. Ironically, it was Dutch colonialism that had politically oriented West Papua *west* towards Indonesia and the Indian Ocean, as opposed to *east* towards Melanesia and Oceania.[22]

West Papuan nationalists rejected Indonesia's position. They made clear distinctions between the racial and ethnic histories of Papua and Indonesia. For example, the RPG argued that "master-slave relations" defined the historical connections between "Asiatic Javanese," Black Papuans, and the Islamic Sultan of Tidore, as Indonesian merchants enslaved Papuans during the Indian Ocean slave trade circa 724 CE.[23]

These voices of dissent were silenced at Bandung. Attended by twenty-nine countries, the talks declared that colonialism was evil. It affirmed that the "subjection of peoples to alien subjugation, domination and exploitation" was a denial of human rights contrary to the United Nations Charter. However, West Papua was the exception. Surkano framed his claims to West Papua as a struggle against Dutch imperialism. As such, Bandung officially resolved to support Indonesia's position on West Papua.[24]

As the conflict between Indonesia and the Netherlands intensified, West Papuan nationalists found themselves in a complicated situation. They pushed for their sovereignty, repeatedly asserting that they were neither pro-Indonesian nor pro-Dutch. In October 1961, they formed a National Congress at Hollandia, and elected a Papuan National Committee (PNC). Given the charge to drive West Papua to independence, the PNC was led by Dorcas Tokoro-Hanesbey, Marcus Kaisiepo, and Nicolaas Jouwe. Days later, it created a flag, an arms, a national anthem, and national names, which it distributed throughout the country as a Manifesto. PNC representative Willem Inuri informed Sydney's *Morning Herald*, "We want our own nation and to rename the territory West Papua." In early 1962, the Partai Nasional (PARNA) announced to the country that in 1970 West Papua would become a Republic.[25]

Dutch residents in Hollandia pondered if West Papua was going to become a "New Congo." Perhaps to assuage these concerns, the Dutch passed an ordinance stating that the new flag could only be raised alongside a Dutch flag of greater height. Still, Netherlands supported West Papuan nationalism as an effort to stave off Indonesia. As such, detractors claimed that the Council was an extension of Dutch liberal politics, downplaying West Papuan nationalism.[26]

In December 1961, Surkano vowed to "liberate the land" from the Dutch. He called for the "total mobilization of the Indonesian people" to invade West Papua. In a national broadcast to one million viewers, he ordered Indonesians to wreck "Dutch efforts to set up a Papua puppet state" by hoisting Indonesia's flag over "West Irian." Reporting in the *Atlanta Daily World*, he exclaimed, "There is no power in this world which can stop us—no fleet, no army . . . when we follow the path which is blessed and approved by Allah. We ask the Dutch what do you march with? At most, your cheese and butter."[27]

Surkano framed the pending invasion as a West Irian Liberation Command. His Ambassador to Australia declared that Indonesia was historically and ethnically entitled to West Irian and that it would not allow it form an independent country with East New Guinea. In February 1962, the *Bermuda Recorder* declared that 10,000 Indonesian volunteers were ready to invade West Papua. Invoking Western prejudices, the paper reported that they were "skilled in the type of jungle warfare required in the wilds" of West Papua.[28]

The PNC retorted that West Papuans were ready to defend themselves against Indonesia. It remarked that there would be an "unending guerrilla war" if Indonesia attempted to occupy their mountains and jungles. It reminded interested parties how only three hundred out of forty thousand Japanese survived the trek across New Guinea during World War II. PNC Vice President Jouwe repeatedly called for Papuans to resist Indonesia with arms if necessary. In January 1962, he challenged Indonesian propaganda that claimed that Papuans would welcome Indonesia's army. "We will welcome them all right," said Jouwe, "but not with hand shakes." Papuans would resist Indonesian rule with everything in their power, including "flights of poisoned arrows." He further stated that his people's "volunteer battalion of jungle fighters" were urging the Dutch for arms. "Because of our fighting prowess," he claimed, "I think we could fight against one hundred Indonesians with five soldiers." Spokesperson Herman Womsiwor agreed—the PNC sought to form a People's Army through finances from Holland. He wanted "warriors equipped with jungle carbines, grenades, light machine guns." Via conscription of Papuans aged sixteen to forty, they hoped to bolster their Papuan Volunteer Corps.[29]

West Papua, Africa, and the United Nations

By 1962, the PNC began to actively seek direct support from Africa. At the PNC's insistence, the Dutch invited African representatives to the United Nations to West Papua to investigate the situation. According to the Council, several African ambassadors declined the invitation because of Indonesian intimidation. Still, in April 1962, ambassadors Frédéric Guirma of Upper Volta and Maxime-Leopold Zollner of Dahomey visited West Papua for two weeks.[30]

Upon their return, Guirma held a press conference on the issue. He concluded that Indonesia's claims to West Papua rested on weak historical grounds. He felt that they were as logical as if Indonesia was to claim Australia and the Philippines. Guirma found it scandalous that seven hundred thousand New Guineans lived in the Stone Age while the United States and Russia sent "satellites to the Moon." The issue was not whether or not New Guinea should go to the Netherlands or Indonesia, but how to elevate "its people to the level of this century." He advocated that the United Nations administer the territory, and after West Papuans had "improved their way of life," a move should be made to complete self-determination.[31]

Guirma's comments were controversial. Guinea's ambassador completely disagreed with him. African American journalist Charles Howard also chastised him: "Why do you, an African, come here and try to propagandize us, on behalf of a colonial power, while the United Nations and the Asian African group are doing all in their power to liquidate colonialism everywhere?" For Howard, it was the attitude of French colonial "puppets" like Guirma and others from the Brazzaville group that stunted Africa's liberation from colonialism.[32]

In Baltimore's *Afro-American*, Howard wrote that Indonesia had appealed to African delegates to the United Nations to help them "restore" West Papua to the Republic. They asked the peoples of Africa "to not heed to the poisonous babble of the Dutch puppets" who made "noises in the interests of their own pockets."[33] Major J. Diamara, a leader of the Indonesian Defense Council, lodged in the United Nations a fine piece of propaganda written on *behalf* of West Papuans. "We, sons of West Irian and representative of West Irian independence fighters, hereby declare to all the peoples of Africa, wherever they may be, that West Irian is an integral part of Indonesia. We, the West Irian Community belong to Indonesia, and since olden times we have spoken Indonesian."[34]

Under the threat of invasion, the PNC launched an international campaign to gather support. It sent delegates to New York, Amsterdam, and cities across Africa. In May 1962, Jouwe took the case of West Papua to the United Nations in New York. Officially a part of a Netherlands delegation, he was very visible in the US media. In July 1962, he stated that Papuans "wanted the same thing the Americans wanted in 1776—freedom and independence." They refused to be "victims of Indonesian blackmail" or be handed down from "one colonial master to another."[35]

The PNC popularized its struggle through the African American press. On

April 14, 1962, the *Pittsburgh Courier's* two-page center spread read, "PAPUANS
SEEK HELP FROM NEGRO BROTHERS AND SISTERS." Tokoro-Hanesbey,
Jouwe, and Kaisiepo informed the paper that Papuans needed assistance from their
global "Negro brothers and sisters" against the "menace of Indonesian imperialism."
This clarion call to the Black world argued that "African Papuans" were a sovereign
Black people. The PNC's pamphlet, *The Voice of the Negroids in the Pacific to the
Negroids Throughout the World*, declared the Melanesian archipelago to be "New
Africa." It stated, "We are living in the Pacific, our people are called Papuans, our
ethnic origin is the Negroid Race. We do not want to be slaves any more." The
PNC informed its "fellow tribesmen of the Negroids throughout the world" that
they were in a "dangerous position." If handed over to their Indonesian enemy, they
would be forced to be slaves. They urged African Americans and African nationals
to exert their influence to have them placed under United Nations supervision.[36]

The article detailed the PNC's program, which was based on self-determination,
rights, and freedom. For the PNC, these were ideals that Black people across the
world fought for. Hence, Papua's quest for liberation was no different than that of
the Africana world. The *Courier* pondered if West Papuans would have a "right to
make their own choice," or whether "the other nations" allow an Asian dictator to
keep them down. The *Chicago Daily Defender* reported that West Papuans wanted
to be free from any form of colonialism.[37]

The PNC's words were poignant, but the photographs that they circulated
arguably had more of an impact. Both the *Courier* and *Defender* published pictures
of the PNC's inaugural 1961 meeting. The images revealed the PNC's red, white,
and blue flag, which was based upon Angganeta's earlier design. One photograph of
a PNC rally on Biak depicted men, women, and children holding placards inscribed
with the phrase "Pampampun"— "WE PAPUANS reject Sukarno and his people."[38]
The demonstrators were dressed in Western clothing, perhaps attempting to challenge misrepresentations of West Papuans as "primitives."

Racist notions of Papua as being of the Stone Age were widely perpetu-
ated through the media. Leon Dennen, in an interview with Jouwe claimed that
it was "tough to be a free Papuan headhunter or the son of one in the age of anticolonialism." The *Chicago Defender* found it to be anybody's guess why the Dutch or
Indonesia wanted backwards West Papua. The *Amarillo Globe Times* claimed that
the "Stone Age habits" of Papuans slowed their transformation to independence,
even though the Dutch had partially repressed headhunting and cannibalism. Papuans spoke two hundred unintelligible languages and lived under poverty and disease. The paper claimed that Indonesia needed West New Guinea like it needed
"the holes Papuans used to drill in enemy skulls to remove the brains for eating."[39]

But while West Papua was being framed as backward and lacking resources,
in 1961, photographs of hundreds of spear-brandishing "stark naked savages" organized in "fighting squads like Zulu Impis" with their "faces made even blacker with

war paint" drove the careers of photographers like Eliot Elisofon. *Life Magazine* published articles about Papua such as "Survivors from the Stone Age: A Savage People That Love War," spliced with photographs taken by Michael Rockefeller. Scientific expeditions to study the world's "rarest anthropological treasure," Papua's "Stone Age natives," bolstered the reputation of Harvard's Peabody museum. Pieces of "New Guinea Primitive art" fetched up to $11,000 at art shows by May Co. Whilshire.[40] What this all demonstrates is how pervasive Western prejudices exhibited towards Oceania—once also held for Africa, Asia, and the Americas—were perpetuated in the pages of Black and white media.

Acts of No Choice

Indonesia landed paratroopers in West Papua in April 1962. Without the consultation of West Papuans, the United States government brokered a New York Agreement that conceded the country to Indonesia. Ratified by the United Nations, it was expected that Indonesia would hold a 1969 referendum on Papuan independence. Now backed by the United States and the United Nations, Indonesia proceeded to colonize West Papua. Writing from New York in 1968, the Freedom Committee of West Papua argued that Indonesia had become "more murderous." Chaired by Jouwe, the Committee included Womsiwor and Secretary General Tanggahma.[41] Through violence, military occupation, intimidation, economic coercion, political incarceration, and propaganda, Indonesia ran the colony like a military fiefdom. According to US officials, its army degraded Papuans because of their "darker skin" and supposed lack of civilization. Charges of genocide were generated by shootings from "trigger-happy, jittery troops."[42]

In 1965, Lodewijk Mandadjan led armed resistance in the mountains of Manokwari with about one thousand fighters. After an Indonesian police brigade was injured, the Indonesian military killed over one thousand persons in an air strike. Its "mopping up operations" netted one thousand World War II weapons with documents connecting them to Operasi Papua Merdeka (Free Papua Organization, OPM).[43] Widely supported, the OPM became West Papua's core opposition to Indonesia. The US State Department found it to be an "all-pervasive revolutionary movement." Loosely organized, it was hard to track down not because it was security tight, but because "everyone talked about it." Reflecting an "amorphous mass of anti-Indonesian sentiment," it had anywhere from between 1,500 and 50,000 members.[44]

As Indonesia's military sought to flush out the OPM, Papaun nationalists coordinated their struggle from outside of the country. Jouwe was based in the Netherlands. In a 1969 report, he stated that thirty armed guerillas were fighting for independence, some armed with only bows and arrows. He reported on numerous killings, arrests and refugees.[45]

By 1967, Marcus Kaisieopo had become President in Exile of the Government of West Papua. In December of that year, he met with Francis Underhill,

Director of the US State Department's Indonesia Affairs. Kaisieopo hoped that the United States could use its influence to ensure the vote occurred fairly. Ironically, Underhill encouraged Kaisieopo to get the support of the Dutch and countries from the Global South since he felt that the views of white nations about colonialism would be arbitrarily dismissed. Kaisieopo responded that the Dutch would not do anything to assure that the referendum would be fairly administered. In addition, Papuan leaders had become "completely disillusioned" of any hope that the Afro-Asian bloc would be helpful—it was "blinded by the 1955 meeting at Bandung" and would not challenge Indonesia.[46]

In January 1968, US political consul Thomas Reynders visited West Papua. He reported that Indonesia was focused on suppressing political unrest. Its presence in West Papua was primarily expressed in the form of ten thousand troops. Despite there being a West Papuan Governor, who Reynders insulted by referring to him as a "sun-dazed frog," Indonesia's General Bintoro *was* the Government of West Papua. He was also rector of Tjenderawasih University, a center of political indoctrination for West Papuan students. Indonesian officials made a concentrated effort to keep Papuans away from UN representatives. According to missionaries, almost everyone in the developed areas of West Papua was anti-Indonesian. There were daily arrests of suspected rebels in Biak, and the military held an unknown amount of political prisoners. Given all of this, most Westerners in West Papua were certain that Indonesia would not win an open election. Violence was inevitable, as nationalists would not accept union without a struggle, and Indonesia would not accept separation. The only question was *how much* violence. Certainly, Indonesia was developing ways to avoid an open election and set the stage for an Act of Free Choice in its favor.[47]

About a year from the referendum, Indonesian foreign secretary Adam Malik suggested that Indonesia use careful groundwork to win the support of sixty "key tribal leaders." This included granting them favors and delivering gifts like clothing, flashlights, tobacco, bead necklaces, tin goods, and sago by C-130 military aircraft. Malik advocated giving amnesty to six political prisoners out of four hundred persons.[48]

In August 1968, US officials summed up Indonesia's precarious task of "designing a form of self-determination that would ensure its retention of West Irian" but yet not appear to be "a flagrant violation" of the human rights of Papuans—obviously, this was not self-determination. Its plan was to avoid universal adult suffrage and create a council with handpicked chiefs and approved restricted voter lists. They reported that the Indonesian government was "wining and dining" these chiefs in Jakarta. Meanwhile, the Dutch pledged not to sabotage Indonesia's plans. Serious opposition from the radical UN Afro-Asian bloc seemed improbable and Indonesia had the backing of moderate African and Asian nations.[49]

West Papuans did have some hope that support would be forthcoming from the United Nations, which had sent Bolivian ambassador Fernando Ortiz-Sanz to ensure that the referendum was held fairly. To Indonesia's disdain, Ortiz-Sanz avowed that he would preside over a completely free election or resign. Critical of Indonesia's handling of the Act, his team included African-Americans James Lewis and Marshall Williams. Both men were totally against Indonesian imperialism, claimed that 95 percent of the country supported independence, and felt that the referendum was a mockery.[50]

According to US officials, Williams "made no secret of the fact that he identified with the Papuans because of his American Negro antecedents." He proudly proclaimed that he was almost declared *persona non-grata* because he openly criticized Indonesia. In one case, Indonesian soldiers ejected him from a UN office during a demonstration because they thought that he was Papuan. The incident in question took place in April 1969, when the OPM organized a one-person, one-vote demonstration in front of Ortiz- Sanz's residence. Troops fired on the crowd of around one thousand persons.[51]

Upon his return to the United States, Ortiz-Sanz felt that at least twenty-five African representatives would not accept the provisions of the Act. In August 1969, as part of an effort to stave off this sentiment, Malik toured Europe and Africa to enlist the support of a number of African states. US officials claimed that OPM leaders abroad used race to mobilize support, arguing that "Brown Indonesia" was oppressing "Black Papua." This political appeal to color speaks to the intentional fashioning of the Black Diaspora across the Global South. Meanwhile, Malik's Africa tour was calculated to use propaganda to counter these operations.[52]

Malik was present for the United Nations' discussions on the Act of Free Choice. Supported by Gabon, Togo, Ghana, and Ecuador, Dahomey's ambassador objected to the short time allotted for the debate. Malik curiously argued the African states understood self-determination in ways that may have applied to Rhodesia. However, he claimed, these states had little understanding of the 1962 New York agreement. Malik asked US officials to convince the African nations to side with Indonesia; US officials were already were discreetly but pervasively pressing them.[53] Of course, the United States government had its own geopolitical interests in Oceania, Southeast Asia, and the Indian Ocean. It had supported Indonesia's push for political independence from the Dutch and saw the nation as a critical Cold War ally against communism.[54] All that being said, the Act of Free Choice passed in Indonesia's favor. Papuan nationalists chided the vote as being an act of "no choice." They continued to press for self-determination internationally while fighting locally.

Negritude in the Pacific
On July 1, 1971, the Revolutionary Provisional Government of West Papua (RPG) declared the country to be independent under President Brigadier General Seth Rumkorem. It claimed that Indonesia had killed over thirty thousand Papuan men,

women, and children since 1963. Tens of thousands of others were fleeing the Indo nesian army and joining the guerillas. The population's intellectual strata found themselves in concentration camps and prisons. The RPG indicated that Papuans risked being placed on reservations like the North American Indians and Aborigines in Australia and could become slaves in their own country. Rumkorem stressed that the Papuan people, the RPG, and its National Army of Liberation would fight "until either their country was freed of the last Indonesian soldiers" or was "the graveyard of its own last child."[55]

By 1975, the RPG claimed to control a territory twice the size of the Nether- lands. They operated schools and two hospitals and had excellent communication with their representatives in Holland and Papua New Guinea. Papuans also lived in exile—five thousand persons in Australia (five hundred were granted asylum), five hundred lived in the Netherlands, and others hid in insecurity amidst the country's dense rainforests. The RPG was represented abroad by Womsiwor, Filemon Jufu- way, and Tanghamma.[56]

In 1971, Womsiwor met with Roy Wilkins of the National Association for the Advancement of Colored People (NAACP). This was somewhat ironic, as Walter White and the NAACP had ardently supported Indonesia's independence struggle against the Dutch.[57] Womsiwor told Wilkins how, in 1969, the RPG had gone before the UN's special committee on decolonization and garnered the support of Gabon, Jamaica, Kenya, Sierra Leona, Tanzania, Dahomey, Central African Republic, Zam- bia, Barbados, Togo, Trinidad and Tobago, Uganda and Guyana, Zambia, and Israel. But as they needed more support, Womsiwor asked if the NAACP could address the case of West Papua at its annual meeting. He provided Wilkins with materials on West Papua's struggle, including a document entitled "African Papuans being slaughtered by Indonesian Government." Sent to Holland from New Guinea, the document claimed that between May and June 1970, Indonesian soldiers killed eighty-five villagers in Biak. This included a pregnant woman. In Bird's Head, free- dom fighters had returned to their villages under amnesty conditions, yet they were still "slaughtered on the beaches." From January to August 1970, 2,053 Papuans were arrested because they challenged the Free Act.[58]

Wilkins was convinced. In 1972, he released a charge to the United Nations on behalf the NAACP, stating that African Americans "knew little or nothing about the situation of their ethnic cousins in West New Guinea." In accordance with its stand against the domination of subject peoples, the NAACP urged the United Nations to grant West Papuans a "hearing on their status with respect to Indonesia." At its 1971 Convention, nearly 2000 delegates and over 1,700 local units voted unan- imously to support West Papua. The same statement was printed in the NAACP's *Crisis* magazine. In 1975, Womsiwor asked the NAACP to call on influential Black congresspersons to get the United States to intervene on their behalf.[59]

The RPG toured Africa in search of allies. They carried literature, documents, and photographs depicting their struggle. This included images of Rumkorem and the National Liberation Army. The RPG argued that if Sao Tome, with a population of eighty thousand, could be promised independence—why not West Papua with its population of eight *hundred* thousand? In 1974, the PGW caught the attention of the African and Mauritian Common Organization (OCM). Formerly known as the conservative Brazzaville group, the OCM invited the RPG to attend their August 1974 conference at Bangui, Central African Republic. Also attending was Senegalese president Senghor. It is likely that this is where the RPG first made direct contact with the iconic architect of *Negritude*. Due to his political invitation and financial support, in July 1975 the RPG opened its coordinating office in Dakar, Senegal.[60]

Senghor became an ardent supporter of West Papua and its Melanesian "neighbor," East Timor. He attempted to have them seated at the 1976 Organization of African Unity's Non-Aligned Coordinating Committee meeting. In a 1976 interview published in the Parisian paper *Le Monde*, Senghor was questioned about his interest in Papua. He stated that Senegal supported "all movements of identification" and primarily *Negritude*, which was "the right of Blacks to work in an independent state for the renaissance and development of their values of civilization." Senghor remarked that Papuans differed from Indonesians by race and culture. They were Black and Indonesians were "a mixture of Black and Yellow races." He also linked Senegal's relationship with the RPG to its support of Palestine's efforts to create a national state; the Palestine Liberation Organization (PLO) also had an office in Dakar. In February 1978, Senghor told Australia's ambassador that he saluted how Australia had granted independence to Papua New Guinea. He felt that the United Nations "had made an enormous mistake in remaining deaf to the demands of Papuans," who stand on their *Negritude* and demanded independence.[61]

US officials found it intriguing that Senghor had given haven to foreign political groups such as the RPG, PLO, the South West Africa People's Organization (SWAPO), and the Moluccans. They believed that Senghor was hoping to enhance his "progressive image," having gotten "good political mileage" for having Senegal be the first Black African state to have a PLO office. Gestures of this nature challenged the idea that he was a conservative. Senghor's support was a closely controlled "vest pocket" operation. He was an "African elder statesman with unparalleled access to, and respect in, western political and intellectual circles." US officials believed that Senghor was intent on earning the trust of radical movements in the Global South, which would theoretically allow him to be leading facilitator between these opposing sides. But they also found that Senghor's fraternizing with "Indonesian separatists" seemed more "adventurous radical chic" than his associations with PLO and SWAPO. Still, they felt that he may have seen these relationships as bridges to Black Diasporic communities that identified with *Negritude*. With the Dutch also concerned, the US State Department wondered if the time was ripe for Indonesia to make overtures towards Senegal to wean its "flirtation with dissident elements."[62]

Without question, Senghor was sincere. Even Wole Soyinka—whose disagreements with Senghor were legendary—understood Senghor's solidarity with West Papua as being a "logical extension of his pan-*Negritude* convictions." For Soyinka, his "obsession with the mapping of the geography of the Black race" took him beyond the African Diaspora of the Americas to the Pacific. Wanting more clarity about struggles of the Black Pacific, he dispatched Carlos Moore to Melanesia. Soyinka claims the he reached the "earliest guerilla encampment of East Timor" and returned to Senegal with a report and photographs taken of his trip.[63]

Moore's path to the region took him through Fiji, where he was hosted by activists Claire Slatter and Vanessa Griffen. Both women were integral in the Pacific Women's Movement, the Nuclear Free and Pacific Movement, and Suva's Pacific People's Action Front (PPAF). They also published the PPAF's newsletter *Povai*, which provided timely and reliable information and analysis on the struggles of Pacific people. The paper's revolutionary content was directly gathered from indigenous struggles across New Caledonia, Australia, Hawaii, Tahiti, Micronesia, Vanuatu, East Timor, New Zealand, and Papua New Guinea. Its March/April 1976 issue included an article on West Papua, remarking how little was known about its "protracted guerilla war against Indonesia since 1965." The brief was based on information provided by Moore, anonymously described as an "outside source in contact" with the freedom fighters. *Povai* also printed an excerpt of a speech that the RPG's Foreign Minister Ben Tanggahma made in Colombo, Sri Lanka's 1976 Non-Aligned conference.[64]

The paper also discussed a February 1976 communiqué by Tanggahma that called on the international community to help both West Papua and East Timor fight against "Indonesian colonial aggression." Tanggahma told the Senegalese paper *Le Soleil* that he had been informed by telephone that Indonesia had bombed villages in the nationalist-controlled zone and killed over 1,600 people. Nationalists responded by killing over four hundred Indonesians, including two officers, and wounding more than eight hundred others. The communiqué denounced the "criminal action of the Indonesian junta and its neo-colonial satellite, Papua-New Guinea." Indeed, it revealed how Papua New Guinea's Foreign Minister Albert Maori Kiki stated that his government would cooperate with Indonesia and refuse sanctuary to the rebels.[65]

The pages of *Povai* demonstrate that Oceanic movements stood in solidarity with West Papua. This was clearly the case in Papua New Guinea, which had obtained independence in 1975 from Australia. *Povai* also described how in February 1976, two hundred students at the University of Papua New Guinea (UPNG) staged a demonstration march to the Indonesia Embassy in Port Moresby. They demanded that the Government supported West Papua and East Timor. These issues were also raised by organizations such as the Women's Action Group, which held a protest against Indonesian imperialism in December 1975.[66]

Students at UPNG had long since expressed this support. By May 1969, its student newspaper *Nilaidat* had become a space of political education on the issue. The paper published an extensive special edition on the political, geographic, historical, economic, and social implications of West Papua. In May 1969, it published a letter that Kaisiepo had sent to the United Nations which described how, between 1965 and 1968, the Indonesian military bombarded West Papua with napalm, burned the houses of dissidents, and killed and tortured adults and children. Kaisiepo claimed that more than fifty thousand innocent men, women and children had been killed in West Papua.[67]

Nilaidat questioned Indonesia's motives surrounding the Act of Free Choice. Disturbed by the reports that Indonesia was bombing West Papua's highlands and sending warships to Biak, it found Indonesia's actions to be "depressingly reminiscent of Italy's enforced subjugation" of Ethiopia in 1936. Reported by *Nilaidat*, UPNG students held a daylong forum about the political and legal implications of the issue. It used the event to gather supplies for children of West Papuan refugees who had fled into Papua New Guinea.[68]

UPNG students also organized a march to the Australian Government house. Over five hundred marchers protested Australia's support of Indonesia, and the United Nations' refusal to assertively address Indonesia's violation of human rights in West Papua. At the Government house marchers sang songs such as "We Shall Overcome."[69] Leo Hannet, president of the UPNG Politics club, led the group. Communications from West Papua were sent directly to him, and he called on Papua New Guinea's spiritual leaders to express their moral support for their western neighbors.[70] Encouraged by West Papua and other issues on decolonization, Hannet and other UPNG students formed the Niugini Black Power Group—a Frantz Fanon–inspired "African Negritude" movement—in 1970.[71] This is only one example of how Melanesian activists embraced Negritude and Black Power in their Pacific struggles. Their references to Senghor and Senegal reflect how Africa played a conceptual and tangible role in these political relationships.

Tanghamma had directed the RPG's Dakar based office since 1975. During a press conference on its founding, the RPG informed media that Papuans were a Melanesian "sub-race of the Black Race." From Senegal, he popularized the West Papuan struggle. For example, he asked Wilkins and Mildred Bond Roxborough to invite him to the NAACP's 1976 national convention. This RPG sought the support of "a strong movement of Black Americans," as it believed that African Americans could influence US and UN policies on West Papuan sovereignty. Tanghamma also reached out to African heads of state. In March 1976, he met with the foreign minister of Ivory Coast and sent a message from Sumkorem to its President, Félix Houphouët-Boigny.[72]

According to the State Department, Tanggahma lived in a large house pro vided by the Senegalese government. The RPG's office staff included a second officer from West Papua, and Tanggahma told an informant that four more colleagues would arrive in the summer of 1976. He also maintained an exceptionally low profile; US and Dutch officials found him to be evasive. When US officials accidently encoun- tered him in the SWAPO office, Tanggahma supposedly withdrew in confusion, say- ing he should not be in contact with diplomats. US officials read this as him trying to keep within the Senegalese government's restrictions placed on him. Whether true or not, his office was adjacent to the residence of the US embassy's communications and records assistant, leading the Department to confidently believe that opportunities "for substantive contact with embassy personnel could arise."[73]

Tanggahma had his own reasons to meet with US personnel. He had unsuc- cessfully hoped to meet with African American Congressman Charles Diggs during his 1976 visit to Dakar. In 1977, Tanghamma visited the US embassy. Stressing US official policy on human rights, he asked for moral and material support for the RPG. He shared with the US ambassador a memorandum, a letter for President Jimmy Carter and a sixty-page document detailing the case of West Papua. Tang- hamma had just returned from an extensive trip to build relationships with Ghana, Liberia, Tanzania, and Mozambique. The ambassador responded gently without commitment.[74]

Unsurprisingly, Tanghamma found most of his support from Black spaces. In February 1976, a group of Black intellectuals, scholars, researchers, and scientists from across the Americas and Africa attended Dakar's Seminar for African Alterna- tives. Tanggahma attended the talks and described West Papua's political history within the context of its struggles against Indonesian and European enslavement and colonialism. In response, the Seminar released a *Declaration of Black Intellec- tuals and Scholars in Support of the People's Struggle of West Papua New Guinea and East Timor Against Indonesian Colonialism*. The document expressed alarm over the reports of Indonesia's "campaign of extermination" against the Melanesian populations of West Papua New Guinea and East Timor. It found it shocking that 165,000 West Papuan Blacks had been killed, imprisoned, or herded into strategic hamlets since 1965, and that 30,000 East Timorese were butchered by the Indonesia since its annexation of East Timor in 1975. It denounced the racist and genocidal acts that Indonesia had bought onto the 2.7 million Melanesians.[75]

The *Declaration* asserted that Melanesians were distinct national commu- nities whose racial, historical, cultural, and political affinities with Africa and the Black world were "beyond question." It understood the armed struggles of West Papua and East Timor as being part of the struggles of all oppressed peoples in Africa, North America, the Caribbean, South America, the Pacific, Asia and the Middle East." It argued that by taking up arms against Indonesian oppression, the twenty thousand guerillas "shedding their blood in a silent isolated struggle" were making a laudable contribution to the emancipation of the Black world. The Seminar resolved to "support to the utmost" the national liberation struggles of West Papua and East Timor. It expressed "unreserved fraternal solidarity" with their brothers: the RPG's National Liberation Army and President Rumkorem, and the Democratic Republic of East Timor's Revolutionary Armed Forces and President Francisco Xavier Do Amaral.[76]

Significantly, the Seminar expressed Indonesia's aggression from a perspective of class, power, and global economics. It considered Indonesia's expansion to be driven by the greed and self-interest of Jakarta's Javanese ruling class, which had also resulted in the deaths of the Indonesian people and was supported by global transnational companies that sought to loot Melanesia's mineral resources. The Seminar was convinced that "without the active mobilization of the Black peoples of Africa, the Caribbean, South America, North America and the Pacific," the "fascist Javanese junta" would be encouraged to enact further acts of genocide.[77]

The *Declaration* called on the Black nations of Africa, the Americas, and the Pacific and other "justice seeking nations" to support West Papua and East Timor. It called on the terrorized 125 million people of Indonesia, "now crushed under the merciless boots of a right wing fascist regime, to rise to their feet and contribute to their own national and social liberation" by aiding these states against a common enemy. It asked the United Nations, the OAU, the Organization of Non-Aligned Nations, the Organization of Afro-Asian Unity, the Arab league, and the Organization of African, Caribbean, and Pacific Nations to compel Indonesia to withdraw its armed forces from West Papua and East Timor.[78]

Interviewed by *Le Monde* during the Seminar, Tanggahma allegedly asserted that West Papuans needed to get rid of Indonesia's guardianship, which was "favorable to yellow supremacy, racist, expansionist, colonialist and fascist."[79] He gave a fascinating interview on the historic struggles of Melanesia to Carlos Moore and journalist Shwana Maglanbayan. Tanggahma defined Melanesians as part of the African family, sharing a common past and destiny with the Black world. He discussed the enslavement of Papuans in the Indian Ocean and Middle Eastern slave trade, enslaved "Black Philippinos" taken to Mexico by the Spanish, African migration into the Pacific, indigenous Black communities in Asia, and blackbirding.[80]

According to Tanggahma, the RPG's ideology was Melanesian nationalism. The Black peoples of Melanesia needed to "determine their own future, and work together with . . . the rest of the Black world to redeem Black peoples from" racial servitude. How would they defeat Indonesia, with its military might, while they had few weapons and material backing? For Tanggahma, this was "a question that our ancestors in New Guinea, in Africa, the Caribbean and the Pacific" must have repeatedly asked themselves "in the face of the invading White man." The only answer was "reliance on the courage, awakening and determination of our people to be free. . . . Reliance on the active and total support of the Black world."[81]

But was it this simple? For Tanggahma, West Papua had received much *sympathy* from the African Diaspora, but it needed "active solidarity" in the form of "concrete material and humanitarian aid." Senegal and Senghor lead the way in this regard.[82] Indeed, the RPG was convinced that if not for Senghor's humanitarianism, they might have been "erased from the face of the planet." He felt that the mere existence of an office in Dakar capable of denouncing "the crimes of Indonesia" had been undoubtedly instrumental in encouraging Sweden to accept West Papuan refugees.[83]

From the US State Department's perspective, the RPG's office in Senegal made strategic sense. While there, its representatives could be in proximity to Black organizers—and potential supporters—who were drawn to Dakar by *Negritude*. The Seminar only seemed to confirm this. As Bermuda's Pauulu Kamarakafego informed the *Black World* in 1976, Black internationalist meetings such as Atlanta's Congress of African Peoples (1970), Senegal's Seminar, 6PAC, and FESTAC were critical spaces of rediscovery between the Black Atlantic, Pacific and Indian Ocean worlds.[84]

Dakar's role as a hub for communication between liberation struggles *within* the South Pacific is striking. This reminds us how the roots and routes of Black internationalism spread across the Global South in ways both unexpected and predictable. The case of West Papua passes through Black communities living in the Harlems of the United States, Netherlands, and West Papua. The surveillance of the Global South speaks through the archives of Senegal, Netherlands, Indonesia, Australia, and the United States.

West Papua remains a colony of Indonesia. In 2010, the Free West Papua Campaign participated in Dakar's World Festival of Black Arts. In opening the Festival, Senegalese President Abdoulaye Wade exclaimed that "West Papua is now an issue for all Black Africans." His comments also welcomed to Senegal the founder of the Free West Papua Campaign, Benny Wanda. It would be interesting to know: while Wanda seeks solidarity from Black communities across the Global South, to what extent are they still, if at all, "Blinded by Bandung?"[85]

Quito Swan is a professor of African Diaspora History at Howard University. The author of Black Power in Bermuda (2010), his research interests include Black Internationalism, global Black Power and racial politics in Oceania. Sponsored by the American Council of Learned Societies, he is 2017–2018 residential fellow at Harvard's Radcliffe Institute for Advanced Study. Research for this article was supported by a 2014 National Endowment for the Humanities Award for University Faculty.

Notes

1.   Provisional Government of West Papua (RPG), "Indonesian Colonialism vs. The People of West Papua New Guinea," 1, Box 8313, West New Guinea, NAACP Papers, Library of Congress.

2. "African Papuans Being Slaughtered by Indonesian Government," NAACP papers; "Nonaligned Nations, Liberation Fronts, Political Leaders, Meetings," July 7 1976, Cable 1976DAKAR04287, National Archives, College Park; *Le Monde,* March 30 1976.

3. Maglangbayan and Moore, "Interview with Ben Tanggahma."

4. See Guridy, *Forging Diaspora.*

5. Malcolm X, "Message to the Grass Roots," 5-6.

6. Lopez, "(Post) global South;" Lumumba-Kasongo, "Rethinking Bandung;" Assie-Lumumba, "Behind and Beyond Bandung;" Jones, *The Muse is Music,* 1.

7. Tate, "Australasian concern over the New Hebrides," Box 219-9, Merz Tate papers; Gravelle, *Fiji Times,* 109; Mortenson, "Slaving in Australian courts: Blackbirding cases, 1869–1871," 1; Horne, *White Pacific,* 34; Maynard, *Origins of Australian Aboriginal Activism;* Crocombe, *Politics in Melanesia;* Robie, *Nationalist Struggles in the South Pacific;* Banivanua Mar, *Decolonization and the Pacific.*

8. Hau'ofa, *We Are the Ocean.*

9. Shilliam, *Black Pacific;* Taketani, *Black Pacific Narrative;* Horne, *The White Pacific;* Solis, "Black Pacific."

10. Levander and Mignolo, "Global South and World Dis/Order"; Milian and Nwankwo, "Interoceanic Diasporas"; Misalucha, "Challenges Facing the Global South"; Harker, "Cavaliers in Paradise"; Banivanua Mar, *Decolonization*; West et al., *The Black International.*

11. Meduna, "Tracking the Lapita Expansion Across the Pacific"; Bedford, Sand, and Shing, *Lapita Peoples: Oceanic Ancestors*; Bedford and Spriggs, "Northern Vanuatu as a Pacific Crossroads."

12. Tate, "Early European Discoveries in the Pacific," 1–2, 4, Box 219–10, Merz Tate Papers.

13. See Serge Tcherkézoff, "A Long and Unfortunate Voyage towards the 'Invention' of the Melanesia/Polynesia Distinction 1595–1832," *Journal of Pacific History* 38:2 (2003): 175–196.

14. Delaney, *Martin Delany,* 482; DuBois, "Bond of Ideals" *Chicago Daily Defender,* 26 September 1942; Cooper, *Voice of Anna Julia Cooper,* 296.

15. Maynard, "In the Interests of Our People," 2; "Sydney Division," *Negro World,* 6 May 1923; Hill, *Marcus Garvey Papers,* Vol 9, 541.

16. "Blacks of Australia Enslaved and Brutalized," *Negro World,* September 20, 1924.

17. "Race Horrors in Australia are Unspeakably Vile," *Negro World.*

18. "Negro Troops Serving on All Fronts," *Cleveland Call and Post.*

19. Tate, "The War Aims of World War I," 521.

20. Tate, "Early European Discoveries in the Pacific," 1–2, 4, Box 219–10, Merz Tate Papers; See Firth, "The Labor Trade in German New Guinea," 51–65; Nelson, *Papua New Guinea,* 66, 123; RPG, "Indonesian Colonialism," 1; Grattan, *Southwest Pacific,* 452–453.

21. Macleod, *Merdeka and the Morning Star.*

22. Grattan, *Southwest Pacific,* 452–453.

23. RPG, "Indonesian Colonialism," 1.

24. Ministry of Foreign Affairs, "Final Communiqué," 168.

25. "A People's Preparations for its Freedom brought to Nought by Indonesia's Blackmail Policy," 20 June 1968, NAACP Papers; AAP Reuters, "Declaration by Papuans," *The Sydney Morning Herald* October 31, 1961; RPG, "Indonesian Colonialism," 2.

26. "Fear New Guinea may become 'New Congo,'" *Chicago Daily Defender,* November 30, 1961; Richard Neff, "Dutch-Indonesia Dispute," *Bermuda Recorder,* January 13, 1962.

27. *Chicago Daily Defender,* April 14, 1962; *Press and Sun-Bulletin,* December 19, 1961;

"Indonesians Told of Logical Base to Attack Guinea," *Atlanta Daily World*, January 5, 1962; Richard Neff, "Dutch-Indonesia Dispute," *Bermuda Recorder.*

28. "New Guinea Crisis Dates Back To 1949 Dispute," *Chicago Daily Defender*, January 23, 1962, 9; "10,000 Indonesian Volunteers Sent to Infiltrate New Guinea," *Bermuda Recorder*, February 2, 1962; *The Age,* January 22, 1962.

29. "Papuans Say Fight Faces Indonesia," *Post-Standard*, December 21, 1961; "Poisoned Arrows Threat by Papuans," *The Age,* January 22, 1962; *The Age*, May 31, 1962.

30. RPG, "A People's Preparations."

31. AAP Reuters, "African Calls Plight of New Guinea Natives a Scandal," *The Age*, May 9, 1962.

32. Howard, "Africans Split on New Guinea Issue."

33. Ibid.

34. Ibid.

35. *The Age*, May 31, 1962; Leon Dennen, "Papuans Want Same, as Most—Their Freedom," *Terre Haute Star*, July 31, 1962.

36. "Papuans seek help from Negro brothers and sisters," *Pittsburgh Courier*, April 14, 1962.

37. Ibid.; *Chicago Daily Defender*, April 14, 1962.

38. *Chicago Daily Defender*, April 14, 1962.

39. Dennen, "Papuans Want Same," *Terre Haute Star*, July 31, 1962; *Chicago Daily Defender*, April 14, 1962; "Stone Age Habits of Papuans Slow Changeover to New Independence," *Amarillo Globe-Times*, October 5, 1962.

40. Elifoson, "New Guinea," 1961 Series I, Writings; Box 58, South Sea Islands Photographs; "The South Seas: Its People, Its Art, May Co, 1963–64," Elifoson Papers, Harry Ransom Humanities Center, University of Texas–Austin.

41. "A People's Preparations for its Freedom," 20 June 1968, NAACP Papers.

42. "Jakarta to State Department," June 9, 1969, POL 19 West Irian, NACP.

43. "Jakarta to State Department," April 27, 1967, NACP.

44. "Jakarta to State Department," June 9, 1969, NACP.

45. *Nilaidat*, May 22, 1969, 1.

46. "Memo of Conversation," 12 December 1967, NACP. See also Macleod, *Merdeka.*

47. "Jakarta to State Department," May 10, 1968, NACP.

48. "Jarkata to State Department," February 29, 1968, April 27, 1968, May 2, 1968, June 18, 1968, NACP.

49. "State Department Report on Implementation of Act of Free Choice," August 9, 1968, NACP.

50. "Jakarta to State Department," July 29, 1968, June 12, 1969, NACP.

51. Ibid; Jakarta to State Department, April 22, 1969, NACP.

52. "Conversation with Ambassador Ortiz Sans," April 25, 1969; "Jakarta to State Department," August 7, 1969; November 19, 1969; NACP.

53. "Memo, Act of Free Choice," November 17, 1969, NACP.

54. See Webster, *Fire and the Full Moon*; and Jones, *Britain, the United States, Indonesia and the Creation of Malaysia.*

55. RPG, "Urgent Appeal to Members of the United Nations," September 1, 1973, NAACP Papers.

56. Ibid.

57. Anderson, *Bourgeois Radicals*, 204–268.

58. Herman Womsiwor to Roy Wilkins, April 29, 1971, National Liberation Council of West Papua, "African Papuans Being Slaughtered by Indonesian Government," NAACP papers.

59. Roy Wilkins to Kurt Waldhcim, January 4 1972; Herman Womsiwor to the NAACP, September 25, 1975; NAACP, "Resolutions Adopted by the Sixty-Second Annual Convention of the NAACP," *Crisis Magazine* (March 1972), 5; NAACP Papers.
60. National Liberation Council of West Papua, "African Papuans Being Slaughtered," NAACP papers.
61. "Nonaligned Nations, Liberation Fronts, Political Leaders, Meetings," 7 July 1976, Cable 1976DAKAR04287, NACP, College Park, MD; "Senegalese President repeats support for West Papua New Guinea Independence," February 4, 1978, Cable 1978DAKAR01024, NACP.
62. "Senegalese Relations with South Moluccans And National Liberation Council Of West Papau/New Guinea," Feb 4, 1976, Cable 1976DAKAR00688, NACP.
63. Soyinka, "Senghor."
64. Griffen, Vanessa, and Claire Slatter, Interview by Quito Swan, November 12, 2014; *Povai*, "Freedom Fighters of West Papua New Guinea," 1.1, March/April 1976, 2; September/October 1976, 8; Pacifica Collection, Library of the University of the South Pacific, Suva, Fiji.
65. "Independence, Liberation Fronts, Foreign Policy Position, Limited War," February 24, 1976, Cable 1976DAKAR01081, NACP.
66. "West Papua," 1.1, June/July 1976, 3; "West Papua New Guinea," 1.3, September/October 1976, 8, *Povai*.
67. *Nilaidat*, Vol. 2, no.. 3, May 22, 1969.
68. *Nilaidat*, Vol. 2, no. 2, May 14, 1969, UPNG Library, Papua New Guinea Collection, Port Moresby, Papua New Guinea.
69. *Nilaidat*, June 6, 1969.
70. *Nilaidat*, May 22, 1969.
71. Hannett, "Niugini Black Power Movement."
72. "Press Release—The Provisional Government of the Republic of West Papua"; "Bernard Tanghamma to Roxborough," Bernard Tanghamma to Roy Wilkins, 12 February 1976, NAACP Papers; "Western Papua New Guinea, a Little Known Rebellion," *Le Monde*, 17 March 1976.
73. "Senegalese Relations with South Moluccans," NACP.
74. Ibid.; "West Irian Dissident Movement Seeks US Support," June 2, 1977; Cable 1977DAKAR03831, NACP.
75. Declaration of Intellectuals and Scholars," 187:2:34, Harold Cruse Papers, Tamiment Library and Robert F. Wagner Labor Archive, New York.
76. Ibid.
77. Ibid.
78. Ibid.
79. "In Western Papua New Guinea . . ." *Le Monde*, 17 March 1976.
80. Maglangbayan and Moore, "Interview with Ben Tanggahma."
81. Maglangbayan and Moore, "Interview with Ben Tanggahma."
82. Ibid.
83. RPG, "Statement to the Press," February 15, 1980, NAACP Papers.
84. "Independence, Liberation Fronts, Foreign Policy Position, Limited War," February 24, 1976. Cable 1976DAKAR01081, NACP; Cobb, "An Interview with Roosevelt Browne."
85. "President of Senegal—'West Papua is now an issue for all Black Africans,'" https://westpapuamedia.info/2010/12/20/president-of-senegal-west-papua-is-now-an-issue-for-all-black-africans/ accessed 10 March 2017.

References

Anderson, Carole. 2014. *Bourgeois Radicals: The NAACP and the Struggle for Colonial Liberation, 1941–1960*. Cambridge: Cambridge University Press.

Hill, Robert, ed. 1983–1991. *Garvey Papers*. Vols 7, 9–10. Berkeley: University of California Press.

Assie-Lumumba, N'Dri. 2015. "Behind and Beyond Bandung." *Bandung* 2, no. 11.

Banivanua Mar, Tracey. 2016. *Decolonization and the Pacific*. Cambridge: Cambridge University Press.

Bedford, Stuart, Christophe Sand, and Richard Shing. 2010. *Lapita Peoples: Oceanic Ancestors*. Port Vila: Vanuatu Cultural Centre.

Bedford, Stuart and M. Spriggs. 2008. "Northern Vanuatu as a Pacific Crossroads: The Archaeology of Discovery." *Asian Perspectives* 47, no. 1: 95–120.

Cobb, Gayleatha. 1976. "An Interview with Roosevelt Browne." *Black World/Negro Digest* 25, no. 5: 32–43.

Cooper, Ana J. 2000. *The Voice of Anna Julia Cooper*. New York: Roman & Littlefield.

Crocombe, Ron. 1982. *Politics in Melanesia*. Suva, Fiji: University of the South Pacific.

Cruse, Harold Papers. Tamiment Library and Robert F. Wagner Labor Archive, New York University: New York.

Delaney, Martin. 2003. *Martin Delany: A Documentary Reader*. Chapel Hill: University Press of North Carolina.

Du Bois, W. E. B. 1942. "Bond of Ideals." *Chicago Daily Defender*. September 26.

Elifoson, Eliot Papers. Harry Ransom Humanities Center, University of Texas-Austin. Austin, Texas.

Guridy, Frank. 2010. *Forging Diaspora: Afro-Cubans and African Americans in a World of Empire*. Chapel Hill: University of North Carolina Press.

Grattan, C. Hartley. 1963. *The Southwest Pacific Since 1900*. Ann Arbor: University of Michigan Press.

Gravelle, Kim. 1983. *Fiji Times: A History of Fiji*. Suva: Fiji Times.

Griffen, Vanessa and Claire Slatter. Interview by Quito Swan. November 12, 2014.

Hannett, Leo. 1971. "The Niugini Black Power Movement." In *Tertiary Students and the Politics of Papua New Guinea*. Lae: Papua New Guinea Institute of Technology.

Harker, Jaime. 2009. "Cavaliers in Paradise . . ." *Global South* 3, no. 2: 1–13.

Hau'ofa, Epeli. 2008. *We Are the Ocean*. Mānoa: University of Hawai'i Press.

Horne, Gerald. 2007. *The White Pacific*. Honolulu: University of Hawaii Press.

Howard, Charles. 1962. "Africans Split on New Guinea Issue." *Afro-American*, June 9.

Jones, Matthew. 2012. *Britain, the United States, Indonesia and the Creation of Malaysia*, Cambridge: Cambridge University Press.

Jones, Meta. 2013. *The Muse is Music: Jazz Poetry from the Harlem Renaissance to Spoken Word*. Chicago: University of Illinois Press.

Levander, Caroline and Walter Mignolo. 2011. "The Global South and World Dis/Order." *Global South* 5, no. 1: 1–11.

Lopez, Alfred. 2007. "The (Post) Global South," *Global South* 1, no. 1.

Lumumba-Kasongo, Tukumbi. 2015. "Rethinking the Bandung Conference." *Bandung* 2, no. 9.

Macleod, Jason. 2016. *Merdeka and the Morning Star: Civil Resistance in West Papua*. Brisbane: University of Queensland Press.

Maglangbayan, Shawna, and Carlos Moore. 1976. "Interview with Ben Tanggahma." *Association of African Historians Newsletter* 1, no. 9.

Maynard, John. 2005. "In the Interests of Our People: The Influence of Garveyism on the rise of Australian Aboriginal Political Activism." *Aboriginal History* 29, no. 2.

Meduna, Veronika. 2015. "Tracking the Lapita Expansion Across the Pacific." *Our Changing World*, August 13.

Milian, Claudia and Ifeoma Nwankwo. 2012. "Interoceanic Diasporas and The Panama Canal's Centennial." *Global South* 6, no. 2: 1–14.

Ministry of Foreign Affairs. 1955. "Final Communiqué of the Asian-African Conference of Bandung." *Asia-Africa Speak from Bandung*. Djakarta: Republic of Indonesia.

Misalucha, Charmaine G. 2015. "The Challenges Facing the Global South." *Bandung: Journal of the Global South* 2: no. 7.

Mortenson, Reid. 2000. "Slaving in Australian courts: Blackbirding cases, 1869–1871," *Journal of South Pacific Law* 4, no. 1. NAACP Papers. Library of Congress: Washington DC.

Nelson, Hank. 1972. *Papua New Guinea*. Middlesex, UK: Penguin Books.

Robie, David. 1989. *Nationalist Struggles in the South Pacific*. London: Pluto Press Australia.

Shilliam, Robbie. 2015. *The Black Pacific: Anti-Colonial Struggles and Oceanic Connections*. London: Bloomsbury Publishing.

Solis, Gabriel. 2014. "The Black Pacific: Music and Racialization in Papua New Guinea and Australia." *Critical Sociology* 41, no. 2: 297–314.

Soyinka, Wole. 2002. "Senghor: Lessons in Power." *Research in African Literatures* 33, no. 4. State Department Cables. National Archives. College Park, Maryland.

Taketani, Etsuko. 2014. *Black Pacific Narrative*. Dartmouth, NH: Dartmouth College Press.

Tate, Merz Papers. Moorland Spingarn Research Center. Howard University: Washington DC.

Tate, Merz. 1943. "The War Aims of World War I and World War II and Their Relation to the Darker Peoples of the World." *Journal of Negro Education* 12, vol. 3.

Tcherkézoff, Serge. 2003. "A Long and Unfortunate Voyage towards the 'Invention' of the Melanesia/Polynesia Distinction 1595–1832." *Journal of Pacific History* 38, no. 2: 175–196.

Webster, David. 2010. *Fire and the Full Moon: Canada and Indonesia in a Decolonizing World*. Vancouver: University of British Columbia Press.

West, Michael et al. 2009. *The Black International*. Chapel Hill: University of North Carolina Press.

West Papua Media. 2010. "President of Senegal–West Papua is now an issue for all Black Africans." https://westpapuamedia.info/2010/12/20/president-of-senegal-west -papua-is-now-an-issue-for-all-black-africans/ (accessed 10 March 2017).

X, Malcolm. 1965. *Malcolm X Speaks: Selected Speeches and Statements*. Edited by George Breitman. New York: Grove.

"Injectable Development"

Depo-Provera and Creation of the Global South

Emily Callaci

In 1972, the United States Food and Drug Administration denied the Michigan-based Upjohn Corporation approval to produce and sell its newly developed inject-able hormonal contraceptive, Depo-Provera, in the United States on the grounds that the drug was not proven to be safe. Depo-Provera simultaneously became the contraceptive of choice for many development experts to send as a form of aid to recently decolonized nations in Africa and Asia. As a network of donors, popula-tion control advocates, and pharmaceutical companies sent vials of Depo-Provera into circulation around the world, the drug's meanings, uses, and political valences morphed. People at various points along this global trajectory were faced with a question: if one of the basic premises of biomedicine was the universality of the body and medical efficacy, what made Depo-Provera unsafe in one part of the world but efficacious in another? What did those women in various global locations, for whom Depo-Provera was considered medicine rather than poison, have in com-mon? In this essay, I track how different people responded to the questions raised by Depo-Provera's uneven global distribution. In doing so, I reveal the multiple ways communities thought about global power and persistent inequality at a moment of historic transition away from a world order structured by the logic of empires and toward a world bifurcated between North and South.

The global dissemination of Depo-Provera contributed materially to the cre-ation of the Global South as a coherent space. Many of the influential thinkers in the

Radical History Review

Issue 131 (May 2018)   DOI 10.1215/01636545-4355145

© 2018 by MARHO: The Radical Historians' Organization, Inc.

world of international development and health in the 1970s believed that population growth was the primary cause of poverty and poor health, and they shared a faith in technological solutions to these problems.[1] Depo-Provera, along with other biomedical contraceptives, was an artifact of their approach. During those years, powerful government, international, and private institutions in the field of population policy—what Matthew Connelly calls the "population establishment"—pursued a policy known as inundation, referring to an intention to inundate poor countries with contraceptives.[2] Advocates of this policy believed that the dissemination of LARCs (long-acting reversible contraceptives), such as intrauterine devices (IUDs) and injectable hormonal contraceptives, would reduce birthrates, thereby alleviating poverty by reducing the ratio of human beings to resources. Historian Randall Packard has argued that, in those years, donors directed funding for health initiatives toward family planning activities at the expense of investments in functional, durable health systems and infrastructures.[3] One of the long-term effects was to further entrench the disparity between the standards of public health systems in different parts of the world.

Yet powerful as they were, the network of donors, policymakers and pharmaceutical companies that sent new contraceptive technologies into global circulation could not dictate the effects, uses, or meanings of these objects. As Michelle Murphy has demonstrated, the invention of synthetic hormones in the 1970s rendered sex and reproduction mutable in new ways, catalyzing struggles over *how* sex would be altered, and on whose behalf. She argues that the same technologies could call together different relationships when used in a feminist health clinic in one part of the world and in a population control program in another. New contraceptives such as Depo-Provera were what Murphy calls "travelling technologies," simultaneously connecting different global locations and transforming meanings and uses as they moved across different political and cultural contexts.[4] The changing ways in which these hormonal technologies were used reveals disconnects between the intentions of donors and recipients, and, at times, the appropriation of technologies for unanticipated ends. For example, as Caroline Bledsoe has demonstrated, West African women have often used biomedical contraceptives, including Depo-Provera, to space children in order to avoid obstetric trauma and protect fertility, with the goal of increasing the number of healthy surviving children in their families.[5] Donors may have shipped Depo-Provera to the Global South in order to curb population growth, but that does not mean that their actions had the intended effect.

Depo-Provera's global history reveals how people began to think of the "Global South" as a coherent space. More than any other pharmaceutical product of the 1970s, Depo-Provera conjured global imaginaries as it travelled. Witnesses at various points along Depo-Provera's global trajectory described it in widely divergent ways: as a lifesaving medicine, an antipoverty vaccine, a rapid-fire automatic weapon, a fertility enhancer, an environmental poison, an addictive sex drug, and as the genocidal tool of a white supremacist conspiracy. Rather than assess the material effects of Depo-Provera, or the veracity of the various claims made about it, I investigate how its global dissemination provoked different modes of global thinking. Stories about Depo-Provera extended far beyond the effect of the drug on individual bodies to raise larger questions about the postcolonial world order. As Claire Wendland has demonstrated, thinking of medicine's stories "as stories," rather than simply asking whether they are true or false, opens up new questions about how power and inequality shape the context of health and healing.[6] Along these lines, I argue that by creating stories and subjectivities around Depo-Provera, communities from different global positions struggled over the shape of the postcolonial world and the power relations that structured it.

The controversies over Depo-Provera in the 1970s reveal three worldviews. First, those in the "population establishment" framed Depo-Provera as a technological fix for two perceived crises: the so-called "population bomb" and high maternal and child mortality rates in poor countries, and they sought to alleviate both of these crises with technology that could reduce the number of pregnancies. For the population establishment, inequality between the Global North and South was accepted as a starting premise, as the naturalized order of the world in which health and economic goals would be articulated. Second, critics and activists argued that not only was Depo-Provera unsafe for individual bodies, but also that its promotion as a fix for poverty intentionally obscured the global historical causes of ill health and inequality. Anti-Depo-Provera activists from around the world articulated a critical counter-mapping of the places where women were offered Depo-Provera, highlighting shared histories of dispossession that linked women in dispersed locations, from the government housing estates of working-class Glasgow, to the medical test sites of San Juan, Atlanta and Chiang-Mai, to the slums of Dar es Salaam. Third, local gatekeepers, including nurses, social workers, and doctors who received Depo-Provera as a form of foreign aid shaped its meaning and uses in contexts of scarcity, uncertainty, and controversy. I focus on one such group of practitioners in Dar es Salaam, Tanzania, who used Depo-Provera and the other resources made available by the population establishment to improvise new health infrastructures, in conditions not of their own choosing.

Travelling Injections

Depo-Provera was created, tested, and marketed in an uneven global terrain on the cusp of a transition from a world order shaped by the logics of eugenics and empire to one shaped by the logics of global population control.[7] The global family planning movement was both a continuation of and a departure from earlier colonial interventions in the reproductive lives of people in colonized territories.[8] For much of its history, European colonial regimes pursued pronatalist policies in an attempt to address labor shortages in colonial industries and extractive economies. As Nancy

Rose Hunt has demonstrated, pronatalist colonial regimes in Africa collected demographic knowledge of subject populations and promoted colonial maternal health programs as the "soft" side of rule, legitimizing the colonial enterprise through the performance of a modernizing benevolence.[9]

In the wake of the decolonization movements of the 1960s, colonial hubris gave way to the intersecting ambitions of private donor agencies, cold war alliances and rivalries, international institutions, and newly sovereign nations. Agents in the United States and Europe no longer operated on mythologies of an imperial mission to "civilize" and "modernize" but rather on the emerging rhetoric of an urgent population crisis. Experts believed that global population growth was approaching critical levels and would result in mass poverty, environmental devastation, and violent conflicts over resources if actions were not taken to reduce population growth rates. Donor agencies, most notably USAID, required countries seeking aid to adopt population control measures as a prerequisite for aid.[10] Several heads of state in Asia enforced top-down coercive population control policies, such as Indira Gandhi, who infamously oversaw mass sterilizations of the poor in Delhi; Suharto, who called for forced sterilizations and IUD insertions in Indonesia; and later, Mao Zedong, whose regime implemented the one child policy in China.[11] By contrast, most African leaders opposed population control measures and instead adopted what Linda Richey has called a position of strategic ambiguity in order to continue to access this valuable source of aid money without committing to population policies that would have been deeply unpopular among their constituencies.[12] When Depo-Provera was invented and tested in the 1960s, its effects took shape unevenly in this changing global terrain.

When injected intramuscularly, Depo-Provera, the commercial name for the drug medroxyprogesterone, works as a contraceptive by preventing ovulation for three to six months, depending on the dosage. Like other synthetic hormonal concoctions developed in the 1960s, the chemistry of Depo-Provera was first used in the treatment of other health conditions, including uterine carcinoma, endometriosis, and recurrent miscarriages.[13] Women who were injected with Depo-Provera to treat recurrent miscarriages experienced infertility for an extended period afterwards as a side effect. This discovery led to its repurposing as a contraceptive.

From the start, Depo-Provera's effects on the body provoked concerns about safety, and successive medical trials did not bring the clarity that Upjohn had hoped for. Trials conducted on beagles suggested that Depo-Provera might cause several harmful side effects including blood clots, breast tumors, and menstrual irregularity.[14] By 1965, human clinical trials were underway in Chiang Mai, Thailand at the McCormick hospital, built by the family of Katherine McCormick, the philanthropist who collaborated with Margaret Sanger to fund research for the birth control pill.[15] Meanwhile, medical trials were ongoing in San Juan, Puerto Rico, which American pharmaceutical companies had fashioned as a kind of "laboratory" for medical testing since the trials of the contraceptive pill in the 1950s.[16] Trials were also carried out from 1972–78 at Grady Memorial Hospital, located in a predominantly Black neighborhood in Atlanta, Georgia, on subjects consisting almost entirely of women who were Black and poor or working class. The FDA ordered the cessation of the Grady trials in 1978 due to concerns about safety.[17] Women who were injected with Depo-Provera experienced several side effects including cessation of menstruation, irregular menstrual cycles, and heavy bleeding. In order to mitigate these effects, doctors sometimes prescribed a monthly estrogen pill for women to take while using Depo-Provera, though many women did not take the supplement because it induced nausea.

One of the most distressing effects of Depo-Provera was the extended and unpredictable period of suppressed ovulation following cessation of the drug, which made it difficult for women to become pregnant. This was especially troubling for women who used contraception not with the intention of having fewer children but with the intention of controlling the spacing of their children. Adding an unintended period of infertility to their childbearing plans could be devastating, especially in situations where a lack of trained medical personnel and patient education meant that many women were not made aware about the effects of Depo-Provera before presenting themselves for an injection.

Upjohn's requests for USFDA approval for the use of Depo-Provera as a contraceptive were repeatedly rejected between its invention in the late 1960s and its eventual approval in 1992, and during those years, women in the United States could use Depo-Provera as contraception only as participants in medical trials, or, in some cases, when doctors prescribed it for off-label use. The lack of FDA approval meant not only that Upjohn could not manufacture or market Depo-Provera as a contraceptive in the United States, but also that government agencies—most importantly, USAID—could not distribute it to other parts of the world as a form of aid.[18] To get around this, Upjohn manufactured the drug in Belgium through a subsidiary company and found its market and distribution network through private donors and purchasing agents, namely the International Planned Parenthood Federation (IPPF) and Pathfinder Fund.[19] Nations with the highest user rates for Depo-Provera included Mexico, Jamaica, Thailand, Sri Lanka, and New Zealand; in the latter, the highest user rates were among Maori women.[20] Feminist activists in London reported that in the United Kingdom, Depo-Provera was prescribed for off-label uses to poor working-class women on government assistance in Glasgow and that it was injected without informed consent into West Indian women in London hospitals when they received their German measles vaccination.[21] On a global scale, Depo-Provera moved from Global North to the Global South, and within stratified national populations towards poor women of color at the same time that the birth control pill was famously revolutionizing the lives of middle-class white women.[22]

Unable to market it in the US, Upjohn saw Africa as a potential market for

Depo-Provera just as newly sovereign African nations were building public health systems on the sparse and uneven foundations left by the colonial era. Upjohn marketed their drug directly to physicians and family planning clinics in Nigeria and in Zaire, leading to concern among clinic staff that the drug was circulating unregulated into the black market.[23] In most cases, Depo-Provera reached new African nations as a form of development aid, eliciting a wide variety of responses. In correspondences with the Population Council, family planning workers in Kenya reported a growing demand for Depo-Provera.[24] In white minority–ruled Rhodesia, Depo-Provera was popular among some women, who could use it without the knowledge of disapproving husbands, but it was also controversial because it was promoted by a political regime that supported white supremacy, suppression of Black birth rates, and the dispossession of Africans of their land. The newly independent government of Zimbabwe banned Depo-Provera in 1981, shortly after ousting the white minority–led state of Rhodesia.[25]

Depo-Provera catalyzed a media scandal in Tanzania in 1973 after the Tanzanian family planning association, UMATI, decided to remove the injection from of its clinics. At the time, Depo-Provera was becoming one of the most widely used contraceptives in Tanzania.[26] In public hearings, UMATI spokespeople insisted that the drug was safe and that the decision to remove it was due to limitations of capacity and personnel: they simply could not conduct proper follow-up with women or control its distribution, and therefore they could not ensure that women understood its effects and were using it correctly. Many members of the public did not believe UMATI's justifications and a media scandal erupted. In the days that followed, the newspapers were filled with anti-Depo-Provera poems, political cartoons, and letters to the editor accusing UMATI of a range of atrocities, including the poisoning and sterilization of Black women, complicity with white supremacists abroad, and the incompetence of its staff. Investigative reporters published rumors that Depo-Provera destroyed the reproductive organs of women, ruined their libido, made their hair fall out, and caused their husbands to divorce them. Though much of what was printed was unsubstantiated, the accusations about Depo-Provera's effects revealed concrete fears about medical vulnerability in an unequal world in which creators and distributors of medicines were not known and visible and could not be held accountable to the public. The scandal incited the Tanzanian government to depart from its earlier stance of strategic ambiguity and to domesticate fears about contraception by incorporating family planning services into its national health service.

The Tanzanian Depo-Provera scandal happened nearly two decades before Upjohn received FDA approval to produce and sell the drug in the United States. The controversies surrounding Upjohn's repeated attempts to gain FDA approval for Depo-Provera encapsulate some of the key debates within second wave feminism in the United States. Wendy Kline has written powerfully about the 1983 US Congressional Board of Inquiry on Depo-Provera, showing how the proceedings raised critical questions about expertise and the body. When, on matters of women's health, the embodied knowledge of women contradicted the scientific knowledge of predominantly male doctors, which would be considered authoritative? How could women stand up for themselves in the face of a male-dominated medical profession, and how would women protect themselves and each other from the profit-driven directives of the pharmaceutical industry? To be sure, these questions are crucial to the history of women's health and second-wave feminism in the United States.[27] Yet only a truncated portion of Depo-Provera's contested history occurred within the borders of the United States. From the start, Depo-Provera's history encompassed the globe. By the time Depo-Provera gained FDA approval in the United States in 1992, it had already circulated the globe, sparking protest and calling together new solidarities and worldviews in its path. The history of Depo-Provera is inherently global in scope.

The Beneficence of the Syringe

Members of the population establishment saw LARCs as a technological fix for two crises: the so-called "population bomb" and maternal mortality. In 1965, Dr. Alan Guttmacher, president of the International Planned Parenthood Federation, travelled to nine African countries to tour family planning and maternal health facilities, and to promote LARCs in Africa. Upon his return, he produced a confidential report that read like the description of a war zone. He described horrific scenes of suffering in hospitals and clinics. He described the stench emanating from unrefrigerated hospital morgues, blood spattered on the dresses of women in hospitals that could not afford hospital gowns for patients, and babies with cleft palates abandoned at the hospital by mothers who could not care for them. He wrote about women pressured by patriarchal traditions to procreate incessantly, leading to dangerous pregnancies and frequent miscarriages. He described nurses with little training performing botched fistulae surgeries and "a breech delivery which sent chills down my spine." Reflecting on what he witnessed, he wrote: "Two verities are uncontestable, 'life is cheap in Equatorial Africa' and 'wives readily replaceable.'" "This," he said, "is the milieu into which we wish to introduce contraception."[28] It was against the comparative horror of these conditions that Depo-Provera was deemed safe.

Like Guttmacher's report, the diaries and travelogues of population establishment doctors reveal how the a priori belief in contraception as a technological solution to poverty shaped their interpretation of the suffering that they saw as they travelled around the world. For these observers, it was maternity, rather than the economic and infrastructural conditions in which maternity took place, that was their target of intervention. What made Depo-Provera acceptable in some places but not others was a belief that the Global South was exceptional and called for its own kind of guerilla health care.

Two years later, at a conference on the theme of "The Role of Family Planning in African Development" held at the University of Nairobi, Guttmacher extolled the virtues of Depo-Provera before an audience of Kenyan doctors and civil servants:

> When I was in Chiang-Mai [Thailand] recently . . . I saw 200 patients going to
> get their injections. It was marvelous to see a competent-looking young nurse
> in a well-starched uniform with a battery of syringes, and to see those patients
> simply walking by or rolling up their sleeves and getting a shot. The nurse could
> have done 100 shots an hour, and this was remarkable, for people had come 50
> miles in order to have the beneficence of the syringe.[29]

In this image, each patient would only need thirty-six seconds of face-to-face time with a health care worker. That worker, Guttmacher would go on to say, need not be a nurse, but could be a "girl" with a high school diploma, trained to administer injections. In Pakistan, he told the audience, they used "Lady Health Visitors" for the implementation of family planning. "They are not nurses/midwives," he said, "they are simply very intelligent high school young women."[30] Hiring "paramedical personnel" was a key component of his vision of contraception inundation. Guttmacher identified Depo-Provera as the most appropriate form of contraception because it was a cheap and efficient way of distributing contraception in a place with little in the way of trained medical personnel and health infrastructure. This vision exemplified Guttmacher's thinking about the relationship between LARCs and medical care for people in the poor nations of the world.

Guttmacher's vision differed markedly from a late colonial-era approach, which included the conceit—albeit never realized—that colonialism would deliver modern health care to the colonies that would eventually approach the standards in Europe.[31] By contrast, stories about the global circulation of Depo-Provera highlighted and accepted inequality and difference as a basic premise. By this logic, health care in Kenya, Thailand and Pakistan should not be seen in relation to health care in Europe, but should instead be lumped together on the basis of their shared infrastructural poverty. For these regions of the world, Guttmacher advocated for LARCs, including Depo-Provera and IUDs, in part because they required little engagement with the women who took them. The birth control pill was easily reversible, in that women had to take it every day and could stop taking it at any time. But women who were on the pill needed to have regular enough contact with a clinic that they could refill their prescription, and the supply chains needed to work so that regular refills arrived in the right places. IUDs and Depo-Provera, by contrast, did not require the same infrastructural sophistication or the same level of day-to-day participation on the part of women. In short, Depo-Provera was not simply an ideal contraceptive: more specifically, it was an ideal contraceptive for poor women.

Guttmacher and his allies had to make a case for why a drug that was deemed unsafe in the country where it was invented was safe for women in Africa and Asia. In 1973, the Population Council convened an ad-hoc committee on Depo-Provera to explore this very question, and invited European development experts working in Africa and Asia to weigh in.[32] One of the leading voices in the promotion of Depo-Provera was Dr. Edwin McDaniels, the head of OB-GYN and family planning at McCormick Hospital in Chiang-Mai, Thailand, where Depo-Provera trials had been carried out under his supervision, and whose work Guttmacher had praised at the Nairobi conference. Born in Thailand to missionary parents, McDaniels started the OB-GYN program at McCormick, and under his direction, Depo-Provera became by far the most widely used contraceptive in the region. McDaniels prepared a manual on Depo-Provera for the Population Council to distribute through their global network, universalizing his experience in Thailand to other populations in the Global South.[33]

In his manual, McDaniels described Depo-Provera as a contraceptive that was especially suited to women in poor countries. He made the case that while doctors in Europe and the United States required women to have a medical examination before being given Depo-Provera, this was not feasible in the circumstances in which he worked. Addressing family planning workers across the world, he wrote:

> In many situations it will be necessary for the decision maker to answer for himself the question: "Given my limitations of time, personnel, and facilities, will I do more good for the community in need of family planning by giving contraceptive services to a large number of women . . . prevent[ing] much maternal morbidity and mortality by the prevention of a large number of unwanted pregnancies (and criminal abortions); or will I do more good by insisting on a more 'professional' course of complete examinations and cancer tests for all women, giving help to fewer women, and possibly risking adverse publicity for the program at the neighborhood or village level?" . . . We feel that furnishing family planning services to a large number of women, without the "luxuries" of general physical and pelvic examination and cancer detection, is more important and fruitful than serving a few, and discouraging many, in an attempt to cling too rigidly to more academic and professional medical standards.[34]

By placing the word "professional" in scare quotes, and labeling cancer screening and physical examinations as "luxuries," McDaniels mapped a world divided in two, with different standards, practices, and rules of medical efficacy in each. This presumption of different medical standards for different populations was echoed widely by policy makers in the population establishment, including director of USAID's Office of Population Reimert Ravenholt, who explained in a USAID memo that the dangers of Depo-Provera must be weighed against the dangers of pregnancy and birth in places without robust public health infrastructure.[35] This calculation became one of the core arguments for proponents of the inundation policy.

For intermediaries like Guttmacher, McDaniel, and Ravenholt, the efficacy of Depo-Provera was based on its ability to work in the *absence* of health infrastructure. From this standpoint, what made a woman suited to one form of birth control or another was not so much her reproductive goals or her body, but rather the infrastructure of the society in which she lived. In promoting the flow of biomedical contraception from the United States and Europe to the Global South, the population establishment mapped a world that naturalized poverty and inequality as a starting principle and designated them problems to be fixed with an injection. Depo-Provera was not just contraception: it was "injectable development."

What made Depo-Provera unacceptably risky for some women but safe for others? What did the women for whom it was deemed acceptably safe have in common? In answering these questions, members of the population establishment made a case for the Global South as an exceptional space with different medical protocols and standards then the Global North. In this sense, the story of "injectable development" obscured historical roots of inequality with a view of the world that naturalized the Global South as a space of biomedical difference.

The Counter-Topography of Anti-Depo-Provera Activism

While population establishment figures like Guttmacher, Ravenholt, and McDaniel identified women living in places with poor health infrastructures as ideal patients for Depo-Provera, critics conjured an alternative map of the world. Like Depo-Provera boosters, they saw a world that was bifurcated between wealthy nations and those who were subject to their agendas and products. Yet rather than defining women in the latter by their material need and their supposed hyperfertility, anti-Depo-Provera activists and critics identified them by their shared histories of colonialism, capitalism, racism, sexism, and poverty. In articulating their protest, they constructed a counter-topography of the world envisioned by the population establishment.[36]

In August 1971, the Tanzanian newspaper *The Nationalist* printed an article by Patricia Rodney entitled "Dangers of Birth Control in Tanzania." She wrote, "I feel it is necessary to write this article firstly as a woman from the oppressed underdeveloped world, secondly as a nurse, and most of all as a mother of three."[37] Rodney was no opponent of family planning and contraception, and in her article she invoked Margaret Sanger as a feminist hero. Yet she linked Depo-Provera's availability in Africa with a history of white supremacy in which poor people of color were exposed to unsafe medical products that white middle-class women were protected from, citing the testing of the birth control pill on Puerto Rican women and poor women of color in the US South as examples. She envisioned solidarity among women who were targeted by such interventions, whose fertility was coopted as a site for the exercise of geopolitical power and experimentation and for whom birth control would be given according to the directives of population control rather than health and bodily self-determination. The export of contraceptives to the Global South, Rodney argued, must be understood within the history of capitalism, colonialism, slavery, and resource extraction. She criticized the population establishment for their view that "poverty is a consequence of large families rather than the product of unjust and unequal distribution of wealth and incomes." Through a critique of Depo-Provera, she exposed latent connections among dispossessed women, oppressed by a powerful global elite that addressed their fertility but not their historical dispossession.

Patricia Rodney, a Black woman from Guyana living in Tanzania, was one of many critics of Depo-Provera in the 1970s. Her own personal global trajectory likely contributed to her perspective. She lived in London in the 1960s with her husband—the Guyanese historian and anticolonial theorist Walter Rodney—before moving to Tanzania, where her husband taught at the University of Dar es Salaam, a famous hub of international leftist intellectuals at the time. Rodney, like other critics, focused less on the safety of Depo-Provera than on the power arrangements that brought Depo-Provera into the bodies of some women rather than others. Meanwhile, in Bangladesh, Farida Akhter, a feminist environmentalist activist, argued that the promotion of contraceptives in what she calls "LACAAP" (Latin America, Caribbean, Asia, Africa, and Pacific) was inextricable from patterns of economic exploitation and coercive population control measures, and that the global circulation of Depo-Provera was a form of pharmaceutical dumping.[38] In Zimbabwe, critics of Depo-Provera linked its promotion for Black women with the broader politics of white supremacy and the expropriation of Black land and wealth.[39] In London, Stella Dadzie, a Black British woman of Ghanaian descent, became one of the leaders of the Campaign Against Depo-Provera. With her fellow activists, she designed and distributed pamphlets that showed a map of the world with the nations where Depo-Provera was available darkened. While a few European countries were included, the majority of the countries filled in were counties in Africa, Asia, and Latin America. This map of the world made visual connections among dispossessed and vulnerable women in all parts of the world. At the same time, it might also be read as a tactic to make the drug seem unsuitable to British audiences by associating it with poor countries with predominantly nonwhite populations. Years later, Dadzie would critique her fellow organizers in the Campaign Against Depo-Provera for emphasizing the need to protect white working-class women in the United Kingdom rather than valuing equally the fate of Black women exposed to Depo-Provera in places like Zimbabwe.[40]

Patricia Rodney's critique of the population establishment also drew on the intellectual movement of international leftist thinkers, including the Egyptian Marxist economist Samir Amin, who argued in a widely cited UNESCO essay entitled "Underpopulated Africa" that the notion of overpopulation was an ideological construct of colonial apologists who blamed poverty on African sexuality and family life, obscuring the colonial roots of African poverty.[41] How one understood the problem of population was a matter of widespread disagreement among intellectuals. Donor agencies, especially the Population Council, sponsored the creation of departments of demography in African universities in order to cultivate scholars who would view population growth as the major obstacle to African economic development. However, to the chagrin of population establishment demographers, university intellectuals in Africa thought about population in ways that did not conform to the agendas of their sponsors, often emphasizing distribution of wealth and the challenge of rapid urban migration instead of fertility rates and population growth. As Cecile DeSweeney of the Ford Foundation lamented in 1975, these African intellectuals saw population as a qualitative problem rather than a quantitative one.[42] Like Patricia Rodney, Amin insisted that an understanding of contraception-as-aid take account of the global circuits through which these technologies flowed. For Amin, it was inequality rather than fertility that was the pressing problem of the postcolonial world order.

Amin's critique resonated in international leftist intellectual circles, disrupting attempts of the population establishment to shape political and economic thought on the continent. These contested population politics came out into the open at the First African Population Conference in Accra, Ghana in 1971, a conference convened by several international agencies in the population establishment, including the Population Council and USAID. While early panels at the conference seemed to conform to the agenda of the conveners, over that weekend, a group of participants including representatives from Europe, North Africa, sub-Saharan Africa, and Latin America collaborated in an attempt to shift the terms of the conference discourse, protesting the poverty and inequality between donor nations and recipients and the power of the former to dictate health and economic policy in the latter. Hector Silva Micellina, a Venezuelan protégé of Amin, began the protest by sharing parts of Amin's UNESCO paper "Underpopulated Africa" during his presentation. The protesters were then barred from participating in the remainder of the conference and USAID representatives responded to "the young leftists" by staging a counter-display of posters meant to demonstrate that overpopulation caused poverty. This attempt to control the terms of the discussion came across to participants as heavy-handed and unconvincing, and Population Council representative L. L. Bean referred to the conference as "a shambles."[43] That same group of protesters staged a second alternative conference in Abidjan, Cote D'Ivoire the following year. Signaling their distance from the rhetoric of population control, they titled their conference "Inter-agency collaboration in family activities."[44]

Anti-Depo-Provera activists drew support and intellectual inspiration from Marxist, feminist, and anticolonial thinkers, and yet their politics also overlapped with those of religious and cultural conservatives. Many Catholic clergy combined opposition to contraception with a pronatalist strand of African nationalist rhetoric, arguing that all contraception was a tool of racism. Others protested Depo-Provera on the grounds that contraception allowed women to be promiscuous and independent—characteristics that they argued were contrary to traditional African gender roles. Though in many ways politically at odds with one another, conservatives and radical feminists alike shared certain tropes to describe Depo-Provera, such as the representation of the drug as a weapon. Rwehikira Bashome, a conservative critic from Tanzania who wrote extensively about the ills of female promiscuity, commented in an editorial for a Dar es Salaam newspaper: "Our enemies do not have to come strafing our villages or bombing our towns. They may come in big cartons of Depo Provera."[45] That militarized imagery was also used in the anti-Depo-Provera materials developed by Stella Dadzie and her collaborators in London, who circulated a pamphlet containing a cartoon image of war planes dropping syringes like bombs.[46]

For critics like Patricia Rodney and Samir Amin, it was only in a world that addressed persistent structural inequalities that Depo-Provera could work as medicine rather than poison. Until those inequalities were addressed, the relative efficacy of new reproductive technologies was beside the point. Rodney, Akter, Dadzie, and other activists opposed Depo-Provera from subject positions from around the globe, yet they envisioned a similar mapping of the world. They engaged in what geographer Cindi Katz calls counter-topography: an intellectual and political project that seeks connections between people in dispersed parts of the world based on shared experiences of global processes. Although each experience of a global phenomenon is situated within distinct local and regional histories and contexts, counter-topography seeks to articulate solidarities across these positions to link them into a shared political project.[47] Anti-Depo-Provera activists looked beyond their own situated knowledge and mapped shared global circumstances—in this case, exposure to Depo-Provera—as a way of articulating new, geographically dispersed political solidarities.

Depo-Provera activated a geographic imaginary in which women in one part of the world became aware of their position in the world vis-à-vis others. In this way, Tanzanian women could envision common cause with poor women in Thailand, white minority–rule Zimbabwe, and the US South. Yet the various maps of anti-Depo-Provera solidarity were not identical. Akhter, for example, defined her imagined community regionally in broad strokes, including Latin America, Asia, Africa, and the Pacific, and excluding Europe and most of North America. For Patricia Rodney and Stella Dadzie, informed by their experience of migration to the stratified cities of the global north, their imagined community included West Indian and African immigrants in London and Black women in the US South, and at times, working-class and poor white women in the Glasgow council estates. Across these various imaginaries, the Global South appears not a stable place on the map, but rather as a mode of mapping that accounts for historical dispossession and its legacies. In anti-Depo-Provera activism, these histories were embodied in the physical experience of vulnerability and exposure.

Anti-Depo-Provera activism was limited in that it did not envision new geographies of accountability or ways of provisioning health care. Its worldview did not account for the small-scale perspective of clinic workers, nor did it include the perspectives of the women who presented themselves at clinics for contraception. For the latter, the global histories of dispossession were not something they could choose to accept or reject but were rather a set of circumstances within which they had to improvise lives, health, and family. To understand these struggles, we turn to those who performed the quotidian work of building public health infrastructure.

Global South Improvisers and the Ambiguous Gift of Depo-Provera

In the 1970s, Depo-Provera stories circulated in many global cities, including Dar es Salaam. By 1969, biomedical contraceptives and family planning workers were moving through the city via the mobile clinic vans of UMATI: the Tanzanian branch of the International Planned Parenthood Federation. At the same time, Dar es Salaam was also a node to many of the intellectuals who opposed Depo-Provera, including those who gathered at the University of Dar es Salaam. University students and Christian and Muslim clergy were among those protesting at clinics during the Depo-Provera controversies. The debates that rocked the Dar es Salaam press and which played out in demonstrations at UMATI clinics appeared as a clash between those that saw Depo-Provera as medicine and those who saw it as a poison.

Most African politicians publicly opposed population control policies. The archives are filled with instances of population establishment representatives expressing frustration at African leaders who did not share their sense of urgency about population growth and family planning. Tanzanians were seen to be especially resistant in this respect. In his diary entry about a visit to Tanzania during his 1965 Africa trip, Alan Guttmacher wrote that when taken to visit Dr. Charles Mtwali, the Permanent Secretary of Health, he was instructed by his handlers to "talk about everything but family planning."[48] A little over a decade later, Dr. R. L. Manning of the World Health Organization wrote to his colleague about the attitudes of Tanzanian policy makers in Dar es Salaam:

The Ministry of Health's expectations . . . from UNFPA [United Nations Fund for Population Activities] are very limited indeed: they essentially want vehicles for the immunization/MCH [maternal and child health] programme and money for inservice training of MCH aides and other health service staff: the central UNFPA theme, better family living with fewer children, is nowhere near their focus of interest."[49]

Lisa Richey has described the Tanzania government's approach to population as one of "strategic ambiguity," signaling cooperation with population control advocates on a global stage while voicing a pronatalist agenda for national audiences at home, all the while refraining from explicit commitments on the issue.[50]

In this context, the Tanzanian health workers who took part in the quotidian work of building health systems were called on to speak and act not only as experts on the efficacy and safety of Depo-Provera and other contraceptives, but also as gatekeepers of Tanzania's relationship with the outside world. In an unequal world, Depo-Provera was an ambiguous gift. Health workers and family planning workers were well aware of the geopolitical reasons why they could ask for and expect to receive long-acting contraceptives like IUDs and Depo-Provera but would be less likely to receive forms of contraception that required women's frequent and willing participation, such as birth control pills and condoms, even when patients preferred the latter. More broadly, while health workers could request and expect to receive LARCs, the same could not be said for assistance to extend piped water or electricity to clinics or maternity wards in hospitals. If they were to improvise health systems, they had to do so within the uneven terrain of what donors chose to make available.

Tanzanian women who accessed biomedical contraception in the 1970s did so through nurses and workers employed by UMATI, which was Tanzania's sole importer of biomedical contraception throughout the 1960s and 1970s.[51] UMATI had a clinic in downtown Dar es Salaam and a mobile van clinic that its health workers drove to different sites in the city to hold open clinic hours. The nurses and social workers employed by UMATI conducted pap smears and pelvic exams, counseled women on family planning, and provided them with various contraceptives, including pills, condoms, IUDs, and, in 1972–3, Depo-Provera injections. The UMATI staff members who circulated through the city of Dar es Salaam dispensing contraceptives were mission-educated Christian women. Having come of age during the late colonial era, they saw themselves as part of a modernizing vanguard that would help transform Tanzania into a modern, prosperous nation.

While their prestigious jobs associated them with a growing Western-educated middle-class African elite, many of UMATI's nurses held beliefs about fertility that differed strikingly from the perspective of donors who contributed the contraception that they distributed, and had more in common with African regional understandings of fertility and the body. Based on her work in the Gambia, Bledsoe identifies the worldview held by many African women, in which obstetric trauma, rather than linear time, is the central determinant of aging and the onset of infertility. In this context, women attempt to space children in order to avoid risky pregnancies, with the aim of prolonging fertility and increasing the number of successful pregnancies over the course of a lifetime.[52] In other words, rather than use contraception to curtail fertility, many African women use it as a tool for cultivating optimal fertility. The retired UMATI nurses that I interviewed expressed this view. When describing early experiences that led them to pursue careers in family planning, they talked about witnessing obstetric traumas of their mothers and sisters in the villages where they were girls, and they saw contraception as a way of cultivating better health for women.[53] Donors prioritized Depo-Provera and the IUD over the contraceptive pill and condoms because they could not be easily tampered with once in the body. By contrast, for UMATI nurses, contraceptive technology was most useful if it was flexible and could help women manage their fertility, often with the result of having a greater number of children and fewer traumatic obstetric experiences.

The 1973 Depo-Provera controversy in Tanzania reveals the position of infrastructure builders in an uneven world of constrained choice. For UMATI nurses, Depo-Provera was not, as Guttmacher saw it, a technological fix to poverty and scarcity, nor was it a poisonous injection given as part of a racist conspiracy to render Black women sterile. Like many of the other forms of biomedical technology exported to the Global South, Depo-Provera was a powerful and imperfect tool to be worked with. Sitting on his veranda on a sunny, cool day in full view of Kilimanjaro, Dr. Mamuya—one of the founding members of UMATI—recalled the hostility and skepticism many Tanzanians expressed towards biomedical contraception over the course of his career.

SM: You ask donors for assistance to build a road, a school, and they won't. They say there is no money. But you ask for contraceptives, you get it, free of charge. Now, why should they want to give us this free of charge something which we don't think is very necessary, and the essentials, they don't give us free of charge?

EC: And how did you respond to those criticisms?

SM: Well, we said . . . they don't give you unless you ask, and we *asked*. . . . We were getting assistance from our federation [IPPF] for the good of the country. We could get money to build clinics, you see. We would get money to pay for people like Ms. Mtawali [an UMATI nurse and educator], Christina Nsekela, and so on.[54]

Mamuya echoed the sentiments of the Tanzanian Minister of Health who did not care about promoting smaller families, but did care about the possibilities of providing vaccines and maternal and child health and sought to do so through the available machinery of the family planning movement. Dr. Mamuya, one of Tanzania's first Western-trained medical doctors, played a prominent role in shaping Tanzania's national health system, and his world was one in which contraceptives were readily available for those who asked for it and roads and schools were not. Local actors like Dr. Mamuya were not in a position to alter the geopolitics but could actively take advantage of them, albeit in highly constrained ways, in order to bring resources to Tanzania. Through their relationship with the population establishment, they enabled the flow of contraceptives and they also built clinics from which to distribute them, receiving grants to train medical professionals like Grace Mtawali,

Maele Kushuma, and Christina Nsekela—all of whom went on to have long careers in nursing and public health after moving on from their work in the family planning movement.

Mamuya's words conveyed the thinking of an improviser, aware of the imperfect world of what was available and positioning himself to build infrastructure on that uneven terrain. Julie Livingston identifies improvisation as the modus operandi of African healthcare workers, like Mamuya. In the cancer ward in Botswana where she conducted her research, rationing, scarcity, and the breakdown of equipment were not exceptional occurrences but part of the everyday practice of medicine. In order to deliver health in such circumstances, they had to improvise with what was available. The Depo-Provera controversy in Tanzania exemplifies an improvisational modus operandi in which resources were scarce, contraceptives plentiful, and health demands great. Nurses and doctors had to navigate different uses and meanings of contraceptives for different audiences from international donors, to the Tanzanian public, and to the clients they met in clinics. In this way, they were simultaneously healthcare workers and public intellectuals, negotiating the boundaries between population control and health care, poison and medicine, for multiple audiences.

Health improvisers operated within a mindset of flexibility, but the mutability of biomedical contraceptives had limits. Depo-Provera was unpredictable. Doctors could not say exactly how long fertility was curbed after an injection. Unlike the pill, which one could stop taking at any time, or the IUD, which a woman could have removed by a medical professional, Depo-Provera stayed in the body once it was injected and could not be adjusted or reversed until it expired. In this sense, it did not work well as a flexible resource, and that is why it caused a scandal. In 1973, Christina Nsekela announced before a gathering of reporters that the Family Planning Association of Tanzania (UMATI) would no longer offer Depo-Provera in its clinics. She explained that while Depo-Provera was not unsafe, it was a powerful drug that impacted fertility and required medical oversight so that women who used it fully understood its effects on their bodies. In a country with a poorly developed public health infrastructure and an extremely low ratio of doctors and nurses to patients, UMATI could not control its distribution or prevent off-market uses and therefore could not ensure that it was being used in a way that would support women's health and reproductive goals. Misuse or misunderstandings about the drug would not only damage patients but would damage the legitimacy of UMATI and an early generation of professional health care workers. For a powerful drug like Depo-Provera to be safe—in order for it to be an instrument of health and not harm—it would need a robust maternal health infrastructure to domesticate it and ensure its proper use. This perspective was the inverse of the perspective of people like Drs. Guttmacher and McDaniels, who argued that it was especially suitable for women in conditions without health infrastructure.

On trial in the Depo-Provera scandal was not so much the drugs themselves as the global position of the emerging cadre of Tanzanian professionals who dispensed them. Protesters accused family planning workers of collaboration with foreign interests on racist plots to reduce the Black population of the world or to use African bodies as guinea pigs for testing dangerous chemicals.[55] Others drew on older regional idioms linking witchcraft and infertility, accusing UMATI nurses of being witches who jealously wanted to preserve their own fertility while using foreign medicines to damage the fertility of others.[56] Some saw UMATI nurses as naïve dupes to a global conspiracy.[57] Critics complained that those dispensing Depo-Provera were poorly trained elementary school teachers and low-level nurses: people who did not have the ability to properly understand how the drugs worked and could not protect patients from their harmful effects. Journalist Benjamin Mkapa, who would later become Tanzania's third president, put these accusations to Christina Nsekela in an interview for a full-page spread in the *Daily News*. He asked her how UMATI was funded, and when she listed foreign donors including the IPPF, he followed up by asking: "Is it therefore the case that you are controlled by the financial purse strings of people in Britain and America who do not have the interest of Tanzanians at heart?" As Nsekela responded to each question, he followed up with more along the same lines, asking about the links between contraception and population control. He asked: "What of the charge that you want to control the population growth?" She replied:

As I said earlier our family planning policy is not oriented towards control of population growth. Our association places great emphasis on pregnancy spacing, but the spacing of pregnancies may or may not limit family size depending on the wishes of the couple. For example if a girl married at the age of 20 and she adopts family planning practices of conceiving a child every two to three years, she may end up with a family of six or seven children by the time she becomes 35 years old. Would you call this control of population growth?[58]

The social relationships around Depo-Provera were at least as controversial as the drug itself. Mkapa's interrogation of Christina Nsekela was not only about Depo-Provera and UMATI but also about an uncertain chain of accountability in a postcolonial world world order.

The Depo-Provera scandal pushed the Tanzanian state to resolve the ambiguity between population control and family planning. They responded by incorporating family planning services into government hospitals, with UMATI reserving its role as sole importer of contraception and as family planning educators. UMATI staff members were deployed to government hospitals to run family planning services as well as to factory floors and military training camps to educate women and men how to plan their families. By placing family planning into government health institutions, the state transformed biomedical birth control from a dangerous foreign substance to a public asset and a medicine. The scandal over Depo-Provera provoked the expansion of state public health infrastructure in order to include family planning. While the population establishment would have had Tanzanians accept Depo-Provera, and the critics would have had Tanzanians reject it, here was a third approach: a mode of improvisational infrastructure building that domesticated ambiguous gifts into social resources.

Conclusion

This essay has framed Depo-Provera as an historical artifact that reveals the creation of the Global South as a spatial concept. Depo-Provera's uneven global itinerary was made possible by a calculation in which some bodies had to be protected from pain, dysfunction, and the risk of infertility and cancer, while other bodies did not. Experts argued that Depo-Provera was suitable for some women both because the dangers of giving birth in poverty were greater than the dangers of Depo-Provera and because the needs of some bodies were evaluated not on their own terms, but in relation to broader aims of population control. This calculation naturalized global inequality and located the cause of and solution to poverty in the reproductive lives of the world's poor. At the same time, the uneven global circulation of Depo-Provera catalyzed alternative mappings of the world, as activists and intellectuals questioned the logic of the population establishment and insisted that the historical causes of inequality be part of the discussion about population and contraception. By using Depo-Provera to tell a story about global power, they made visible the connections and potential solidarities between geographically dispersed women. Depo-Provera, perhaps more than other pharmaceutical product of its time, sparked global imaginaries.

Though politically at odds, both boosters and critics of Depo-Provera participated in the creation of a taken-for-granted mapping of the world. It made sense to Guttmacher and McDaniels to think of Thailand, Pakistan and Kenya as part of a single space of health intervention. Anti-Depo-Provera activists like Rodney and Dadzie saw a more complex world map, illuminating connections between women in Tanzania and Zimbabwe, but which also included women in specific urban neighborhoods in Atlanta, Glasgow, and London, all of whom shared experiences of vulnerability, dispossession, and potential solidarity. These multiple interpretations of Depo-Provera's global trajectories do not reveal a single blunt bifurcation of the world into two distinct territories but rather competing modes of thinking about global inequality. We might, therefore, think of the "Global South" not as a place but rather as a mode of global thinking that continually maps and remaps the world in the service of different visions of the future.

Neither the world maps imagined by population control advocates nor those of anti-Depo-Provera activists could represent the lived experiences and itineraries of women who presented themselves for Depo-Provera injections. Many women chose Depo-Provera despite the dangers and the larger geopolitical injustices

embedded in the travelling injections. Could these technologies be purified of genealogies that included racism, population control, and a naturalization of poverty, and
be used to deliver health? That was a question that was not answered from the vantage point of the world map but rather from the vantage point of the clinic. Nurses
and health workers engaged this vantage point on a daily basis as they improvised
women's health care from the imperfect set of tools available to them. They had
to continually navigate the precarious boundary between population control and
family planning as they interacted with multiple audiences, from heads of powerful and wealthy international institutions to patients in the mobile family planning
clinics. Meanwhile, for women who contemplated using contraceptives to control
their fertility, the question of whether Depo-Provera was a poison or a medicine was
not an abstract question about world population but a practical question about how
to bring health to their bodies and their families from within a position of vulnerability and constraint. For them, to live in the Global South was to live in a space of
improvisation.

Emily Callaci is assistant professor of African history at the University of Wisconsin, Madison.
She is the author of *Street Archives and City Life: Popular Intellectuals in Postcolonial Tanzania*
(2017). She is currently working on a second book about the history of contraception and the family planning movement in Africa.

Notes

1. Packard, *A History of Global Health*, 105–8, 184–5.
2. Connelly, *Fatal Misconception*, 155–94.
3. Packard, 186.
4. Murphy, *Seizing the Means of Reproduction*, 12–3.
5. Bledsoe, *Contingent Lives*.
6. Wendland, *A Heart for the Work*, 6–7.
7. Murphy, *The Economization of Life*.
8. Thomas, *Politics of the Womb*; Hunt, *A Colonial Lexicon*, 237–80; McCurdy, "Urban threats," 212–33.
9. Hunt, *A Colonial Lexicon*, 237–80; Allman, "Making Mothers," 23–47; Summers, "Intimate Colonialism," 787–807.
10. Packard, part 5.
11. International Planned Parenthood Federation, *Family Planning in Five Continents*; Tarlo, *Unsettling Memories*; White, "The Origins of China's Birth Planning Policy," 250–78.
12. Richey, *Population, Politics, and Development*, chapter 2.
13. Marks, *Sexual Chemistry*, 60–115; May, *America and the Pill*, 12–34.
14. Kline, 97–125.
15. George B. Baldwin, "The McCormick Family Planning Program in Chiang Mai, Thailand," *Studies in Family Planning* 9 (12), December 1978, 300–12.
16. Laura Briggs, *Reproducing Empire: Race, Sex, Science, and U.S. Imperialism in Puerto Rico*, 109–41.
17. Kline, *Bodies of Knowledge*, 120–2.
18. Bunkle, "Calling the Shots?" 237–302.

19. Ibid.

20. Ibid.

21. Wellcome Library Archives, SA/PAT/D/14 Contraception; Black Cultural Archives, Stella Dadzie Papers, 1/1/38.

22. Marks, *Sexual Chemistry*; Elaine Tyler May, *America and the Pill*.

23. For example, Upjohn hosted luncheons at the Kinshasa family planning meeting. "Kinshasa Postpartum Program, March 7–9, 1974," 1974. Rockefeller Archive Center, Population Council Records (hereafter RAC/PC), Box 358, Folder 3460 Montague, Joe, Country File- Africa- General- Postpartum Program. In Nigeria, Upjohn marketed Depo-Provera directly to physicians. RAC/PC, Box 228, Folder 2122, Depo-Provera, Ad-Hoc Committee, 1973–1974; RAC/PC, Box 228, Folder 2122, Depo-Provera, Ad-Hoc Committee, "Memorandum," from David Gwatkin to Anna Southam, October 8, 1969; RAC/PC, Box 228, Folder 2122, Depo-Provera, Ad-Hoc Committee, "Request for Literature on Depo Provera." See also Tola Pearce, "Reproductive Practices and Biomedicine."

24. RAC/PC, Box 228, Folder 2122, Depo-Provera Ad-Hoc Committee, 1973–74, James J. Russell to Dr. Sheldon Segal, November 15, 1969.

25. Kaler, "A Threat to the Nation," 347–76.

26. Between January and November 1973, the Dar es Salaam branch of UMATI reported 647 new users and gave 4,133 follow-up injections. RAC/PC, Box 357, Folder 3445, Montague- Country File- Tanzania- Institutional Development- University of Dar es Salaam, 1973–1974.

27. Kline, *Bodies of Knowledge*, 97–176.

28. Alan Guttmacher, "Confidential Report on Equatorial African Trip," 1965. Sophia Smith Collection, Planned Parenthood Federation of America papers (hereafter SSC/PPFA), Box 202, Folder 15.

29. Alan Guttmacher, "The Role of Family Planning in African Development," University College, Nairobi, Kenya, December 13–16 1967, (London: IPPF, 1968).

30. Ibid.

31. Hunt, *A Colonial Lexicon*, 3–6.

32. RAC/PC, Box 228, Folder 2122, Depo-Provera, Ad-Hoc Committee, 1973–1974.

33. Edwin B. McDaniel, "Mini-manual." RAC/PC, Box 228, Folder 2122, Depo-Provera, Ad-Hoc Committee, 1973–1974.

34. Ibid.

35. Untitled, Wellcome Library Archives, SA/ICM/L/1/4/1, Reimert Ravenholt, MD, MPH, Director, Office of Population (1966–79).

36. I borrow the term counter-topography from geographer Cindi Katz. See Katz, "On the Grounds of Globalization," 1213–34.

37. Mrs. P. Rodney, "Dangers of Birth Control in Tanzania."

38. Farida Akhter, *Depopulating Bangladesh*.

39. Kaler, "A Threat to the Nation," 347–76.

40. Interview with Stella Dadzie by Rachel Cohen, June 2011, for Sisterhood and After: The Women's Liberation Oral History Project, British Library.

41. Samir Amin, "Underpopulated Africa."

42. Cecile DeSweeney made this observation following a trip to Africa in 1975. Dr. Cecile DeSweemer, "Position Paper," Ford Foundation, Lagos. RAC/PC, Box 124, Folder 1182.

43. L. L. Bean, "Diary Notes, December 9–18, Accra, Ghana, The First African Population Conference," 1971. RAC/PC, Box 76, Folder 723, Ghana: Correspondences, Reports, Studies: African Population Conference, Accra, Dec 9–18, 1971.

44. Ghana: Major, Benjamin, (Dr.) 1971–72, Trip Report, Abidjan, 26–29 March, 1972. RAC/PC, Box 77, Folder 725.
45. Rwehikira Bashome, "Contraceptives Are Evil to Our Society."
46. Black Cultural Archives, Stella Dadzie Papers, 1/1/38.
47. Katz, "On the Grounds of Globalization," 1213–34.
48. Alan Guttmacher, "Confidential Report on Equatorial African Trip," 1965. SSC/PPFA, Box 202, Folder 15.
49. Dr. R.L. Manning, WR, Dar es Salaam, to Comlan Quenum, MD, January 1, 1976. World Health Organization Archives, P13/372/9 TAN- Population and Family Planning, Tanzania.
50. Richey, *Population, Politics and Development*, Chapter 2.
51. Kaler and Watkins, "Disobedient Distributors," 254–69.
52. Bledsoe, *Contingent Lives*, 1–34.
53. Interview with Maele Kushuma, December 21, 2010, Dar es Salaam; Interview with Amy Mfinanga, January 3, 1011, Moshi; Interview with Grace Mtawali, December 26, 2010, Dar es Salaam; Interview with Christina Nsekela, December 6, 2011, Mbeya.
54. Interview with Dr. Sifuel Mamuya, January 3, 2011, Marangu.
55. Rwehikira Bashome, "Depoprovera: A Long Overdue Withdrawal"; Deogratias Masakilija, "The Pill Scandal Uncovered."
56. Interview with Grace Mtawali, December 26, 2010 Dar es Salaam; Interview with Amy Mfinanga, January 3, 2011, Moshi.
57. "UMATI Yaeleza Ukweli juu ya Sindano ya Depo-Provera," *Uzazi Bora* 3, 1973.
58. Benjamin, Mkapa, "Mrs. Nsekela Talks to Ben Mkapa: Umati Does Not Want to Control Birth Rate."

References

Akter, Farida. 1992. *Depopulating Bangladesh: essays on the politics of fertility*. Dhaka, Bangladesh: Narigrantha Prabartana.

Allman, Jean. 1994. "Making Mothers: Missionaries, Medical Officers and Women's Work in Colonial Asante, 1924–45." *History Workshop* 38: 23–47.

Amin, Amir. 1971. "Population Policies and Development Strategies: Underpopulated Africa." Dakar, Senegal: UNESCO.

Baldwin, George B. 1978. "The McCormick Family Planning Program in Chiang Mai, Thailand." *Studies in Family Planning* 9, no 12: 300–12.

Bledsoe, Caroline. 2002. *Contingent Lives: Fertility, Time, and Aging in West Africa*. Chicago: University of Chicago Press.

Briggs, Laura. 2003. *Reproducing Empire: Race, Sex, Science, and U.S. Imperialism in Puerto Rico*. Berkeley: University of California Press.

Bunkle, Phillida. 1993. "Calling the Shots? The International Politics of Depo-Provera." in *Racial Economy of Science: Towards a Democratic Future*, edited by Sandra Harding. Bloomington: Indiana University Press, 237–302.

Connelly, Matthew. 2008. *Fatal Misconception: The Struggle to Control World Population*. Cambridge, MA: Harvard University Press.

Guttmacher, Alan. 1968. "The Role of Family Planning in African Development," University College, Nairobi, Kenya, December 13–16 1967. London: IPPF.

Hunt, Nancy Rose. 1999. *A Colonial Lexicon: Of Birth, Medicalization and Mobility in the Congo*. Durham, NC: Duke University Press.

International Planned Parenthood Federation. 1979. *Family Planning in Five Continents:*

Africa, America, Asia, Europe, Oceania. London. International Planned Parenthood Federation.

Kaler, Amy. 1998. "A Threat to the Nation and a Threat to the Men: The Banning of Depo-Provera in Zimbabwe." *Journal of Southern African Studies* 24, no. 2: 347–76.

Kaler, Amy and Susan Cott Watkins. 2003. "Disobedient Distributors: Street-Level Bureaucrats and Would-Be Patrons in Community Based Family Planning in Rural Kenya." *Studies in Family Planning* 32, no. 3: 254–69.

Katz, Cindi. 2001. "On the Grounds of Globalization: A Topography for Feminist Political Engagement." *Signs* 26, no. 4: 1213–34.

Kline, Wendy. 2010. *Bodies of Knowledge: Sexuality, Reproduction and Women's Health in the Second Wave*. Chicago: University of Chicago Press.

Marks, Lara V. 1999. *Sexual Chemistry: A History of the Contraceptive Pill*. New Haven, CT: Yale University Press.

Massey, Doreen. 2002. "Globalization: What Does it Mean for Geography?" *Geography* 87, no. 4: 293–6.

May, Elaine Tyler. 2010. *America and the Pill: A History of Promise, Peril, and Liberation*. New York: Basic Books.

McCurdy, Sheryl. 2001. "Urban threats: Manyema women, low fertility and venereal diseases in British colonial Tanganyika, 1926–36." In *"Wicked" women and the reconfiguration of gender in Africa*, edited by Dorothy Hodgson and Sheryl McCurdy, 212–33. Portsmouth, NH: Heinemann.

Murphy, Michelle. 2012. *Seizing the Means of Reproduction*. Durham, NC: Duke University Press.

Murphy, Michelle. 2017. *The Economization of Life*. Durham, NC: Duke University Press.

Packard, Randall M. 2016. *A History of Global Health: Interventions into the Lives of Other Peoples*. Baltimore: Johns Hopkins University Press.

Pearce, Tola. 1995. "Reproductive Practices and Biomedicine: Cultural Conflicts and Transformations in Nigeria." In *Conceiving the New World Order: The Global Politics of Reproduction*, edited by Faye Ginsburg and Rayna Rapp. Berkeley: University of California Press.

Richey, Lisa Ann. 2008. *Population, Politics and Development: From Policies to Clinics*. New York: Palgrave Macmillan.

Summers, Carol. 1991. "Intimate Colonialism: The Imperial production of Reproduction in Uganda, 1907–1925." *Signs* 16, no. 4: 787–807.

Tarlo, Emma. 2003. *Unsettling Memories: Narratives of the Emergency in Delhi*. Berkeley: University of California Press.

Thomas, Lynn. 2003. *Politics of the Womb: Women, Reproduction and the State in Kenya*. Berkeley: University of California Press.

Wendland, Claire. 2010. *A Heart for the Work: Journeys through an African Medical School*. Chicago: University of Chicago Press.

White, Tyrene. 1999. "The Origins of China's Birth Planning Policy" in *Engendering China: Women, Culture and the State*, edited by Christina Gilmartin, et al. Cambridge, MA: Harvard University Press, 250–78.

The Political Economy of Regions

Climate Change and Dams in Guyana

Sarah E. Vaughn

In July 2011, I accompanied a group of state-sponsored civil engineers on a visit to a canal construction site on Guyana's Atlantic coast. It was a muggy afternoon, and they hoped to have foremen complete the construction of a canal's embankment before the storm clouds broke. The construction site was overrun by uneven layers of peat soil. I walked with the engineers as they inspected the terrain to identify where it was impractical to build. Hours later, foremen reinforced sections of the canal's embankment with large sheets of industrial fiber-plastics. Krishna, an engineer at the site, was frustrated with the complications they faced. In an interview with me this engineer explained: "We want this to be done. . . . You know before the next big flood. So whatever it is we are doing . . . you know we can't wait like the slaves. . . .Wait for twenty years and wait for [the soil] to compress."

Krishna's invocation of slavery testifies to his anxieties about how science serves goals not entirely of its own making. He recognizes that civil engineering is intertwined with changes in society and global capitalism. Nonetheless, he is responsible for canals that are unreliable and that pose a challenge to his very sense of expert practice. The canal Krishna refers to is part of a World Bank–funded climate adaptation project intended to improve the drainage capacity of the country's largest earthen dam, the East Demerara Water Conservancy (EDWC). To build the canal, engineers have updated hydraulic models to account for climate-related rainfall and sea-level rise. But in whatever ways climate adaptation may draw attention to what

Radical History Review

Issue 131 (May 2018)   DOI 10.1215/01636545-4355157

© 2018 by MARHO: The Radical Historians' Organization, Inc.

Ulrich Beck calls a "world at risk," its territorializing imperatives remain tied to place-based knowledge. For engineers like Krishna, climate adaptation efforts produce not only specific understandings of (post)colonial development, but also of space.

This article charts the role damming practices play in rescaling the geopolitical interests of engineers in Guyana. Based on archival and ethnographic research conducted between 2009 and 2011, it focuses on engineers' responses to a disastrous flood in 1934, the first flood in recorded history to compromise the EDWC. I argue that even the discourse of technical specialists rested on ideas about regionalism. By damming for local flood hazards, engineers recognized their failure to fully mobilize the plantation agriculture which had provided an economic base for the rest of the (British) Caribbean. At the same time, their ideas about the formation of a regional political economy were subject to variations over time because of these flood hazards. Engineers, in other words, are political actors because they produce geographic frameworks for relating development to a changing climate. By tracing the work of these engineers, this article attempts to understand what climate change can tell us about the pasts and futures of regional identity in the Global South.

In what follows, I outline the Guyanese case of damming in relation to theoretical debates about scale and region formation. I then briefly document the origins of the EDWC and the translocal expertise of which it was a part. I then outline how the 1934 disaster compromised the EDWC's drainage and the way engineers mobilized technico-political ideas about regionalism. Their mobilization was informed by the colony's participation in the 1938 Moyne Commission, which called for, among other things, "West Indian Federation" through agriculture. In the final part of the paper, I explore how contemporary proposals for climate adaptation create new regional networks through which engineers relate histories of development and disasters to climate change.

Regional Formations

This article builds on cross-disciplinary debates that treat regions as socio-environmental spaces that are mobilized through political struggle.[1] I contribute to these debates by examining the multiscalar effects of climate change on the regional identities of experts in the Global South. In doing so, I explore the ways the technical labor of engineers transforms the material arrangements through which regions are experienced and contested.

Throughout Guyana's history, dams have stood in as symbols of modernization. As historian Walter Rodney detailed with fervor, the country's coast is notoriously unruly and difficult to dam because it is below sea level and subject to biannual wet seasons.[2] At the same time, engineers have aspired to account for why damming in Guyana creates differences in its economic performance compared to other states in the Caribbean. Their aspirations have centered on one specific technique, river basin damming, which conceives of the head of a river as the source of hydraulic systems. This technique has served as a means to not only rationalize water management but to permit the structural reform of land tenure and in some cases mineral resource extraction. This is perhaps unsurprising given the countless studies that detail how engineers' institutional policies for national-level water management reinforce particular ideas about nature's commodification.[3] But in Guyana, engineers have faced a recurring problem. Because of climate-related flooding, they have had to reinvent their ideas about what it means to be economically part of the Caribbean as they modify dam design measures. Hence, damming practices illustrate that regions do not have fixed spatial boundaries, because they are formed by power-laden processes of knowledge exchange and consumption.

Scholars in human geography have long noted that regions denote a place between the national and local scale, but that this place is much more than a territorial unit.[4] In light of globalization in the 1980s and 1990s, many scholars studied regions by analyzing how networked forms of telecommunication, travel, and neoliberal trade made cities less politically and culturally distinct from one another.[5] Others demonstrated that these networks had the reverse effect. Market-based approaches to urban reform only intensified existing socioeconomic inequalities within cities, thereby reinforcing regional differences between them.[6] These contradictory outcomes revealed that the formation of regions is dependent on people's performed and collective identity with a place.[7] The political clout of a region, its fiscal robustness or plight, and its accessibility of resources obviously do not equally characterize the experiences of its residents. As Ash Amin summarizes, "[Regions] are temporary placements of ever moving material and immanent geographies, as 'hauntings' of things that have moved on but left their mark . . . as contoured products of the networks that cross a given place."[8]

Indeed, the meanings people attribute to regional boundaries vary across activities and cannot be imposed in a monolithic way.[9] This insight has not been lost on scholars tracking the political responses of states in the Global South to climate change. Studies center on how human vulnerability to climate change is related to globalization and inequality in the historic and current emissions of greenhouse gases. Yet, as Mike Hulme notes, the institutional negotiations of the IPCC[10] prioritize the "goal of a stabilized global climate as the centerpiece of policy."[11] Through these negotiations, the various opinions of state bureaucrats working in the Global South have been marginalized, and in some cases assumed to be always already against emission reductions.[12] These negotiations have led Dipesh Chakrabarty to argue that "there is no corresponding 'humanity' that in its oneness can act as a political agent" to manage climate change.[13] In this regard, disputes over such issues as climate justice remain tied to the various economic—as opposed to technoscientific—interests of states in the Global South.[14] Consequently, while climate change has spurred a new region-based awareness about uneven development, it is symptomatic of globalization's historical antagonisms.

The Guyanese experience of damming is one case in point. Engineers have historically mobilized translocal engineering expertise as a response to climate-related flooding. Engineers' repair of the EDWC after the 1934 disaster is emblematic of this mobilization. But the repair of the dam did not provide a technical or long-term remedy for Guyana's trouble with floods. Instead, engineers became increasingly entangled in dam projects that espoused economic models for Caribbean regional development, thereby normalizing place-based climatic risks. This spatial reordering of economy influenced the ways in which engineers perceived themselves as knowledgeable of flooding. In turn, discourses about regionalism became crucial instruments of power that into the present inform political contestations about climate adaptation and its viability in Guyana.

A Prelude to Regionalism

Before there were dams, human settlers experimented with only a handful of infrastructures to hold back flood waters. Well over seven thousand years ago, the Warao an Amerindian fishing community, constructed large shell mounds that protected their land. With the migration of Dutch planters and African slaves from the colony's forested interior to the coast in the seventeenth century, canals became the dominate infrastructure for flood control. While the Dutch set up plantation estates that displaced existing Amerindian settlements, they did rely on Amerindian trade routes along rivers to dig canals.[15] This organization supported the development of land around what planters called empoldering, a relatively low-tech but labor-intensive method for reclaiming land from the sea. When the colony changed hands to the British in 1803, planters expanded the Dutch grid while heavily investing in a seawall to protect the capital city of Georgetown and its ports.[16]

By the 1830s, planters called for a new system of flood control that could challenge what they perceived as predatory land tenure that resulted from slave emancipation in the British Empire. Land titles were granted to freedmen and to those newly arrived indentured laborers who stayed in the colony instead of returning to India at the end of their contracts.[17] But many of their land plots were located off the canal grid and so were often vulnerable to sabotage by planters. In turn, freedmen and indentured laborers devised elaborate methods to access and drain water, such as digging side trenches that cut across each other's land plots. At the same time, planters competed for levies to go toward the construction of roads, sea defenses, and canals near or on their estates. This fragmented process of land settlement led planters to urge the governor to hire consulting engineers from Britain to build a large dam to service the flood control and irrigation needs of the entire coast.[18] Over twenty-two square miles, the EDWC was dug in 1877 from a swamp on the edge of savannah. Constructed at a high elevation, water from the Mahaica River channeled into it and drained into adjacent canals that fed into Georgetown and the coast's ten largest estates.

While local land disputes continued to influence the way the EDWC was financed, correspondence between engineers around the world informed its daily management. The EDWC's design was known as a "gravitation scheme" because its drainage was dependent on a steep slope. This design was first perfected by the Royal Corps of Engineers in the 1840s around efforts to provide water to a growing urban population in Glasgow.[19] By 1850, there were one thousand British engineers in the diaspora, some of whom were designing gravitation schemes for geographies that spanned from Colombo to Hong Kong.[20] With varied ecologies and political institutions that did not easily assimilate to the gravitation scheme, engineers modified and did not completely abandon indigenous damming structures.[21]

Yet, in a New World context like British Guiana where gravitation schemes were often the only visible evidence of damming, what counted as "successful" engineering was not obvious. William Russell, the consulting engineer hired for the EDWC's construction, took inspiration from newspaper articles about dams along the Nile to perfect his soil and river surveys. His enthusiasm was further bolstered when a colleague told him about a trip to California where he saw a technique called "beavering"—stacking grass and logs to heighten dam walls. By the 1880s, Russell's work crew was beavering the EDWC. He wrote about their efforts in the Guianese natural history journal called *Timheri*—a Carib word meaning *petroglyph*.

Beyond a narrow appreciation for design, Russell wrote about his ambitions to piece together the history of the Guianese floodplain. In the 1882 article "Farming and Irrigation" he complained that Dutchmen created canals that functioned

simply as highways for opening up sections of the colony, affording both navigation and drainage. But none of these works can be described as *conserving* fresh water. . . . Further, no one now living can give any account of this work or when it was done. . . . I am not astonished to find so few marks of water conservation in the Dutch time, because, as a nation, they have been more famed for keeping off water than for conserving it; and in the Holland of to-day no large works are to be found for impounding water for Guiana [Suriname], with its two wet and two dry seasons, said to have been more regular in the past than at the present day.[22]

British Guiana's absence of ruins had a number of implications. The most obvious was engineers' decision to use rain gauges to monitor water levels in the EDWC's system. With rain gauges, they could broaden their point of reference about flood control from the particularities of seasonal crop rotations to hydrology. At the same time, dams were a colonial invention that had origins in the piecemeal processes of land dispossession that characterized settler colonialism, slavery, and indentured servitude. To this end, Russell argued that not all forms of "national" engineering expertise were equivalent because there was no one who could remember where land was taken or repurposed. He intimated that a kind of regional approach to

damming that analyzed historic river and weather patterns was needed. The prob
lem however, is that while Russell cared a lot about the kind of data collection coordinated between Dutch and British engineers, he was seemingly less concerned
with *how* data was circulated to improve flood control. This was a matter not
only about dam design, but as engineers would later learn, also the management
of disasters.

Geographies of Federation

The EDWC remained engineers' crowning achievement into the early twentieth
century, with only one other gravitation scheme, the Bonasika Water Conservancy,
built in the colony. Their expertise was tested, however, in January 1934. It was the
first time the EDWC was compromised by flooding from a simultaneous rainstorm
and high tide. Engineers and flood victims reported seeing cracks along the EDWC's
embankment and living "through a situation fraught with terror."[23] A flood commission was established by the governor to assess the EDWC's damages. Upon initial
inspection, engineers feared that adding more fascine structures would "loosen its
top soil and [allow] water readily to percolate through."[24]

 Parting with Russell's approach to beavering, the engineers affiliated with
the flood commission requested that the governor fund the construction of a new
drainage canal to use during storms. The decision also proved to be amenable to non-
engineers on the commission, including the politician Hon E. A. Lukhoo founder of
the British Guiana East Indian Association (BGEIA). He argued that with the construction of a storm drainage canal, the governor could establish more settlements
for small landowners near the EDWC. At the same time, he noted the dismal reality
of this proposition. Even with "fortified lands," small landowners and their propri-
etors would run into debt paying for the maintenance of the storm drainage canal
and associated pumps. He argued, "If you sell your lands several times over again
you would still not be able to meet these obligations."[25] Throughout its existence, the
BGEIA focused on raising public awareness about the role of Hindu/Muslim culture in the South Asian Diaspora and strategies for political emancipation. But the
1934 disaster highlighted other concerns for E. A. Lukhoo. Damming had become
an important symbol of anticolonialism at the same time that it exposed the ways in
which people's identification with a place could be redefined by disasters.

 The 1934 Flood Commission might thus be understood as having resonance
with other social crises in the wider Caribbean at the time. There were a series
of labor riots, strikes, and looting that swept through Trinidad, Jamaica, St. Vincent, British Guiana, British Honduras, and Barbados between 1936 and 1938. A
committee, chaired by Baron Moyne, was appointed to investigate these events.[26]
In preparation, the colonial office established the West Indies Development and
Welfare Organisation and research councils to fund British and West Indian academics to complete "social science" studies about the riots.[27] Over the course of

fifteen months, the Moyne Commission held numerous public forums and completed 370 interviews. The final report concluded that West Indian development was being blocked by the supposed moral and cultural failings of the West Indian family unit—particularly households headed by single Black mothers. These conclusions, while steeped in European middle-class assumptions about respectability and social reproduction, also assumed "material betterment," were conditioned by West Indians themselves.[28] The Moyne Report, in its quest to uncover a regional understanding of the "social," reduced political personhood to environment and geography to development.

The West Indian envoys representing the commission included men from a variety of political, class, and racial-ethnic backgrounds. Other than being of West Indian ancestry, the characteristic that drew them together was the "command, however rudimentary, of the language and culture of Imperial Power."[29] They argued that "once an exceedingly philanthropic institution" that oversaw the abolition of slavery, "[the colonial office] had yield to the idea of pecuniary profit and colonial exploitation."[30] Playing the long game for a referendum on independence, envoys openly debated whether a federal body should administer free trade between the colonies and agricultural marketing organizations.[31]

They were skeptical about the role federation could play, if any, in solving what many glossed over as the British West Indies' geography problem. Trinidadians were the most indifferent to the idea of federation, noting the island's need to diversify the economy around mineral extraction, especially oil. Jamaicans, particularly those championing what they called a Fabian understanding, put the issue of economy in the starker terms of spatial scale. They looked forward to economic diversification but noted that each colony had its own "stage of development" to consider:

The islands are very far apart, and I think our stages of development are not
identical. The structure of Jamaica is very different to Barbados or Trinidad, or
British Guiana. What might be admirable here would not be advisable there.
We [Jamaicans] are big enough and sufficiently alive to our problems to deal
with them here.[32]

Indeed, the British West Indies was expansive in both size and distance. Hence, the envoys' technical work not only involved negotiating ambitious trade agreements but creating an up-to-date geographic database of the region. A reviewer for the international science journal *Nature* agreed with the Jamaican envoys: while he praised the Moyne Report for its "remarkable" and "exhaustive breadth" of information, it was accompanied by what he called an "inadequate map."[33] At a scale of "fifty-five miles to an inch the Leeward and Windward groups . . . appear as little more than dots on the vast expanse of the Caribbean. . . . The need for cartographical aid is all the more necessary because of the scattered distribution of the British West

Indies."[34] The maps, the envoys surmised, would help them visualize trade routes and the colonies' differences in stages of development.

Nonetheless, the central assumption of the Moyne Commission was that regional economic integration could be achieved by first expanding peasant agricultural production. The colonies faced a slew of obstacles reaching this goal—from plant disease epidemics, dependence on low-tech farming machinery, to a high rate of labor outmigration. The envoys argued that all of these problems could be fixed with time and investments in state of the art technology. British Guiana, however, was the only colony singled out for being less than fit to expand peasant agriculture because of its intractable drainage.

The envoys proposed that engineers in British Guiana should not undertake additional land settlement schemes around the EDWC until more extensive soil and river surveys were completed. The report summarized: "The British Guiana system does not involve one great outfall like the Fens of Eastern England, the problem of silting at the various small outfalls, with comparatively small discharge and low silt-removing power, is an extremely serious one."[35] The envoys' prognosis was grim. Either the cost of drainage would "be undertaken as an irrecoverable Colonial charge," or Royal Engineers would have to be permanently stationed on Guiana's coast, even after independence, to monitor flooding.[36]

"Practical Considerations"

For engineers in British Guiana, the Moyne Commission offered a devastating critique of their large-scale damming techniques. On the one hand, by definition, dams could do little to control the "natural" siltation of rivers or even made siltation worse. On the other, the horrific flooding in 1934 prevented engineers from relating to dams solely through the language of development and specifically small-scale/peasant agriculture. Flooding took on a more active materiality, one caught up in the loss of human life and the erosion of the built environment. Development, in other words, was not experienced the same way by engineers working in British Guiana as by the Moyne Commission envoys. Instead, development was a contested claim about Caribbean, or regional identity.

The Moyne Commission's conclusions suggested that the gears of capitalist machinery, including peasant agriculture, could be made amenable to the management of social crises and related environmental disasters.[37] Regional identity, in other words, was defined not only by the data engineers collected but by their understandings of the causal relationships between floods and dam design.[38] The concept of regionality in this sense constantly animated struggles over decolonization and the figure of the engineer in its unfolding.

By 1952, engineers decided to follow the advice of the Moyne Commission and expand the EDWC's network with the construction of the agricultural Mahaica-Mahaicony-Abary (MMA) Scheme. Named after coastal rivers, the MMA Scheme was based on an approach called river basin damming. An interconnected system of canals would control the dams' water flow at "intermediary" points along the rivers' paths to the Atlantic Ocean. The dams were to "spread across the rivers, to join the land on the higher land on both sides [of the dams] and thus form a shallow reservoir."[39] In addition, the dams were designed to overlap with the irrigation grid of an existing rice field which was started in 1942 and covered eleven thousand empoldered (and diked) acres, of which four thousand were cultivated.

Events surrounding the rise of nationalist and anticolonial movements underscored the MMA Scheme's importance.[40] Colonial authorities surmised that "expansive flood protection" was the only way to "give more people the feeling of having a real stake in the country."[41] This pledge to freedom through flood control was a response to escalating tensions, particularly between Afro-Guianese and Indo-Guianese laborers, over growing underemployment in the sugar sector. At the same time, colonial authorities looked to create conditions that would protect the interests of British-based sugar corporations after independence. They envisioned that the MMA Scheme's system of individual leasehold titling for selective cash crop rotations would lessen these tensions.[42] The MMA Scheme's administrative planning also reflected that of the dams in a newly independent India, with the consulting engineer citing the Damodar Valley Cooperation and its small-scale land settlements as his inspiration.

In the MMA Scheme's Stage 1 Report, engineers explained that the dam was a realistic venture if only because of the meticulous rainfall data engineers kept since the 1870s under William Russell. The data showed "abnormal" periods of dry and wet weather in the East Coast region, which lead the MMA's head engineers to believe that riverine areas with fairly deep peat soils were "well-nigh impossible to drain" and were thus effectively avoided in design efforts.[43] For instance, he estimated the changes in velocity (flow) of water in open channels due to topography, tides, and the elevation of river basins. He called these calculations ways to "govern flood relief by practical considerations," by designing dam embankments, channels, and banks that were purposefully oversized and extremely flat. With these dimensions in mind, the head engineer proposed to add two drainage canals to the EDWC.

Thus, river basin damming was dependent on calculative techniques that could flatten space into administrative areas bounded by rivers. Unlike the gravitation scheme, river basin damming was a distinctively American invention first conceived by engineers managing the Tennessee Valley Authority (TVA). They envisioned using the water from rivers for multiple purposes, from irrigation and flood control to hydropower development. The history of the TVA's influence on the formation of high modernist aesthetics and planning in the decolonizing world is well documented.[44] A handful of scholars have even related these geographies to those of dispossession in the United States, particularly among poor and landless Blacks in the TVA district.[45] We also know that the TVA approach to damming relied heavily on a spatial logic and procedure of data collection. Rainfall data had to be collected from the "total area" of rivers, not just in the dam, for damming to be effective.

TVA engineer Arthur Morgan, in his tome *Dams and Other Disasters*, explains that Army Corps engineers resisted the TVA approach when it was first proposed. Along the Mississippi River, levees and not dams were their preferred choice for flood control. Morgan argues that because engineers did not travel to the "top catchments" of rivers and set up rain gauges, they had developed a reliance on dams for irrigation alone. One engineer complained that multipurpose dams "were like the 'combination tool,' the joy of the inventor but the despair of the user."[46] But with more *and* different kinds of rainfall data, Morgan argued, engineers could learn to anticipate the user's despair with engineer review boards—independent of the Army Corps—that could periodically monitor the network of dams. Morgan surmised that with a targeted approach to data collection followed changes in engineers' attitudes toward the circulation and use of data across society.

Similar concerns informed the MMA Scheme's management. A technical board comprising sugar and rice barons, agronomists, engineers, surveyors, hydrologists, politicians, and pedologists oversaw the dams' construction and were responsible for reporting to the Minister of Agriculture. In turn, the board's meeting minutes became the point of reference for engineers to schedule when to open sluice gates in the event of a flood or drought. But in 1949, engineers were ordered by the governor to stop surveying rivers after sugar barons delayed legislation in parliament, fearing that the scheme would take away their labor supply during dam construction. The head engineer allegedly grew disillusioned and "resigned in disgust," leaving the project stalled until the governor could find a replacement.[47]

His resignation signaled that the MMA Scheme was troubled by much more than pernicious structures of plantation employment. By the mid-1950s, the colony was already training cohorts of native-born engineers. Robert Victor Evan Wong, S. S. Narine, Phillip Allsopp, and author Wilson Harris were included. After completing qualifying examinations in the colony, they went to university in the United Kingdom, followed by internships under the direction of consulting engineers back home. Racialized tactics of hiring and promotion informed their professional arrangements on projects such as the MMA Scheme. Their status as "indigenous" engineers meant that dams became components of intraclass conflicts and aspirations that galvanized a working class as much as the nonwhite middle class. Known as the "Queens College Boys," this labor force reimagined mobility, political belonging, and who counted as an engineer. They were, in Michelle Stephens's view, charting masculine geographies that mobilized Caribbean imaginings of the self that operated on an affective level across the jurisdictions of transnational and colonial expert cultures.[48] Indeed, by the time soil and river surveys for the MMA Scheme started again in the early 1960s, it was headed by an engineer of a well-off Guianese family of Portuguese decent.

From engineers' perspectives, the technical demands of river basin damming shaped how and when scientific, political, and economic bureaucracies ignored or coordinated with one another. Far from environmental determinism, dams depended on engineering expertise that could respond to (and less so predict), the violent ebb and flow of flood waters. River basin damming, therefore, conducted through various ideological props, induces forms of subjectivity—such as engineer, small landowner, Moyne Commission envoy, and flood victim—that tenuously collide and elide with one another. Through the day-to-day work of dam design, engineers made powerful arguments that technoscience produces a Caribbean regional identity. Perhaps this is the point we can glean from the MMA Scheme's head engineer who called his job an effort to "govern by practical considerations."

River basin damming made clear that colonial independence in the British West Indies could unfold at different speeds and times across the region. Moreover, river basin damming tied notions of political personhood to the human capacity to live with disastrous flooding. The Moyne Report, apart from British Guiana, makes no mention of the infrastructure other West Indian colonies would need to deal with the hurricanes, droughts, and floods that supposedly contributed to the region's differences in "comparative prosperity."[49] Engineers' rainfall data and river surveys offered important rejoinders to Moyne Commission envoys' anxieties about the potential quagmires of West Indian federation. Accordingly, river basin dams in British Guiana allowed engineers to enact a kind of strategic regionalism, even as their work sustained colonial binaries of space and territory, freedom and power.

Disaster, Redux

With independence in 1966, engineers faced the immediate task of securing international aid to build the MMA Scheme's three dams. When the government took on a socialist agenda (1970–1985), it lost support from lenders and fell into massive debt. Consequently, only one dam, the Abary Dam, was completed during socialism, while many engineers migrated in search of work in North America and other parts of the Caribbean. An engineer who worked on the Abary Dam noted in an interview with me how his assumptions about the tight coupling of development and damming quickly crumbled under socialism:

In those days things were fairly orderly. But then we went through a period when there wasn't much money . . . and things were really bad. . . . When things started to go bad financially we still had the infrastructure which was good but we did not have money to maintain the structures. When you nationalize major industries in your country the big corporations and superpowers of the world tend to pressure you and I think that's what happened to the government. . . .

It all revealed that we had more work to do than money. So if you aren't maintaining adequately things get progressively worse. It meant that farmers were not able to pay for their irrigation and drainage rates and they were calling for services. Some were saying because they weren't getting adequate services they wouldn't pay. Well, if you don't pay you can't get services! And if you are not maintaining your infrastructure adequately something is actually happening; it's getting worse. Coupled with that a lot of engineers left the country. We had brain drain. I don't think we ever saw the recovery of that. . . . Many were trained abroad in England, the Netherlands, Cuba. . . . But it's only right now [after the disaster] that we have started to recover and people want to come back to help.

This engineer's comments return to the question William Russell posed when the EDWC was initially planned. What are the stakes of a world based in damming and what kinds of data facilitate their production or erasure of a given place? With the socialist transition in the early 1990s, engineers began to explicitly answer this question. The government partnered with the American Army Corps of Engineers to update water balance surveys of the EDWC. In addition, funding from the World Bank for agriculture marketing programs became institutional capital engineers drew on to garner support from parliament to fund the MMA Scheme dams.

While engineers in Guyana embarked on a path toward liberalization, a global anti-dam movement had already gained momentum. The movement revealed that the damages created by TVA-inspired dams are not specific to projects but the technology itself. In many cases, critics argued that because dams contribute to the extensive desiltation of rivers, they tend to have the most impact on agriculture-based livelihoods.[50] Scholar-activists as diverse as Patrick McCully and Arundhahti Roy have argued that anti-dam movements are, at their core, protests against the impacts of globalization on the world's poor. The United Nations' 1998 World Commission on Dams agreed as much when it charted the complex networks of global aid and construction financing that support dams in developing, Global South contexts. The report highlights, "The beneficial effect on local communities is often transient due to the short-lived, pulse impact of the construction economy on dam construction sites. Careful planning may, however, enhance the 'boom' phase and lead to long-lasting benefits."[51] But the extent to which displacement and economic "boom" phases are processes that overlap in time and space is not always clear cut.

In Guyana, no opposition by that time coalesced around the MMA Scheme dams.[52] Some scholars point to racial party politics and the postsocialist ascent of a majority Indo-Guyanese government as stifling democratic opposition from the majority Indo-Guyanese agrarian class.[53] This may be a reason for the absence of an anti-dam movement, but it may not be the only reason. As I have argued elsewhere, farmer-based water associations play a central role in not just water allocation but engineers' daily work.[54] Championed for replicating the legal framework of those in

Andhra Pradhesh—India's "rice bowl"—the farmer-based water associations govern the payment of user fees and canal repairs. Nonetheless, engineers have been critical of these arrangements. Because MMA dam construction (and repair) is highly dependent on grant-based development projects, farmers in everyday practice are the primary actors monitoring minute changes in drainage. Engineers, in turn, have become used to thinking in a mode of flood response instead of preparedness. They have focused on researching macro-scale flood-related processes, such as siltation and coastal erosion cycles, when they can broker support from organizations such as the World Bank.[55]

Even still, engineers' assumption that river basin damming can be sustained through farmer-based water associations has been put to the test in recent decades. In March 1997–1998 a drought was associated with the strongest El Niño cycle in Guyana's recorded history. The severity of the drought resulted in the President declaring a state of emergency as rivers dried up and dams experienced salience intrusion approximately 48–64 km upstream of the coastal rivers. The dam's low water levels contributed to a shortage of drinking water and the quarterly production of rice and sugar fell by 35 and 13 percent, respectively. But it was the disastrous 2005 flood that pushed engineers to once again reconsider the EDWC's design.

Between December 2004 and February 2005, multiple storms resulted in over sixty inches of rain flooding Guyana's Atlantic coast.[56] The storms were unprecedented compared to engineers' records which estimated nine inches as the average monthly rainfall. The storms affected 62 percent of the nation's population (roughly 520,000 people), leaving them stranded in three to five feet of water for weeks.[57] Timing the release of water from the EDWC into canals was crucial. If water was released when the tide was high, Georgetown would have been inundated not only with water from the EDWC but with seawater as well. Recognizing the short timeframe they had before water would overtop the EDWC, engineers decided to release water into the Mahaica River. While this strategy provided relief to Georgetown, it further exacerbated flooding in rural communities.

A few months after the disaster, the Ministry of Agriculture solicited support from the World Bank's Global Environment Fund for help. The Fund provided resources for engineers to update the EDWC's hydraulic models and to build a storm drainage canal similar to the one proposed after the 1934 disaster. They have also pursued a program in mapping the country's drainage grid and installed automatic sensors to collect data about the EDWC's real-time and storm water levels. Alongside these shifts in engineering, the canal has sparked protests. Farmers displaced for its construction fear that it is only a temporary solution to flooding—which, since the disaster, they view as an increasingly unpredictable threat to their livelihoods in cash crops (e.g. tubers and rice)—while advocacy groups such as the Guyana Human's Rights Association (GHRA) have called for the state to provide those displaced with permanent assistance for flood relief and land for resettlement. What should we make of these charges? The engineers' and the GHRA's responses do not necessarily offer solutions to intergenerational injustices brought on by colonizing processes of damming and land settlement schemes. What's more, their responses only further demonstrate that regional models of development have been historically shaped, and in many instances undermined by a changing climate.

Conclusion

What makes Guyana's case so striking is that when engineers first proposed modifications to the EDWC in 1934, they were "adapting" to a changing climate but might not have known it—at least they did not describe it as such. Engineers in British Guiana had trouble convincing Moyne Commission envoys that dams were worth continued investment. Through their participation with the Moyne Commission, they learned that dams could shape political attitudes about regional identity. Thus the 1936 and 2005 disasters are events that may not only index climate change: They have created multiple pathways for mobilizing the political economy of a region.

Indeed, contemporary forms of biopolitical security such as climate adaptation also signal a definitive commitment to regionalism. For instance, Guyana and Suriname are a handful of non-island states that are members of the Alliance of Small Island States (ASIS), while thirteen other Caribbean island states are members as well. The ASIS mobilizes around states' vulnerability to sea-level rise and their historic experiences of purported underdevelopment. Such organizations represent states in the Global South as a region of disparate terrestrial/atmospheric/ marine-scapes. Unlike the efforts of past colonial projects such as the Moyne Commission, these regional relations are not necessarily territorial. They coalesce around the political treaties and negotiations associated with carbon emissions. Hence, climate change has not only shaped new understandings of risks impacting the Global South but also the sociomaterial boundaries that comprise it as a region of states.

For instance, the rate of sea-level rise is six times that of the global average in Guyana. Salt water intrusion from the Atlantic poses a threat to the health of both rivers and agricultural lands.[58] The concurrent efforts of engineers researching the deep histories of peat soils and mangrove ecosystems to build more resilient drainage channels for the EDWC reveal as much. Research programs with explicit appeals to climate adaptation have also been undertaken in the West, in places like New Orleans, New York City, and New Jersey since Hurricane Katrina and Superstorm Sandy.[59] In many respects, the technical goals of climate adaptation have circumvented traditional political diagnoses about what counts as development.

So while climate adaptation may be an altogether new mode of governance, states in the Global South for quite some time have prefigured the West's climatological future. Comaroff and Comaroff offer a similar diagnosis of the "contemporary order of things" arguing that the "raw materials" of the Global South become "Theory" for the West.[60] They focus on the complex flows of finance capital and of

Africans struggling to creatively get by while etching out strident critiques of neo-liberalism. For instance, the "informal economies" in pharmaceutical drugs are not incidental to but are in many cases pretenses for Euro-American commerce and Western pharmaceutical investments in Africa. The Global South thus provides a wellspring of theory for anticipating the future workings of the world at large. However they might be imagined, Comaroff and Comaroff argue, the borders between the West and the Global South are quiet unstable, and so too the value of the raw materials that circulate in and across them.

What is most important about Comaroff and Comaroff's analysis for climate adaptation is that raw materials can have political effects on the spatial distribution of expertise in the Global South. As Guyana's finicky rivers and soils indicate, climate adaptation is dependent on engineers' place-based knowledge about flood hazards and its uptake across global governing institutions. Recent work by scholars writing about the Global South and its built environment get at this point. AbdouMaliq Simone reminds us that life in the Global South is not a "depleted" version of life in the West but simply "a different form—that constantly lives under specific threats and incompletion."[61] For Simone, cities particularly in Africa and Asia are examples of where built environments—slum housing or broken water pipes—become novel arrangements for human living. Importantly, then, people's sense of place and (affective) attachments to it are not independent of their experiences of vulnerability. This means that living with climate change requires a deep skepticism about the sociomaterial processes that bound and mark a place. And if a discourse about the Global South emphasizes difference, then one must consider how that difference gets caught up in the circulation of place-based knowledge.

This article has attempted to chart the circulation of place-based knowledge and the various historical processes through which climate change has impacted expertise. It has demonstrated that climate change shapes engineers' debates about regionalism and regional political economy in Guyana. Engineers are central figures in these debates, not only because of their scientific acumen but because their work exposes that addressing development and climate change requires negotiating a spatial politics that is sensitive to issues of globality as much as transregionality. The task at hand for critical scholarship of the Global South is to understand how (non)expert practices create regions in ways that powerfully reorder environmental subjectivities and ways of life under climate change.

Sarah E. Vaughn is an assistant professor of anthropology at the University of California, Berkeley. She is currently writing a book titled *Engineering Vulnerability: An Ethnography of Climate Change and Expertise.*

Notes

I would like to thank the reviewers and editors for their generous feedback and comments. I am, of course, solely responsible for any of the article's errors or limitations. This article would not have been possible without generative insights of my field informants, particularly those engineers affiliated with Guyana's Ministry of Agriculture and the firms CEMCO and SRKN'gineering.

In addition, the writing of this article would have not been possible without the support of the Yale School of Forestry and Environmental Studies's James & Mary Pinchot Sustainability Fellowship.

1. See Jones and Riding, *Reanimating Regions*; and Gupta and Ferguson, *Anthropological Locations*.
2. Rodney, *A History of the Guyanese Working People, 1881–1905*.
3. See Swyngedouw, "Technonatural Revolutions"; and Mitchell, *Rule of Experts*
4. See Agnew, "From the Political Economy of Regions to Regional Political Economy"; Thomas, Harvey, and Hawkins, "Crafting the Region."
5. See Lash and Urry, *Economies of Signs and Space*; and Scott, *Regions and the World Economy*.
6. See Massey, *World Cities*; and Amin and Thrift, *Cities*.
7. See Passi, "Place and Region."
8. Amin, "Regions Unbound: Towards a New Politics of Place," 34.
9. Jones and MacLeod, "Regional Spaces, Spaces of Regionalism."
10. Intergovernmental Panel on Climate Change.
11. Hulme, "Geographical Work at the Boundaries of Climate Change," 6.
12. Verbitsky, "Just Transitions and a Contested Space: Antarctica and the Global South."
13. Chakrabarty, "Postcolonial Studies and the Challenge of Climate Change."
14. See Beer, "Climate Justice, the Global South, and Policy Preference of Kenyan Environmental NGOs."
15. For a detailed history of Dutch colonial settlement and trade with Amerindians see Benjamin, "A Preliminary Look at the Free Amerindians and the Dutch Plantation System in Guyana during the Seventeenth and Eighteenth Centuries": 1–21; and Whitehead, *Lords of the Tiger Spirit*.
16. Rodway, *The Story of Georgetown*.
17. A significant number of indentured laborers also arrived from Portugal, China, and West Africa but were not granted the same land arrangements at the termination of their contracts. For an extended discussion about land tenure and labor in the transition to and postemancipation era, see Adamson, *Sugar Without Slaves*.
18. Kirke, "The Early Years of the Lamaha Canal"; Bellairs, "Twenty Years' Improvements in Demerara Sugar Production, Part II." Structures similar to dams were present in the colony before the EDWC. However, they were moat-like and usually encircled a single estate across a narrow strip of land. For a description of planters' and small-scale landowners' drainage systems, see Rodney, *A History of the Guyanese Working People, 1881–1905*.
19. Broich, "Engineering the Empire."
20. For comparative analyses of civil engineering during the late nineteenth-century British Empire, see Anderson, "Colonial Connections and Consulting Engineers 1850–1914"; Buhanan, "The Diaspora of British Engineering"; and Cookson-Hills, "The Aswan Dam and Egyptian Water Control Policy, 1882–1902."
21. Joyce, *The Rule of Freedom*; Mrázek, *Engineers of a Happy Land*.

22. Russell, "Farming and Irrigation," 97.

23. Sufferer, "Letter to the Editor: Flood Conditions."

24. Second Legislative Council, "Report by the Floods Investigation Committee, 1934."

25. Sufferer, "East Coast: Havoc Mahaicony/Village Devastated."

26. West Indian Royal Commission, *The Moyne Report.*

27. Bush, "Colonial Research and the Social Sciences at the End of Empire."

28. Thomas, "The Violence of Diaspora"; Austin-Boos, *Jamaica Genesis.*

29. John L. A. Guerre, "The Moyne Commission and the West Indian Intelligentsia, 1938–39," 154.

30. Ibid., 136.

31. The West Indian Moyne Commission, *The Moyne Report*, 256–60.

32. Guerre, "The Moyne Commission and the West Indian Intelligentsia, 1938–39," 141.

33. Fitzgerald, "The Moyne Report on the West Indies Region."

34. Ibid., 254.

35. The West Indian Moyne Commission, *The Moyne Report*, 307.

36. The West Indian Moyne Commission, *The Moyne Report*, 307–8.

37. For other colonial examples of the tight coupling between rationalities of emergency, social crisis, and agriculture, see Stoler, *Along the Archival Grain*; and Davis, *Late Victorian Holocausts.*

38. The distinction between a feeling and demand for causality is an important one for engineers. Engineers in British Guiana were long invested in a theory of uniform velocity (e.g., Manning's Formula) that took into account the impacts of water pressure on the structural foundations of dams. Nonetheless, the demands on engineers to use this theory to make political justifications for certain projects, such as the MMA Scheme, cannot be overstated. For a similar appraisal about causality, politics, and theory-building among kinds of technoscientists, see Barad, *Meeting the Universe Halfway.*

39. Clark, *The Economic Development of British Guiana*, 202.

40. For an overview of events related to the rise of nationalist movements, see Jagan, *The West on Trial.*

41. Colonial Office, *Report of the British Guiana Constitutional Commission 1954*, 21.

42. Camacho, *The Mahaica-Mahaicony-Abary Water Control Project.*

43. Clark, *The Economic Development of British Guiana*, 203.

44. Scott, *Seeing Like a State*; Ekbladh, "Mr. TVA"; D'Souza, *Drowned and Dammed.*

45. Grant, *TVA and Black Americans.*

46. Morgan, *Dams and Other Disasters*, 266.

47. Smith, *British Guiana*, 92–3.

48. Stephens, *Black Empire.*

49. The West Indian Moyne Commission, *The Moyne Report*, 9–28.

50. Patrick McCully, *Silenced Rivers.*

51. World Commission on Dams, *Dams and Development*, 99.

52. Under the socialist government engineers planned a large hydro-electric dam near the Venezuelan border. The plan never materialized after (inter)national advocacy groups and the Venezuelan government pressed the World Bank to stop its construction. They feared that the dam would have flooded four thousand five hundred Akawaio and Arekuna off their land. Geography undoubtedly played an important role in this decision, as Venezuela looked to protect its border from an ongoing border dispute with Guyana. The relative "remoteness" of Amerindian livelihoods from coastal plantations, suggested that the

dam would have been a hindrance in the initial stages of development in the area. In recent years, the government has again proposed a hydro-electric dam but in a different part of the interior. For an appraisal of damming and alternatives to plantation-centric worldviews, see Price, *Rainforest Warriors.*

53. Hintzen, *The Costs of Regime Survival.*
54. Vaughn, "Reconstructing the Citizen."
55. For a broader analysis of Caribbean neoliberal developmentalism, oppositional politics, and the formation of place-based agricultural sciences see Crichlow, *Negotiating Caribbean Freedom.*
56. Eric Blommestein, *Guyana.*
57. Ibid.
58. Narayan, "Climate Change Impacts on Water Resources in Guyana."
59. Collier, Cox, and Grove, "Rebuilding by Design in Post-Sandy New York."
60. Comaroff and Comaroff, *Theory from the South*, 3.
61. Simone, "The Uninhabitable?," 136.

References

Adamson, Alan. 1973. *Sugar Without Slaves: The Political Economy of British Guiana, 1838–1904.* New Haven, CT: Yale University Press.

Agnew, John. 2000. "From the Political Economy of Regions to Regional Political Economy." *Progress in Human Geography* 24, no. 1: 101–110.

Amin, Ash. 2004. "Regions Unbound: Towards a New Politics of Place." *Geografiska Annaler* 86, no. 1: 33–44.

Amin, Ash, and Nigel Thrift. 2002. *Cities: Reimaging the Urban.* Cambridge: Polity Press.

Anderson, Casper. 2011. "Colonial Connections and Consulting Engineers 1850–1914." *Engineering History and Heritage* 164, no. 4: 201–209.

Austin-Boos, Diane J. 1997. *Jamaica Genesis: Religion and the Politics of Moral Order.* Chicago: University of Chicago Press.

Barad, Karen. 2007. *Meeting the Universe Halfway: Quantum Physics and the Entanglement of Matter and Meaning.* Durham, NC: Duke University Press.

Beck, Ulrich. 2008. *World at Risk.* Cambridge, UK: Polity Press.

Beer, Christopher Todd. 2014. "Climate Justice, the Global South, and Policy Preference of Kenyan Environmental NGOs." *The Global South* 8, no. 2: 84–100.

Bellairs, Seaforth M. 1892. "Twenty Years' Improvements in Demerara Sugar Production, Part II." *Timheri: The Journal of the Royal Agricultural and Commercial Society of British Guiana* 4: 1–21.

Benjamin, Anna. 1992. "A Preliminary Look at the Free Amerindians and the Dutch Plantation System in Guyana during the Seventeenth and Eighteenth Centuries." *Guyana Historical Journal* IV & V: 1–21.

Blommestein, Eric. 2005. *Guyana: Socio-Economic Assessment of the Damages and Losses Caused by the January-February 2005 Flooding.* Georgetown: ECLAC-UNDP.

Broich, John. 2007. "Engineering the Empire: British Water Supply Systems and Colonial Societies, 1850–1900." *Journal of British Studies* 46, no. 2: 346–65.

Buhanan, R. A. 1986. "The Diaspora of British Engineering." *Technology and Culture* 27, no. 3: 501–24.

Bush, Barbara. 2013. "Colonial Research and the Social Sciences at the End of Empire: The West Indian Social Survey, 1944–57." *The Journal of Imperial and Commonwealth History* 41, no. 3: 451–74.

Camacho, R. F. 1960. *The Mahaica-Mahaicony-Abary Water Control Project: Stage 1, the Control of the Abary*. Georgetown, Guyana: Drainage and Irrigation Department.

Chakrabarty, Dipesh. 2012. "Postcolonial Studies and the Challenge of Climate Change." *New Literary History* 43, no. 1: 1–18.

Clark, Harrison. 1953. *The Economic Development of British Guiana: Report of a Mission Organized by the International Bank for Reconstruction and Development*. Baltimore: Johns Hopkins Press.

Collier, Stephen J., Savannah Cox, and Kevin Grove. 2016. "Rebuilding by Design in Post Sandy New York." *Limn*7. https://limn.it/rebuilding-by-design-in-post-sandy-new-york/.

Colonial Office. 2003. *Report of the British Guiana Constitutional Commission 1954*. Edited by Odeen Ishmael. Georgetown, Guyana: GNI Publications.

Comaroff, Jean L., and John Comaroff. 2016. *Theory from the South: Or, How Euro-America is Evolving Toward Africa*. New York: Routledge Press.

Cookson-Hills, Claire. 2013. "The Aswan Dam and Egyptian Water Control Policy, 1882–1902." *Radical History Review* 116: 59–85.

Crichlow, Michaeline A. 2005. *Negotiating Caribbean Freedom: Peasants and the State in Development*. Lanham, MD: Lexington Books.

D'Souza, Rohan. 2006. *Drowned and Dammed: Colonial Capitalism and Flood Control in Eastern India (1803–1946)*. New Delhi: Oxford University Press.

Davis, Mike. 2002. *Late Victorian Holocausts: El Niño Famines and the Making of the Third World*. New York: Verso Books.

Ekbladh, David. 2002. "'Mr. TVA': Grass-Roots Development, David Lilienthal, and the Rise and Fall of the Tennessee Valley Authority as a Symbol for U.S. Overseas Development, 1933–1973." *Diplomatic History* 26, no. 3: 335–74

Fitzgerald, Walter. 1946. "The Moyne Report on the West Indies Region." *Nature* 157, no. 3983: 254–55.

Guerre, John L. A. 1971. "The Moyne Commission and the West Indian Intelligentsia, 1938–39." *The Journal of Commonwealth Political Studies* 9: 134–57.

Gupta, Akhil and James Ferguson. 1997. *Anthropological Locations: Boundaries and Grounds of a Field Science*. Berkeley: University of California Press.

Grant, Nancy. 1990. *TVA and Black Americans*. Philadelphia: Temple University Press.

Hintzen, Percy C. 2006. *The Costs of Regime Survival: Racial Mobilization, Elite Domination and Control of the State in Guyana and Trinidad*. Cambridge: Cambridge University Press.

Hulme, Michael. 2007. "Geographical Work at the Boundaries of Climate Change." *Transactions of the British Institute of Geographers* 33, no. 1: 5–11.

Jagan, Cheddi. 1997. *The West on Trial: My Fight for Guyana's Freedom*. Kingston, Jamaica: Hansib Publishing.

Jones, Martin and James Riding, eds. 2017. *Reanimating Regions: Culture, Politics, and Performance*. New York: Routledge.

Jones, Martin and Gordon MacLeod. 2004. "Regional Spaces, Spaces of Regionalism: Territory, Insurgent Politics and the English Question." *Transactions of the British Institute of Geographers* 29, no. 4: 433–52.

Joyce, Patrick Joyce. 2003. *The Rule of Freedom: Liberalism and the Modern City*. New York: Verso.

Kirke, Henry. 1893. "The Early Years of the Lamaha Canal." *Timehri: The Journal of the Royal Agricultural and Commercial Society of British Guiana* 7: 284–99.

Lash, Scott and John Urry. 2002. *Economies of Signs and Space*. London: Sage Publications.

Massey, Doreen. 2007. *World Cities*. Cambridge, UK: Polity Press.

McCully, Patrick. 2001. *Silenced Rivers: The Ecology and Politics of Large Dams*. London: Zed Books.

Mitchell, Timothy. 2002. *Rule of Experts: Egypt, Techno-Politics, Modernity*. Berkeley: University of California Press.

Morgan, Arthur. 1971. *Dams and Other Disasters: A Century of the Army Corps of Engineers in Civil Works*. Westford, MA: Porter Sargent Publishers.

Mrázek, Rudolf. 2002. *Engineers of a Happy Land: Technology and Nationalism in a Colony*. Princeton, NJ: Princeton University Press.

Narayan, Kailas. 2006. "Climate Change Impacts on Water Resources in Guyana." In *Climate Variability and Change: Hydrological Impacts*, edited by Siegfried Demuth, 413–18. Wallingford, UK: International Association of Hydrological Sciences.

Passi, Anssi. 2004. "Place and Region: Looking through the Prism of Scale." *Progress in Human Geography* 28, no. 4: 536–46.

Price, Richard 2012. *Rainforest Warriors: Human Rights on Trial*. Philadelphia: University of Pennsylvania.

Rodney, Walter. 1981. *A History of the Guyanese Working People, 1881–1905*. Baltimore: Johns Hopkins University Press.

Rodway, James. 1997. *The Story of Georgetown*. Georgetown, Guyana: Guyana Heritage Society.

Russell, William. 1882. "Farming and Irrigation." *Timheri: The Journal of the Royal Agricultural and Commercial Society of British Guiana* 1: 87–99.

Scott, Allen. 1998. *Regions and the World Economy: The Coming Shape of Global Production, Competition and Political Order*. Oxford, UK: Oxford University Press.

Scott, James. 1999. *Seeing Like a State: How Certain Schemes to Improve the Human Condition Have Failed*. New Haven, CT: Yale University Press.

Second Legislative Council, "Report by the Floods Investigation Committee, 1934." Georgetown, Guyana: The 1934 Flood Commission.

Simone, AbdouMaliq. 2016. "The Uninhabitable?: In Between Collapsed Yet Still Rigid Distinctions." *Cultural Politics* 12: 135–54.

Smith, Raymond T. 1962. *British Guiana*. London: Oxford University Press.

Stephens, Michelle Ann. 2005. *Black Empire: The Masculine Global Imaginary of Caribbean Intellectuals in the United States, 1914–1962*. Durham, NC: Duke University Press.

Stoler, Ann Laura. 2010. *Along the Archival Grain: Epistemic Anxieties and Colonial Common Sense*. Princeton, NJ: Princeton University Press.

Sufferer. 1934. "East Coast: Havoc Mahaicony/Village Devastated." *The Argosy* January 9, 1934.

———. 1934. "Letter to the Editor: Flood Conditions." *The Argosy* January 10, 1934.

Swyngedouw, Erik. 2007. "Technonatural Revolutions: The Scalar Politics of Franco's Hydro Social Dream for Spain, 1939–1975." *Transactions of the British Institute of Geographers* 32, no. 1: 9–28.

Thomas, Nicolas J., David C. Harvey, and Harriet Hawkins. 2013. "Crafting the Region: Creative Industries and Practices of Regional Space." *Regional Studies* 47, no. 1: 75–88.

Thomas, Deborah. 2009. "The Violence of Diaspora: Governmentality, Class Cultures, and Circulations." *Radical History Review* 103: 83–104.

Vaughn, Sarah E. 2012. "Reconstructing the Citizen: Disaster, Citizenship, and Expertise in Racial Guyana." *Critique of Anthropology* 32, no. 4: 359–387.

Verbitsky, Janes. 2014. "Just Transitions and a Contested Space: Antarctica and the Global South," *The Polar Journal* 4, no. 2: 319–34.

West Indian Royal Commission. 2010. *The Moyne Report.* Kingston, Jamaica: Ian Randle Publishers.

Whitehead, Neil. 1988. *Lords of the Tiger Spirit: A History of the Caribs in Colonial Venezuela and Guyana 1498–1820.* Dordrecht, Netherlands: Foris Publications.

World Commission on Dams. 2000. *Dams and Development: A New Framework for Decision Making.* London: Earthscan Press.

A City Called Mirage

Kiluanji Kia Henda

An Introduction, by Marissa J. Moorman

Kiluanji Kia Henda is an artist born and based in Luanda. The images—five photographs—and text that appear here are drawn from the work entitled *A City Called Mirage*. The full exhibit, curated by Kari Conte from work originally commissioned by the Sharjah Art Foundation, comprised a four-channel video installation and three interconnected photographic series that ran at the International Studio and Curatorial Program in Brooklyn between June 27 and October 6, 2017. Kia Henda produced this work between 2014 and 2017 during artistic residencies in Jordan and the United Arab Emirates and has shown it in various combinations in Lisbon, Portugal, and Naples, Italy.

Kia Henda's earlier work, like *Icarus 13* (2008) and *Balamuka-Ambush* (2010), deeply unsettles what we think of as the past. Photographing old monuments and weaving new fictions around derelict buildings, Kia Henda subverts, renarrates, and innovates on and in Angola's public history. This work tugs at the category of the postcolonial. His ironic framing captures, for example, a towering bronze of Angolan Queen Nzinga Mbandi in waiting at the old colonial military fort, staking her ground in front of the diminutive figure of Dom Afonso Henriques, the first king of Portugal, who was deposed from his public plinth in Luanda over forty years ago. Kia Henda's lens takes the measure of the nation against the brutality of the erstwhile colonial ruler. At the same time, amidst Luanda and Angola's postwar dis-

Radical History Review

Issue 131 (May 2018)   DOI 10.1215/01636545-4355209

© 2018 by MARHO: The Radical Historians' Organization, Inc.

repair, the statue of Nzinga Mbandi looms grandiose. The past troubles the present; the nation cannot rest easy.

A City Called Mirage turns to the future. This work takes the desert as a blank slate, as a place where dreams are built. The desert is where, as a video inter-title demands, "from the demarcation of space, a place emerges." But there is more space than place. The outlines of construction frame emptiness (Figures 2, 3, 4), notional lines float unmoored (Figure 5), and we glimpse labor (Figure 1).[1]

Framing emptiness operates at two levels. Dubai has been utilized as a model for the new Luanda, which Angolan elites, empowered by an oil boom, imagine could be a "Dubai on the Atlantic." Kia Henda sees the ultimate city in the desert as also figuratively arid and laments more broadly the thoughtless application of foreign models—Dubai today, Marx yesterday—while still holding up the ideal of cultural exchange. Here, and secondly, we can say Kia Henda is framing emptiness again, this time the hollowness of aesthetics imbued with ideology. Turning to the desert, he hoped to escape the grip of Angolan history and politics. But Kia Henda claims to have failed in that. He found, instead, a new vector of politics.[2] In this very failure he traces a seam traversing Global South aesthetics, binding difference across distance: the impossibility of artistic expression free of politics. He engages in a practice that joins together new lines of consciousness as he witnesses and records, for example, the precarity of the Pakistani and Bangladeshi guest workers in the Middle East without promising them freedom or a sturdier solidarity.

Birth, Life, and Death of the City, *A Statement by Kia Henda*

The city was conceived without knowing where exactly its foundations would take root. The main concern was the dream to raise a colossal line of horizon which could brush against the invisible mantle of the sky. So it did not matter whether its col-umns stood on land or in the sea. Conceived as a talisman, the city caused delirium due to the artificial gleam in the three-dimensional video of its outline. Even with the tops of its buildings enveloped by clouds, the metropolis's materialization was one of the greatest representations of the emptiness of the subsoil. Inverted, its image would be an endless crater in the southern hemisphere; inside out, a coast without beaches. The material extracted to construct the city covered the land with its own entrails, and the prototype of a terrestrial paradise was born by a caesarean that never healed.

The precipitous design of its buildings pierced the landscape and fragmented it. The bones were of steel and the skin of glass. The city grew out of a dream, and its costly adornments turned it into an enormous bauble. Its ideal of happiness was distorted, since it had been ineffective in fulfilling its primary purpose of providing a home. The city was sterile. A series of impenetrable cubes and cylinders reflected the pale figures of its passers-by in the facades.

The impalpable comfort printed on the postcard gleamed, while the constructed walls were suddenly invaded by emptiness. Putting all of the square feet of abandoned tiles together, a new concrete-covered desert had been born. This sight was more disturbing than the cruelty of the desert, since nothing between the empty walls of a building abounds in greater quantity than desolation. It was known that the city fed on a viscous liquid, a powerful solution in the metal veins of a gigantic mechanical artifact. This liquid gradually dried bit by bit and was insufficient to make its heart beat. The city slowly succumbed to its unsustainable artificiality. Its windows shattered and were blown by the wind into the sand and coral, returning the crystallized shine that had been stolen from them. The erected steel of the buildings had converted itself into a huge skeleton that was so enigmatic that many asked if the city had ever actually existed or was merely the description of the mirage of a delusional poet in the battle to survive the desert of our existence. Leaving its ruins was like freeing oneself of a corpse. It was embarrassing and almost painful to have to reconstitute the facts of its physical death. With the city demolished and cut into pieces, the rubble was thrown into a pool of water at the corner of another city coming to life.

CURATED SPACES provides a focus on contemporary artists whose work addresses social, historical, or political subject matter.

Figure 1

Figure 2

Figure 3

Figure 4

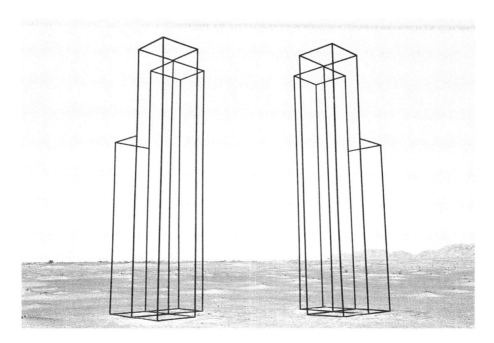

Figure 5

Kiluanji Kia Henda (born 1979, Luanda) is a Luanda-based artist, working across photography, video, and performance. He has exhibited at institutions including Tate Liverpool, 2017; SCAD Museum, Savannah, 2016; Centre Georges Pompidou, Paris, 2016; National Museum of African Art—Smithsonian Institution, Washington DC, 2015; Tamayo Museum, Mexico, 2012; and Arnolfini, Bristol, 2012. He participated in the 2015 Triennal: *Surround Audience*, New Museum, New York; Dakar Biennale, 2014; Bienal de São Paulo, 2007; Venice Biennale, 2007; and the Luanda Triennale, 2007. He is the winner of the 2017 Frieze Artist Award and the 2012 National Prize for Art and Culture awarded by the Angolan Ministry of Culture.

Notes

1. Lusona, the plural of sona, are Chokwe (an eastern Angolan population) sand drawings that communicate social expectations, a complex esoteric knowledge system, and political critique. They are simultaneously technical, mathematical, and aesthetic.
2. ISCP studio talk, August 23, 2017.

China and the Global South

A Geostrategic Perspective

Ronald C. Po

In his book *The China Dream*, which was published in 2010, Liu Mingfu predicted that the twenty-first century would belong to China.[1] One year later, Xi Jinping proclaimed on several occasions that his country was ready to foster China's dream of enhancing its international status in the new century. Since then, this ambitious China Dream (or China's Rise) has caused unease among the existing superpowers. This is particularly true for the United States, which has long been leading the world and directing the global order. Within the United States there has even existed a narrative, which is literally entitled "China's threat," that aims to crack down on the nature of the "China Dream." American politicians and intellectuals consider the China Dream a conspicuous symbol of the country's ambition as a maritime and global power across the Pacific Ocean.[2] These politicians predicted that China would use all means to break though the "two island chains"—which consist of Japan, South Korea, Taiwan, the Philippines, and Guam, and which were purposively set up by the Americans—and become the new Pacific giant threatening to usurp the dominant role of the American powerhouse. Without a doubt, the Chinese government has become much more ambitious than in previous decades. However, I am reluctant to side with those analysts who embrace the "China's threat" discourse and who regard the China Dream as being equivalent to its aspiration of rising as a Pacific power. Instead, I argue that in facilitating the China Dream, over the next few decades, the Chinese government is and will be more interested in engaging with the Global South than with any other region of the world, particularly

Radical History Review
Issue 131 (May 2018)   DOI 10.1215/01636545-4355233
© 2018 by MARHO: The Radical Historians' Organization, Inc.

In its military engagement in Africa and the Indian Ocean. Xi Jinping and his cabinet are truly interested in squarely situating China's position within these Southern territories and in ensuring its dominant role among a series of developing, though at the same time rapidly rising, economies. Even though the Pacific Ocean is no less geopolitically and strategically salient, this paper suggests that the Pacific has not been prioritized as the foremost strategic theatre by the Chinese Communist Party. In the paragraphs that follow, I will justify my observation by briefly explicating China's intensifying military engagement in the region throughout the twentieth and twenty-first centuries.

Before moving onto the military aspect, however, we have to understand that even though China's foreign policy has evolved since 1949, one policy that has not changed much is its close attachment to the regions of the world around the South China Sea and the Indian Ocean.[3] In fact, throughout China's history, Chinese traders and politicians interacted with peoples from Southeast and South Asia (the *nanyang* sector).[4] The number of overseas Chinese that have settled in these countries is the highest among all other Euro-American nations. In formulating China's foreign policy, Mao, Deng, and Jiang all stressed that China would firmly stand on the side of the people of the Third World and that it would preserve world peace.[5] By "Third World," these three leaders meant Southeast Asia and the region around the Indian Ocean—today two significant components of the Global South. From a historical perspective, since the early 1950s, Beijing's status as a key actor, if not a genuine leader, in the developing world is traceable and undeniable.

The Chinese government is one of the most proactive actors in transforming the geostrategic pattern of the Global South. In addition to its naval presence in the South China Sea, which has become a heated topic in recent years, China has also projected a considerable level of military engagement on the African continent—an topic that has not yet been sufficiently studied.[6] Security interests in Africa are driven by the economic growth of Chinese enterprises there. In turn, Beijing's primary goals are to promote and safeguard its investments and its citizens who have settled overseas and continue to do so. As a result, since the 1970s, China's military infrastructure has been built and supervised by its own personnel in Sudan, Zimbabwe, and Uganda. Many other African countries, such as Nigeria and Kenya, have also acquired fighter aircrafts and escorting destroyers from China. In fact, China's military equipment is currently being used by more than two-thirds of African countries (fifty-one countries on the continent). According to a recent study conducted by the Institute for Strategic Studies in London, China has been making remarkable inroads into the African defense market, reflecting significant growth in Beijing's influence and investment in the Global South. A cluster of African countries, such as Algeria, Angola, Nigeria, Chad, Equatorial Guinea, Gabon, and Ghana, are "regular emergent buyers" consuming a great deal of Chinese military exports. Beyond an official level, it is notable that Chinese-manufactured weapons and ammunition have also spread across Africa through illicit trade and smuggling. These weapons have been found in the hands of both private armed groups and government forces in places like South Sudan, Darfur, and the Central African Republic. One the one hand, it is quite obvious that these imports of illegal armaments from China have facilitated serious human rights violations in Africa; one the other, we have to take into account that interactions between China and the Global South do not merely take place on a visible, formal level, but also on a hidden, unregulated scale.

An even more significant step that China decided to take through the existing China Dream matrix—an emphasis of which is to rise up and expand peacefully (*heping jueqi*)—is its significant and aggressive establishment of military locations in Africa. In 2015, for instance, China had signed a ten-year contract to set up its first overseas military base in the east African nation of Djibouti. Even though the Chinese Defense Ministry reiterated that the military outpost will be a logistics and supply center to help China better engage in the world, such a strategic move is noticeably a military installation and is very much about Chinese experimentation. This is also substantial evidence illustrating that China is becoming a more important player in the Southern hemisphere. Additionally, since 2008, the Chinese navy has been patrolling and battling piracy in the Gulf of Aden, taking up the role of a global maritime police force in the disputed sea zone.[7] By pushing its military engagement deeper into Africa and its surrounding seawater, it is obvious that China is representing itself as a leader capable of ensuring harmony, peaceful coexistence, and security in the Global South.

In short, the China Dream or China's Rise cannot be examined without looking at the country's military engagement with the Global South. And those who think that the China Dream is equivalent to China's rise in the Pacific region are making a strategic mistake. To lead the world, China first needs to lead the Southern hemisphere. More than half the world's population lives in the South and, as Henry Kissinger believes, the global system is undergoing a fundamental change. The actualization of the China Dream will take Chinese wisdom and vision. And in the creation of an Asian era and an Asian model, China must first accomplish its China Dream in the Global South to lead the new century.

Ronald C. Po is assistant professor in the Department of International History at London School of Economics. His research focuses on the history of late imperial China and global maritime studies. His forthcoming book with Cambridge University Press is entitled *The Blue Frontier: Maritime Vision and Power in the Qing Empire*.

Notes

1.   Mingfu, *Zhongguo meng*.
2.   See, for example, Yee, *China's Rise*; Yee and Storey, *China Threat*; and Vairon, *China Threat?*
3.   See Robinson and Shambaugh, *Chinese Foreign Policy*; and Lanteigne, *Chinese Foreign Policy*.
4.   For an impressive study, see Geoff Wade, ed., *China and Southeast Asia*.
5.   Char, "Aspiring to be a Global Power," 63.
6.   See, for example, Hayton, *The South China Sea*; Hui-Yi Tseng, *Rethinking South China Sea Disputes*; and Jenner and Truong Thuy, *The South China Sea*.
7.   Zhu, *China's New Diplomacy*, 33–34; Rotberg, ed., *China into Africa,* 163–70.

References

Char, James. 2016. "Aspiring to be a Global Power: China's Activism in the Global South." In *Diplomatic Strategies of Nations in the Global South: The Search for Leadership*, edited by Jacqueline Anne Braveboy-Wagner. New York: Palgrave Macmillan.

Hayton, Bill. 2014. *The South China Sea: The Struggle for Power in Asia*. New Haven, CT: Yale University Press, 2014.

Hui-Yi Tseng, Katherine. 2017. *Rethinking South China Sea Disputes: The Untold Dimensions and Great Expectations*. New York: Routledge.

Jenner, C. J., and Tran Truong Thuy, eds. *The South China Sea: A Crucible of Regional Cooperation or Conflict-Making Sovereignty Claims?* Cambridge: Cambridge University Press.

Lanteigne, Marc. 2016. *Chinese Foreign Policy: An Introduction*. New York: Routledge.

Mingfu, Liu. 2010. *Zhongguo meng: Hou Meiguo shidai de daguo siwei yu zhanlüe dingwei*. Beijing: Zhongguo youyi chuban gongsi. [English translation: 2015. *The China Dream: Great Power Thinking & Strategic Posture in the post-American Era*. New York: CN Times Books.]

Robinson, Thomas W., and David Shambaugh, eds. 1994. *Chinese Foreign Policy: Theory and Practice*. Oxford, UK: Clarendon Press.

Rotberg, Robert I, ed. 2008. *China into Africa: Trade, Aid, and Influence*. Washington DC: Brookings Institution Press.

Vairon, Lionel. 2013. *China Threat?: The Challenges, Myths, and Realities of China's Rise*. New York: CN Times Books.

Wade, Geoff. 2009. *China and Southeast Asia*. 6 vols. New York: Routledge.

Yee, Herbert S, ed. 2002. *China's Rise—Threat or Opportunity?* New York: Routledge.

Yee, Herbert, and Ian Storey, eds. 2002. *China Threat: Perceptions Myths*. New York: Routledge Cruzon.

Zhu, Zhiqun. 2010. *China's New Diplomacy: Rationale, Strategies and Significance*. Surrey, UK: Ashgate Publishing Limited.

When a Dragon Changes Its Colors

Governance Implications of the New Sino-Southern African Relations

Phineas Bbaala

China and Southern Africa in the Early Days

Since its establishment as a Republic in 1949, China has led efforts to strengthen ties among the developing countries of Africa, Asia, and Latin America in an attempt to establish a Southern Bloc respectful of fundamental human rights and capable of fighting against perceived injustices in global relations. Sino-African relations are a branch of the broad South-South relations which gained prominence in mid-1950s when most developing countries were fighting for their independence and equal treatment in the global order dominated by the North. Riding on its own history of humiliation by the Allied Forces, China widely spoke of its support for the emancipation of all occupied and oppressed nations and peoples around the world.[1] The Afro-Asian Conference held in the Indonesian city of Bandung was the first major interactive forum between China and Africa. The five principles of mutual respect for sovereignty and territorial integrity, mutual nonaggression, noninterference in another country's internal affairs, equality and mutual benefit, and peaceful coexistence embedded in China's foreign policy seemed to resonate with the African dream of freedom and self-determination. Thus, the late President Julius Nyerere, of Tanzania once stated that not only did African countries need to unite among

Radical History Review
Issue 131 (May 2018)   DOI 10.1215/01636545-4355245
© 2018 by MARHO: The Radical Historians' Organization, Inc.

themselves, but they should also elevate China's role on the international stage as the spokesperson of the developing world. [2]

While China supported Africa's liberation struggles from colonialism and other forms of imperialism, Africa championed the recognition of China at the United Nations. This was the backdrop for Taiwan's recognition as the official and only government of the whole of China by the United States and its allies. However, passage of United Nations General Assembly resolution 2758 on October 25, 1971, recognizing the People's Republic of China, not Taiwan, as the sole legitimate government of all China removed a major hurdle from China's way to the outside world, effectively providing the highway to its *zouchuqu*[3] (Going out) policy. The large number of newly independent countries in the General Assembly, which already had warm ties with Beijing, gave China an advantage during the meeting.[4]

In Southern Africa, the liberation movements in Mozambique, Angola, Namibia, South Africa and Zimbabwe received varied Chinese support.[5] During apartheid in South Africa, China always voted in favor of Security Council resolutions aimed at ending apartheid and accelerating the independence of Namibia, including the stopping of air raids and other terrorist activities conducted by the apartheid regime in Southern Africa.[6]

China's financing and construction of the 1,860 kilometre–long Tanzania-Zambia Railway (TAZARA)[7] sought not only to consolidate the independence gains of the two countries but to also aid the liberation struggles in Mozambique, Angola, Namibia, South Africa and Zimbabwe, whose Africanist movements had operations in Dar es Salaam and Lusaka.[8]

The challenging terrain on which the railway had to be laid and the determination of the Chinese engineers to accomplish the project on time were indeed manifestations of China's early commitment to mutually beneficial relations with Africa. Other than the fact that the stretch on which the railway was to pass was thick with virgin forests home to dangerous wild animals and insects, it was also swampy and sandy. During the construction of the railway, seventy Chinese workers lost their lives.[9] In Figure 1, Chinese engineers defiantly use heavy trucks to

Figure 1: Extracting a Railway? Chinese Contractors Clearing Up the Bed of the Railway in Early 1970s. *World Affairs Press.* 2015. *A Monument to China-Africa Friendship: Firsthand Account of the building of the TAZARA,* 21.

Figure 2: Early Days of
Comradeship: Chinese
Contractors with the help of
local People, Laying Tracts
on the Piers with Track-
laying Cranes in the 1970s.
*World Affairs Press. 2015.
A Monument to China-
Africa Friendship: Firsthand
Account of the building of
the TAZARA, 201.*

overcome a swampy surface and human sludge underneath to prepare the bed of the railroad tracks. The trucks were a part of the heavy machinery that had been shipped from China to Africa through the coast town of Dar es Salaam in Tanzania specifically for the $455 million railway project.[10]

Tanzania and Zambia are two countries linked, *inter alia*, by mountains, escarpments and rivers which the railway had to cross. The images in Figure 2 depict the ingenuity and difficulty with which the construction of the railway had to overcome such barriers. The images in the photograph also show that the construction of the railway called for teamwork between the Chinese workers and Africans. This is notwithstanding the fact that the Chinese handled most of the technically challenging tasks whilst their African counterparts provided manual support. Interestingly, to bridge communication barriers, Chinese workers, whose number had risen to about 16,000 at the peak of the project, and Africans had developed a common working communication which they called "TAZARA language"—a combination of some Chinese and Swahili words.[11]

China and Southern Africa in the New Millennium

After two decades of near absence in the region, China reemerged in southern Africa with a policy focusing on resource exploration and exploitation. Through its *Zouchuqu* policy, China identified this resource-rich region as one of its major target areas for accessing resources and finding market for Chinese goods and contracts for Chinese construction firms. On its return to Africa at the turn of the new century, China's seemingly insatiable appetite for Africa's resources and its search for market and business opportunities are fueling conflict and poor governance on the continent. Although China-Africa relations were originally meant to foster peaceful coexistence, global equity and fair play, some of China's recent engagements with the continent raise questions not only of neocolonialism but of blatant interference with the governance of countries in which it has strong economic interests.

There is also the view that China is using its policy of noninterference to seek acceptance in resource-rich, populous African countries where competition for resources among major global powers and the emerging economies of BRICS (Brazil, Russia, India, China and South Africa) has been rife—a twenty-first century scramble for Africa. Such policy pronouncements tend to give China an unfair advantage in competing for the continent's resources and markets.[12] A careful examination of some of the aspects of China-African relations suggests that China at times seems to support pariah regimes by seeking stronger ties with resource-rich countries that violate the human rights of their citizens and clamp down on voices of dissent. The power structures in most of these countries seem favorable to the modus operandi in China's foreign policy. For instance,

Regimes within these countries tend to base their power in extensive patronage networks and control major assets through personal shareholdings, often held by close relatives. . . . Some of these 'neo-patrimonial regimes' have consistently appeared at the bottom of Transparency International's Corruption Perception Index, namely, Angola (1457th out of 179 in 2007), Congo-Brazzaville (153rd), and Equatorial Guinea and the Democratic Republic of Congo (joint 168th).[13]

Elsewhere, amid state violence against irate citizens following an announcement of the election results of the March 29, 2008 election, widely believed to have been rigged, a Chinese vessel delivering weapons to Zimbabwe was on Southern African waters just a fortnight into the conflict. The vessel, identified as the MV *"An Yue Jiang,"* was caught on camera by local and international media attempting to offload military wear destined for Zimbabwe outside the port of Durban in South Africa. This news caused a stir, as

local and international media investigations revealed that the ship was owned by a Chinese parastatal, the Chinese Ocean Shipping Company. It had been at Durban harbor's outer anchorage from 10 April 2008. It was carrying cases of weapons and ammunition in six containers. The delivery address was the Zimbabwe Defense Force, Causeway, Harare. The point of origin on the cargo manifest was Beijing, China.[14]

Consequently, the images of the vessel ignited an international campaign of solidarity for the people of Zimbabwe who were already targets of postelection state violence. The entry of new weapons into the cash-strapped brutal regime would undoubtedly contribute to increased bloodshed as opposition supporters mounted spirited protests against the results of a sham election.

Evidently, while the China of yesteryear contributed immensely to the liber-

Figure 3: Beyond the Rhetoric: Vessel Delivering Chinese Weapons to Zimbabwe Marooned off the South African Coast. Daily Mail, April 19, 2008. Available on http://www.dailymail.co.uk/news

ation of all oppressed peoples in southern Africa and beyond, on the basis of South-South solidarity, the resource-hungry China of the twenty-first century is willing to violate human rights by providing support to repressive regimes it has business deals with in the region. In Figure 3, the Chinese ship is seemingly stranded on the waters of southern Africa as watchful civil society organizations successfully pressured the South African government not to allow it to offload the weapons at the Durban port. The brown rectangular containers suspected to house the weapons are visible.

As Zambia prepared for the 2016 general election, the leading independent tabloid, *The Post* revealed a $192 million loan that the government had secretly acquired from China for procurement of security wares.[15] The election, in which the governing Patriotic Front (PF) controversially and narrowly beat the opposition United Party for National Development (UPND), was the bloodiest in the country's electoral history. The well-equipped Zambia Police used violence to enforce public order and deny the opposition the right to mobilize support ahead of the election. *The Post* was officially forced into liquidation by the state in 2016 for alleged failure to settle tax debts. In the Democratic Republic of Congo where trade with China was estimated at $4,185 billion at the end of 2014, some forty people were reportedly killed while hundreds others were arrested following President Joseph Kabila's refusal to retire at the end of his last team in office in December 2016.[16] As Claude Kabemba notes, while China enjoys accolades from the Congolese ruling elite, they face constant protests from citizens because of the nature of China-Congo relations, which funnels most of the benefits from Chinese mining deals to a few corrupt individuals connected to the ruling structure at the expense of the ordinary people. [17]

Conclusion

Because its resource interests are threatened, despite the rhetoric of noninterference, China is directly intervening in certain conflicts on the African continent. The difference between Chinese and Western intervention is the scope of transparency and the manner of execution. While Western intervention tends to be widely publicized and seeks international coalitions and alliances, Chinese intervention is con-

cealed. Outside southern Africa, Chinese intervention has been reported in Nige
ria's oil-rich Niger Delta region and South Sudan where Chinese multinationals are
exploring oils and gases. With the ever-increasing number of undemocratic regimes
in resource-rich African countries looking east for development aid, China is poised
to cash in while laundering its international image as an "All-Weather Friend" of the
African people. While pariah regimes like Zimbabwe and the Democratic Republic
of Congo are happy to cling on to power through Chinese support, Beijing is cleverly
using them to sign trade deals that promote Chinese economic interests. Not only
are these countries condemned to Sino-dependence but, in some instances, they
receive aid that threatens to reverse hard-fought democratic gains.

Phineas Bbaala teaches development administration and public finance in the Department of
Political and Administrative Studies at the University of Zambia. He researches and writes on
Governance and International Economic Relations. He is the author of *Emerging Questions on
the Shifting Sino-African Relations* (2015) and many other journal articles and book chapters.

Notes

1.   Lieberthal, *Governing China*, 56–60.
2.   Hongwu, "Fifty Years of Sino-African Cooperation Relations," 24–56.
3.   *Zouchuqu* is a Chinese word that means "going out."
4.   Van Beek, "China's Global Policy and Africa," 389–408.
5.   Pere, "China," 1–7.
7.   Shulan, "Reflections of China's Assistance to Zambia in Hongwu," 376–78.
8.   People's Republic of China, *A Monument to China-Africa Friendship*, 7.
9.   Ibid., 10.
10.   Hongwu, "Fifty Years of Sino-African Cooperation Relations," 24–56.
11.   Ibid.
12.   Roughneen, *Influence Anxiety*.
13.   Transparency International, Corruption Perception Index, 2007. Cited in Alden and Alves, "China and Africa's Resources," 18.
14.   Fritz, "People Power."
15.   *The Post Newspaper*, May 9–11, 2015.
16.   *The Guardian*, December 31, 2016.
17.   Kabemba, "China-Democratic Republic of Congo Relations," 3–4.

References

Alden, Chris, and Ana. C Alves. 2009. "China and Africa's Resources: The Challenges and
     Implications for Development and Governance." South African Institute of International
     Affairs, Occasional Paper No. 41.
Daily Mail, April 19, 2008. http://www.dailymail.co.uk/news.
Fritz, Nicole. 2009. "People Power: How Civil Society Blocked an Arms Shipment for
     Zimbabwe." South African Institute for International Affairs, Occasional Paper No. 36.
Hongwu, Liu. 2009. "Fifty Years of Sino-African Cooperation Relations: Background, Progress,
     and Significance." In *Fifty Years of Sino-African Cooperation: Background, Progress, and
     Significance—Chinese Perspectives*, edited by Liu Hongwu and Yang Jiemian. Kunming,
     China: Yunnam University Press.

Kabemba, Claude. 2016. "China-Democratic Republic of Congo Relations: From a Beneficial to a Developmental Cooperation." *African Studies Quarterly* 16, nos. 3–4, 73–88.

Lieberthal, Kenneth. 2004. *Governing China: From Revolution through Freedom*. New York and London: Norton and Company.

People's Republic of China. 2015. *A Monument to China-Africa Friendship: Firsthand Account of the Building of the TAZARA*. Beijing: World Affairs Press.

Pere, Garth L. 2012. "China". In *Region Building in Southern Africa: Progress, Problems and Prospect*, edited by Chris Saunders, Gwinyayi A. Dzinesa, and Dawn Nagar, 284–85. London: Zed Books.

Roughneen, Simon. 2006. "Influence Anxiety: China's Role in Africa." *ISN Security Watch*. http://www.isn.ethz.ch/news/sw/details.

Shulan, Zhao. 2009. "Reflections of China's Assistance to Zambia" in *Fifty Years of China-African Cooperation: Background, Progress and Significance—Chinese Perspectives on Sino-African Relations,* edited by Liu Hongwu and Yang Jiemian, 376–78. Kunming, China: Yunnam University Press.

The Guardian, December 31, 2016. http://www.theguardian.com/world/2016/dec/31/.

The Post Newspaper, May 9–11, 2015.

Transparency International, Corruption Perception Index. 2007. Transparency International, *Corruption Perception Index*. <http://www.transparency.org/policy_research/surveys _indices/cpi/2007>.

United Nations Security Council. November 15, 1985. *Fortieth Year, 2629th Meeting*. New York.

Van Beek, Ursula J. 2011 "China's Global Policy and Africa: A Few Implications for the Post-crisis World." *Politikon, South African Journal of Political Studies* 3, no. 8: 389–408.

"The Year of China in South Africa"

Two Scenes from Johannesburg

Mingwei Huang

Johannesburg is a key site in which the "China in Africa" story unfolds. Going back to nineteenth-century immigrant shopkeepers and indentured gold miners, Johannesburg is home to the largest and oldest Chinese diasporic community in Africa and also houses a population of "new" migrant entrepreneurs who arrived since the early 2000s, coming in search of upward mobility unavailable to them in post-reform China.[1]

Scene 1. The Chinese and South African governments declared 2015 "The Year of China in South Africa," which culminated in Johannesburg hosting of the sixth Forum on China-Africa Cooperation meeting.[2] That year at OR Tambo airport, Bank of China advertisements covered multiple walls and conjured the largesse of Chinese investment and infrastructure in Africa. One lining a walkway outlined continental China and Africa filled with images of wildlife and highways; they were connected with a red ribbon—a BRICS-era Silk Road—while the rest of the world disappeared into white space. The image proposed a Sino-African world order, a South-South future produced by two economic powerhouses straddling North-South boundaries.[3]

Scene 2. That same year, I worked at one of Johannesburg's China Malls—wholesale and retail centers for low-end Chinese imports, and where Zimbabwean and Malawian economic migrants can find employment without papers. A story that stuck with me was of a Chinese trader who was found strangled to death in her shop, the register empty and her body rolled up in a bolt of fabric she imported and sold.

Radical History Review
Issue 131 (May 2018)   DOI 10.1215/01636545-4355257
© 2018 by MARHO: The Radical Historians' Organization, Inc.

Figure 1. Bank of China advertisement when leaving the international terminal of O.R. Tambo International Airport. Photograph by author.

The suspects were her two Malawian workers, one new, the other an employee of six years. The story was perplexing: the methodical plotting of a murder, the dreadful intimacy of strangulation, the deliberate wrapping of her body in the very thing the workers handled. In the weeks to come, the story was the talk of the mall. Among Chinese traders, her death further confirmed the presumed ruthless criminality of African workers. For many undocumented, underpaid, and overworked workers, the exuberance for revenge was unspeakable yet palpable all the same. Apart from the sensationalism of violence, the story became mythology not because it was an exceptional event, as I initially thought, but because it was the extreme actualization of everyday tensions between bosses and workers.

These fraught intimacies and encounters are as much a part of the "Year of China in South Africa" story as diplomacy and finance. Sino-African economic and geopolitical relations transform everyday lives in ways different from the Beijing-Johannesburg imaginaries, and "South-South" is a discourse more often invoked from locations of the powerful than the ordinary. Sharing a geopolitical space-time, these scenes are connected and symbolically linked. The China Mall is a highly visible site of bilateral trade that hosts Chinese and South African governmental delegations. In 2013, President Jacob Zuma himself inaugurated the new arch-way in Chinatown where "new" migrants live. With the prevalence of the trope of "China's rise" in Africa, these scenes show it is anything but uniform, singular, or uncontested.

I juxtapose these sites to complicate the grand "China in Africa" narratives of triumphant South-South economic cooperation, and the opposite, Africa as "China's Second Continent." At the heart of anxieties about "China in Africa" is the decline of US imperialism whereby "geopolitical anxieties over new South-South alliances are really about China's place in the world rather than Africa's 'place-in-the-world.'"[4] Accordingly, the "China in Africa" narrative is fundamentally one of China "in/of"

Figure 2. An ordinary scene from a China Mall. Photograph by author.

the Global South. Yet the question remains: can China—on the fringes of the Global South—be considered an empire in postcolonial Africa?[5] Aihwa Ong and Donald Nonini's ungrounded empire is productive for making sense of power and domination on the edges of neoliberal global capital in the South among nonstate actors. In this framing of empire, Chinese transnational practices form "deterritorialized and protean structures of domination" that "collude with the contemporary regimes of truth and power organizing the new flexible capitalisms and modern nation-states, but also act obliquely to them."[6]

As *Theory from the South* and *Ungrounded Empire* contend, there is a *sui generis* character to Afromodernity and Chinese transnationalism that diverges from Euro-American capitalist modernity even as they emerge from the same world-historical forces. The upward mobility of Chinese excluded from the windfall of market reform relies on exploiting the labor of African migrants disenfranchised by structural adjustment. If the Global South is the "harbinger of Future-History," these scenes forecast Southern futures: of traders and global financiers seeking new frontiers, racialized labor regimes without white bosses, and flexible forms of South-South domination undertaken in the very name of the South.

Mingwei Huang is a PhD candidate in American studies at the University of Minnesota, Twin Cities. She is completing a dissertation on contemporary Chinese migration in South Africa and the intimacies of racial capitalism.

Notes

I would like to thank the anonymous reviewers, editors, and special issue editors for their suggestions, especially Pamila Gupta and Christopher Lee for their encouragement over the past few years. Many thanks to Jigna Desai, Karen Ho, Jamie Monson, Melissa Lefkowitz, and Jay Schutte for their comments on drafts. This research was funded by the Wenner-Gren Foundation. I am ever grateful for the Center for Indian Studies at the University of Witwatersrand for providing me with an intellectual home.

1. Huynh, Park, and Chen, "Faces of China," 288–89.
2. China has been South Africa's largest trading partner since 2010, with a trade volume of R270 billion in 2013. Part of this relationship manifests in the export of low-quality, low-cost, mass produced goods from China since the early 2000s whereby China Malls all over Johannesburg are at the epicenter of this phenomenon. The Department of Trade and Industry estimated R70 billion spent on Chinese imports between January to June that year, numbers which are likely conservative. Read, "China Mall overhaul"; Anthony, "South Africa and China."
3. South Africa is a regional hegemon and economic powerhouse between North and South, but China, as Jean Comaroff and John Comaroff note, is the "most portentous player of them all" as it "has interpolated itself into both north and south without being truly either, all the while promising, some time off into the future, to alter the political economy, and the geo-sociology, of the entire planet." We might, then, marginally situate China-South Africa as "South-South." Comaroff and Comaroff, *Theory from the South,* 46.
4. Sylvanus, *Patterns in Circulation,* 170.
5. My use of "empire" is in the spirit of the "imperial turn" within American Studies. Adapting this term to the Sino-African context, I deploy empire as a capacious analytic that enables a critique of power. I am interested in theorizing and critiquing contemporary structures of global inequality that are difficult to categorize as empire in the postcolonial South-South context. These flexible forms of empire operate outside of the historical relationships between metropolitan centers and colonies, through military domination, or in state policy.
6. Ong and Nonini, "Chinese Transnationalism as an Alternative Modernity," 20.

References

Anthony, Ross. 2016. "South Africa and China: Behind the Smoke and Mirrors." *Mail & Guardian*, January 11. http://mg.co.za/article/2016–01–11–south-africa-and-china-behind-the-smoke-and-mirrors.

Comaroff, Jean and John L. Comaroff. 2012. *Theory from the South, or, How Euro-America is Evolving Toward Africa*. Boulder and London: Paradigm Publishers.

French, Howard. 2014. *China's Second Continent: How a Million Migrants Are Building a New Empire in Africa*. New York: Alfred A. Knopf.

Huynh, Tu T., Yoon Jung Park, and Anna Ying Chen. 2010. "Faces of China: New Chinese Migrants in South Africa, 1980s to Present." *African and Asian Studies* 9: 286–306.

Ong, Aihwa and Donald Nonini. 1997. "Chinese Transnationalism as an Alternative Modernity." In *Ungrounded Empires: The Cultural Politics of Modern Chinese Transnationalism,* edited by Aihwa Ong and Donald Nonini, 3–38. New York and London: Routledge.

Read, Brigette. 2014. "China Mall overhaul." *Wits Journalism China-Africa Reporting Project,* March 4. http://china-africa-reporting.co.za/2014/03/chinese-mall-overhaul/.

Sylvanus, Nina. 2016. *Patterns in Circulation: Cloth, Gender, and Materiality in West Africa*. Chicago: University of Chicago Press.

The Zairian Avant-garde

Modes of African Modernism

Sarah Van Beurden

In December of 1974, Zaire's president, Mobutu Sese Seko, went on a diplomatic visit to China. Traveling with him was a selection of the works of a group of modern Zairian artists who called themselves the *Avant-gardistes zaïrois*. The paintings and sculptures were intended to help promote the cultural image of the Zairian state under the leadership of Mobutu. The visit was symbolic not only of Mobutu's political desire to form alignments with powerful nations in the Global South, but it also hints at the growing role of modern art in Zaire's engagement with the Global South.

The *Avant-gardistes zaïrois* were a group of young Zairian artists who had united in 1973 with the goal of creating a new kind of modern Zairian art. In their manifesto, they called for an art "blessed with a young blood [and] animated by a magic spirit. We wish to have our art recover its autonomy and its intrinsic personality."[1] The group included roughly ten members, all of whom were connected to the Fine Arts Academy in Kinshasa. Among them were sculptors Liyolo Limbe M'Puanga and Tamba Ndembe, the painters Lema Kusa, Mokengo Kwekwe, Mayemba ma Nkakasa and Mavinga ma Nkondo Ngwala, as well as ceramicist Bamba Ndombasi. The movement was short-lived: although it was never officially disbanded, it fell victim to squabbles and tensions by the mid-1970s. Nonetheless, the group served as a catalyst for the development of a Zairian visual modernism, and several of the participants were influential through their long careers as art teachers. Far less well known than Nigerian and Senegalese visual modernisms, the history of this group of artists nonetheless offers an interesting addition to the growing litera-

Radical History Review

Issue 131 (May 2018)   DOI 10.1215/01636545-4355269

© 2018 by MARHO: The Radical Historians' Organization, Inc.

ture on African modernisms. Zairian modernism's relationship to the development of the Global South invites the question of whether this particular global context is lacking in the histories of other African modernisms.

The history of the Mobutu regime's cultural politics of *authenticité* loom large in the background of the activities of the *Avant-gardistes zaïrois*. Declared the official state policy in 1971, *authenticité* attempted to reorient the country's cultural identity to so-called authentic indigenous African values, with the professed goal of ending the cultural alienation created by the colonial experience. The most visible practices associated with *authenticité* were marches and public spectacles that included dancing and singing, and new practices, such as the adaptation of "Africanized" names and clothing. Many colonial monuments were also removed from the cityscape of the capital. For a brief period in the early 1970s, *authenticité* had an impact among artists and intellectuals, among them the *Avant-gardistes*, who sought an artistic expression of the ideology.[2]

The visual and thematic language these artists shared is in part based on their training at the colonial art academy in Leopoldville (the city that later became Kinshasa,) but it evolved through their commitment as *Avant-gardistes zaïrois* to the development of a new kind of modern art and through the ways in which this movement became embedded in the Zairian state and its ideology of *authenticité*. The bulk of their artistic production came in the form of paintings, sculptures (particularly in wood and bronze), and ceramics. Two-dimensional work, like that of Mayemba, Mavinga and Lema Kusa, became characterized by the use of rich colors, a certain visual rhythm or repetition, and flowing yet angular lines in the depiction of bodies (fig. 1). Sculptors like Liyolo fluctuated between rounded and abstracted bodily forms (figs. 2 and 3) and a style that combined angular shapes with lanky fluidity. The same intersection between abstract forms and rounded and elongated bodies characterized the ceramic work (figs. 4 and 5). The work was often vaguely folkloric or historical in inspiration, rarely allowing for an exact identification of specific so-called traditional styles.

There is an affinity with other African, particularly Senegalese, modernisms visible in much of the work, particularly in its color palette and use of shapes and volumes. This connection was paralleled by personal and professional contacts. The students of the Academy of Fine Arts of Kinshasa, and many later *Avant-gardistes* in particular, were represented in the FESTAM 1966 exhibition in Dakar, and although only a few were able to travel there, the news reporting and accompanying publications encouraged an imagined community of African artists and a modernist language, one that would serve as a source of inspiration for the Zairian *Avant-gardistes*. (Of course, the Mobutist politics of *authenticité* at large also bear the stamp of the example of Senghor's cultural politics.[3])

The upsurge in publications on African modernism of the last decade or so has rightly been concerned with the exclusionary narrative established by the canon

Figure 1 Mayemba mosaic at Nsele presidential compound in Kinshasa (Detail from photo by Willy Kerremans, s.d. Collection of Royal Museum for Central Africa)

of art historical scholarship. In response, scholars of Africa have been dismantling the false universalism of Western modernity, which casts African modernisms as derivative, instead claiming a plurality and globality of modernisms and arguing for multiple centers as opposed to a center-periphery model. Some of this literature is attempting to change the very definition of modernism by contesting the exclusionary mechanisms therein, or by relocating the origin of modernisms to African colonies.[4]

The example of the Zairian *Avant-gardistes* highlights another global context in which the history of these modernisms need to be seen: not only that of other modernisms within Africa, but also more broadly of cultural diplomacy and art markets in the Global South. These Zairian artists circulated and worked in a context that was attuned to opportunities and cultural trends across Africa and into Asia. As explained above, evidence for the African framework in which these artists situated themselves can be found in their visual language, and their awareness of the Global South as a market is clear from their travels and sales. It was a function of their ever-growing closeness to the Mobutu regime, and the latter's desire for

Figure 2: Liyolo, Torse (1974) on display at the artist's home gallery in
Kinshasa. In the background are several photographs of his international
travels and exhibitions. (Photo by the author, 2016)

Figure 3 Liyolo, *Elle Est la Nature* (1975) on display at the artist's home gallery in Kinshasa. (Photo by author, 2016)

cultural legitimation, that several of them accompanied him on official state visits. The renewed relationship with China, for example, opened up a new market, both for sale and exhibition.[5] For some of the artists, these relationships had quite some longevity. The bronze sculptures of Liyolo found a market in China, and later Japan, that exists to this day.[6] The entry of artists like the *Avant-gardistes Zaïrois* in the Chinese art market occurred at a moment in which Chinese modern art itself, under the influence of the centralized cultural politics of the Cultural Revolution, was undergoing a visual and political evolution, with the establishment of an official art of the revolution.[7] On the part of both the Zairian and the Chinese states, there was an ideological opening towards other authoritarian regimes and their accompanying cultural representations.

Figure 4 Bamba Ndombasi, *Envoi* s.d [1970s] (Photo Collection
of the artist)

As indicated by the brief examples above, placing the *Avant-gardistes zaïrois*
in the political and economic context of the Mobutu regime's cultivation of connections in the Global South, and in the artistic context of other African modernisms,
allows for a much more complete image of their work and activities to emerge. It
also raises questions about scholarly tendencies to discuss modernisms within the
confines of national cultural economies, or those of the Global North. Instead, a
closer look at other global patterns of contact and circulation allow for the histories
of modernisms in the Global South to shift away from being anchored to artistic life

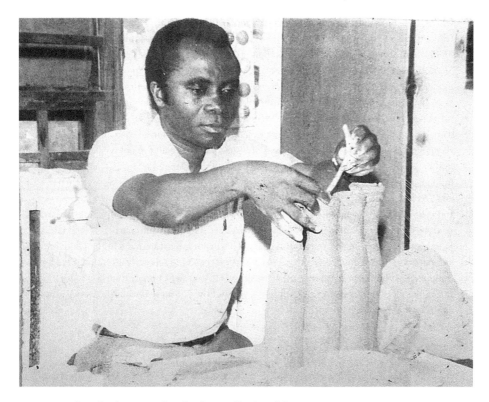

Figure 5 Bamba Ndombasi at work, s.d. (Photo Collection of the artist)

and art markets in the Global North. Although Global South cultural diplomacy and art markets allowed individual Zairian artists to expand markets and audiences, the Zairian-Chinese example also highlights how these exchanges and cultural agendas contributed to a consolidation of authoritarian cultural agendas, and hence, a history of linked Global South authoritarianisms.

Sarah Van Beurden is associate professor of history and African American and African Studies at the Ohio State University. She is the author of *Authentically African: Arts and the Transnational Politics of Congolese Culture* (2015).

Notes

This essay is part of a larger project on cultural planning, generously supported by the Max Planck Institute of the History of Science in Berlin. Thanks to Ruth Sacks for help locating image one.

1.   Quoted in Badi-Banga, *Contribution*,118.
2.   Interview with Liyolo by author, January 25, 2016, Kinshasa, Congo; interview with Bamba Ndombasi by author, January 27, 2016, Kinshasa, Congo.
3.   For more on this see: Van Beurden, *Authentically African*,107–13.
4.   See, for example: Salah M. Hassan on Sudanese modernism (Hassan, *Ibrahim El Salahi*);

Olu Oguibe on South African and Nigerian modernism (Oguibe, "The True Location");
Chika Okeke-Agulu on postcolonial Nigerian modernism (Okeke-Agulu, *Postcolonial
Modernism*); and Elizabeth Harney on Senegalese modernism (Harney, *In Senghor's
Shadow*). See also the 2010 special issue of *South Atlantic Quarterly* on African
modernism. On the relocating of the origin of modernism, architecture scholars have
been particularly influential. See, for example, the work of Gwendolyn Wright on colonial
urbanism in French empire in Africa (Wright, *The Politics of Design*) and Johan Lagae's
work on the Belgian Congo (Lagae, "De Kolonie als Architectuurlaboratorium").

5.   Zairian president Mobutu, in the context of his pursuit of nonalignment, visited China twice
in the early seventies: once in January 1973 and again in December 1974. The presence and
influence of Chinese officials in Kinshasa grew in tandem. Crawford Young and Turner, *Rise
and Decline*, 370–71.

6.   Interview with Liyolo by author, January 25, 2016, Kinshasa. There is interesting research to
be done on the circulation of the work of African artists in Asia, and particularly in China,
Japan, and Korea from the 1970s until today. This history of art markets in the Global South,
and particularly in China, has only recently started receiving scholarly attention. See, for
example, Karchenkova, Komarova, and Velthuis "Official Art Organizations," 78–101.

7.   For the modern art scene in China in the 1970s and the Cultural Revolution, see Andrews,
Painters and Politics, 314–376.

References

Andrews, Julia. 1994. *Painters and Politics in the People's Republic of China, 1949–1979.*
Berkeley: University of California Press.

Badi-Banga ne Mwine, Célestin. 2002. *Contribution à l'étude historique de l'art plastique
zaïrois modern.* Kinshasa, Congo: Editions Malayika.

Harney, Elizabeth. 2004. *In Senghor's Shadow. Art, Politics and Avant-Garde in Senegal,
1960–1995.* Durham: Duke University Press.

Hassan, Salah M. 2012. *Ibrahim El Salahi: A Visionary Modernist.* Washington, DC: Museum
of African Art.

Karchenkova, Svetlana Komarova Nataliya and Olav Velthuis, 2015. "Official Art Organizations
in the Emerging Markets of China and the Russia." In *Cosmopolitan Canvases: The
Globalization of Markets for Contemporary Art*, edited by Olav Velthuis and Stefano Baia
Curioni. 78–101. Oxford, UK: Oxford University Press.

Lagae, Johan. 2002. "De Kolonie als Architectuurlaboratorium? Bouwen in Belgisch Congo
1885–1960." In *Vreemd Gebouwd*, edited by Stefaan Grieten en Jo Braeken, 467–90.
Turnhout, Belgium: Brepols.

Okeke-Agulu, Chike. 2015. *Postcolonial Modernism: Art and decolonization in Twentieth
Century Nigeria.* Durham, NC: Duke University Press.

Oguibe, Olu. 2005. "The True Location of Ernest Mancoba's Modernism" *Third Text* 19, no. 4:
419–26.

Turner, Thomas. 1985. *The Rise and Decline of the Zairian State.* Madison: University of
Wisconsin Press.

Van Beurden, Sarah. 2015. *Authentically African: Arts and the Transnational Politics of
Congolese Culture.* Athens: Ohio University Press.

Wright, Gwendolyn. 1991. *The Politics of Design in French Colonial Urbanism.* Chicago:
University of Chicago Press.

Portrait of a Thai Country Singer

Pumpuang Duangjan

Pahole Sookkasikon

The impact that Thai country singer Pumpuang Duangjan (1961–1992) has had on the people of Thailand and Thai popular music from the late-1970s and onward cannot be underestimated: her music and unique voice passionately conveyed the troubles of many underrepresented Thais—in particular, women, the working class, and those residing beyond the borders of Bangkok. Said to have a melodic voice that was "hair raising" (or, "ขนลุก"), Duangjan's sound was hauntingly tender and nasal, conveying the rich emotions of her music.[1] Lyrically, the singer called upon everyday struggles, privileging stories based upon ordinary characters—peasants, lorry drivers, struggling farmers, and sex workers—while speaking to themes that reflected the migratory patterns of countryfolk in addition to issues of infidelity, pain, and desire.[2] As her music emphasized the quotidian, Pumpuang Duangjan gained popularity as she came to be known by her fans as the "Queen of Luk Thung" (Figure 1),[3] heralding a new era for Thai popular music.[4]

As such, drawing upon the historical and long-standing relationship between Duangjan and Thailand partially uncovers the formation of Thai gender and sexuality through 1980s Thailand and the Global South. Thailand's history, its culture, and its overarching assumptions of Thainess and Thai character have been informed by a patriarchal, nationalist, and monarchial discourse, a rhetoric chiefly cultivated by the kingdom's capital, Bangkok.[5] This fixed idea of Thainess was premised on the romanticized axiom that Siam was never formally colonized, and it proselytized this identity as free from outside influences though still heavily informed by the

Radical History Review
Issue 131 (May 2018)   DOI 10.1215/01636545-4355281
© 2018 by MARHO: The Radical Historians' Organization, Inc.

Figure 1. Known for her beauty and unique style of singing, Pumpuang Duangjan was loved by thousands and celebrated as the "Queen of Luk Thung"

upper-classes. Additionally, Thailand's road to modernization, while participating in the global economy, further led the nation to encourage foreign investment, industrialization, and tourism with relatively few regulations.[6] These infrastructural changes ultimately led many Thais—particularly the poor, the rural, and countless women—to be dispossessed by globalization, further alienating them while simultaneously creating a rift between classes and sexes. Yet Duangjan's music challenged the homogenizing foundations of Thainess and the hierarchies held within the nation-state. By narrating the stories of those impacted by development and modernization, Duangjan's music defied restrictive pleasures and dominant idealizations of an overarching Thai identity, underscoring the hardships and lives of the rural and the marginal as supremely significant.[7]

Pumpuang was born on August 4, 1961 to poor sugarcane farmers from the city of Suphan Buri. Like many others at the time, the financial woes of her family forced the young Duangjan to leave primary school, taking to the fields alongside her family. She was illiterate yet adept at memorizing lyrics, and she participated in many local singing competitions, catching the attention of a visiting band who brought her to Bangkok where she found fame from the late 1970s onward. Once settled, Pumpuang Duangjan began modernizing the musical genre of *luk thung* into a dance-ready form that popularized her with fans nationwide, so much so that every concert was packed with people from all over Thailand (Figure 2). Her sound was distinctively country, marked by a strong and emotional vibrato and further pronounced by her lyricism, making her an icon to the people because her music spoke of the harsh realities faced by those overshadowed by development (Figure 3).[8] As she sang about the lives and aspirations of everyday Thais, Duangjan's fans found her to be approachable and loving, and she was celebrated as one of their own.[9] However, though she was loved by millions, Pumpuang's career was marred by people in her life who coercively deprived her of her earnings to the extent that

Figure 2: Crowds from all over Thailand would come to see Duangjan perform as she sang emotionally about the lives, trials, and desires of everyday Thais.

she could not afford treatment for systemic lupus erythematosus (SLE).[10] She died at the age of 31 in 1992 but has been celebrated ever since.

What cannot be undermined is the influence that Pumpuang Duangjan's music has had on millions of Thais, specifically women and farmers who identified with the singer and her struggles even long after her death.[11] For example, Duangjan's famous song, "นักร้องบ้านนอก," or "The Country Singer," spoke of a Thainess detached from the one conceived by those in power. The song articulates the daily concerns of the rural poor, specifically privileging the struggles that many rural women had in Bangkok. Almost autobiographical, "The Country Singer" speaks of a woman who longs to be a singer, even despite the warnings of other villagers. In the capital, the singer struggles to find wealth and fame as life becomes more difficult, diverging sharply from glamourous fantasies of a cosmopolitan Bangkok. As the singer sees a flock of crows flying home at twilight, she begins missing the pastoral and the rice fields that once defined *home*. Bangkok becomes a place of uncertainty, filled with exploitation and regret. The narrator questions her place in the

Figure 3: Duangjan serenades her fans with her elegiac and emotive voice.

megalopolitan, wondering if return is ever possible. In this sense, the elegiac lyrics symbolically critique dominant idealizations of Thainess, underscoring how cultural development and economic transformation for the nation-state were primarily due to the labor and sacrifice of thousands of rural women.[12] The song ends with the narrator professing that she will "endure" for her people, emblematically highlighting debates of how capitalism and modernity have continually impacted Thailand, specifically its most defenseless citizens.

The significance of "นักร้องบ้านนอก" cannot be overstated: it speaks to the contemporary experiences of thousands of Thais, especially women, while reconstituting Thainess beyond its mainstreams definitions. Ara Wilson writes that development and the global economy has had a profound impact on Thai sex and gender systems, arguing that "capitalist development in Asia has relied heavily on women's work," further making invisible the ways that modernization has greatly altered Thainess and intimate realms—gender, sexuality, and ethnicity.[13] For Duangjan to speak on such complicated matters begs us to reflect on the price marginal communities pay under the weight of global integration. Her music, as a remembrance, offers hope and solidarity to the Thai people, exploding the limitations of Thai belonging by recentering the collective, the countryside, and the seemingly forgotten.

Pahole Sookkasikon is a PhD candidate in the department of American studies at the University of Hawaiʻi at Mānoa. His dissertation examines the ways that contemporary Thai popular culture and performance queer notions of Thainess informed by the Western economies of desire as well as nation-state practices of respectability in addition to its heteronationalist interests.

Notes

My heartfelt thanks to Mark Padonngpatt for his helpful comments on this essay.

1. "ตามตำนาน I EP.13 I ราชินีลูกทุ่ง 'พุ่มพวง ดวงจันทร์' I Full HD," YouTube video, 26:58, posted by "NOW26," November 8, 2016, https://www.youtube.com/watch?v=AWjgt-kPZFo.
2. Ridout, *The Rough Guide to Thailand*, 839.
3. Jirattikorn, "Lukthung," 24–50.
4. *Luk Thung* is a genre of Thai country music that was popularized after World War II and is typically associated with the Thai countryside and those living in rural communities outside of Bangkok. It is often thought of as "low-brow" and music that lack elegance in relation to popular forms of music and culture celebrated in Thailand's capital. Scholars (Siriyuvasak 1990) have noted the poeticism written into the genre, noting that its style is simple and down-to-earth, drawing upon the rural as the genre's focal point. In other words, what makes the musical category of *luk thung* unique and notable are the ways that it calls attention to the rural as its subject matter, confronting urban life and the socioeconomic and culture splits brought upon conditions that separate both the countryside and its residents from Thailand's main metropoles.
5. Winichakul, *Siam Mapped*, 3–5.
6. Wilson, *Intimate Economies of Bangkok*, 19.
7. Jaiser, *Thai Popular Culture Volume I*, 168.

8. Lockard, *Southeast Asia in World History*, 182.
9. "ตามตำนาน I EP.13 I ราชินีลูกทุ่ง 'พุ่มพวง ดวงจันทร์' I Full HD," YouTube video, 26:58, posted by "NOW26," November 8, 2016, <https://www.youtube.com/watch?v=AWjgt-kPZF0>.
10. "ตามตำนาน I EP.13 I ราชินีลูกทุ่ง 'พุ่มพวง ดวงจันทร์' I Full HD," YouTube video, 26:58, posted by "NOW26," November 8, 2016, <https://www.youtube.com/watch?v=AWjgt-kPZF0>.
11. Lockard, 181.
12. Mills, *Thai Women in the Global Labor Force*.
13. Wilson, 21.

References

Jaiser, Gerhard. 2012. *Thai Popular Culture Volume I: Thai Popular Music*. Bangkok: White Lotus Press.

Jirattikorn, Amporn. 2006. "Lukthung: Authenticity and Modernity in Thai Country Music." *Asian Music* 37, no. 1: 24–50.

Lockard, Craig. 2009. *Southeast Asia in World History*. Oxford, UK: Oxford University Press.

Mills, Mary Beth. 2006. *Thai Women in the Global Labor Force: Contested Desires, Contested Selves*. New Brunswick, NJ: Rutgers University Press.

Ridout, Lucy. 2009. *The Rough Guide to Thailand*. London: Rough Guides.

Wilson, Ara. 2004. *Intimate Economies of Bangkok: Tomboys, Tycoons, and Avon Ladies in the Global City*. Berkeley: University of California Press.

Winichakul, Thongchai. 1994. *Siam Mapped: A History of the Geo-Body of a Nation*. Honolulu: University of Hawai'i Press.

"ตามตำนาน I EP.13 I ราชินีลูกทุ่ง 'พุ่มพวง ดวงจันทร์' I Full HD," YouTube video, 26:58, posted by "NOW26," November 8, 2016, https://www.youtube.com/watch?v=AWjgt-kPZF0.

Hollywood, the Global South, and *Total Recall* (2012)

Keith B. Wagner

Written off as a typical Hollywood science fiction film, Len Wiseman's 2012 *Total Recall* can also be perceived as a spatial analogy for the Global South. In Wiseman's depiction of the Global South, he uses a Hollywoodized megacity, one which is shot almost entirely on studio sets and rendered by computers: a digital city that is a curious amalgamation of real Global South societies and an underdeveloped futurity that should not be ignored. Although I focus entirely on *Total Recall*, other Hollywood blockbusters such as *Cloud Atlas* and *Babel*, as well as certain blockbuster films from the Global South such as *Metro Manila* from the Philippines, *Elite Squad: The Enemy Within* from Brazil, and *District 9* from South Africa, now work within and against visualizing the structural unevenness of power, capital, and people across cities in the world. As a consequence, I view *Total Recall* as not simply depicting two futuristic megacities—one generic and prosperous in the United Federation of Britain or "UFB," located in the British Isles and Western mainland of Europe, and the other, named the Colony or "New Asia," as more dystopian. Rather, through this urban dichotomy, *Total Recall* communicates the spatial politics of the South as a cinematic invention itself that has helped to "acquire visibility on the global scene in an assertion of its autonomy, partial autonomy," even if this urban space is imagined.[1] In urban studies, Faranak Miraftab and Neema Kudva argue that cities from the Global South can be conceptualized through a range of social forces that they explicate chiefly as the "changing migration patterns and large

Radical History Review

Issue 131 (May 2018)   DOI 10.1215/01636545-4355293

© 2018 by MARHO: The Radical Historians' Organization, Inc.

scale population movements to changes in geopolitical power and the technologies of infrastructure, communication and manufacturing" that all bolster the validity of this concept and illustrate its institutional merit to replace the antecedent term the "Third World" city.[2] In applying Miraftab and Kudva's Global South city concept, I believe *Total Recall* goes some way to imagining the "rising cultural and cinematic importance of emerging cities and the urban regions, which now compete with long established hubs" in the Global North.[3]

To explicate this cinematic imagining happening in both Hollywood and the Global South and to rethink this creative capacity on a global scale, I coin the term Aesthetic Cooperation among Developing and Developed Countries (ACDDC). Briefly put, the ACDDC is a play on the Global South's historical progeny at the 1978 Global South Conference on the Technical Cooperation among Developing Countries—known as the TCDC—held in Buenos Aires, Argentina. At this historic meeting, 138 countries adopted the Buenos Aires Plan of Action, which favored a new creative capacity for developing countries to solve their economic and political problems through self-reliance and collaborative partnerships with themselves and the North.[4] The ACDDC is instructive, I believe, because it stresses an aesthetic hybridity beyond any one style and any one conception of our many North and South urban metropoles found on screen.[5]

In its narrative construction, Wiseman's millennial reboot represents a substantial departure from Philip K. Dick's original 1966 short story, "We Can Remember It for You Wholesale," and Paul Verhoeven's 1990 postmodern film adaptation entitled *Total Recall*. *Total Recall* centers on Earth in the late twenty-first century and not on an off-world colony on Mars; Dick's Mars rebellion was symbolic and conscious of the independence movements in Africa and Asia during the Global Cold War, while Verhoeven's kitschy Mars remained less concerned with addressing this allegory. However, it is not just the old colony powers that Wiseman's film is concerned with; rather, he is preoccupied with the Global South as an alternative paradigm that is opposed to neocolonialism and can be understood by way of my ACDDC coinage. In effect, *Total Recall* depicts a divided anthropocene, longitudinally split between the UFB and the Colony. The residents of the Colony travel to the UFB to work in factories and perform service jobs, traveling in a massive gravity elevator running through the Earth's core colloquially referred to as "China Fall." The image of the Colony from the future Global South is one of the megacity, full of multilingual citizens, polycultural spaces, and amalgamated, rain-soaked architectural forms that range from dilapidated Mexican-style Brutalism to globalized Favelas. In opposition to the Colony, UFB's cinematic representation is articulated as a repressive federation of states, with its capital city London and simulacrum Big Ben and Parliamentary Building put on display and interwoven into a larger set of airy, neoclassical architecture.

The Colony, though, still carrying with it the Third World jingoism of our late

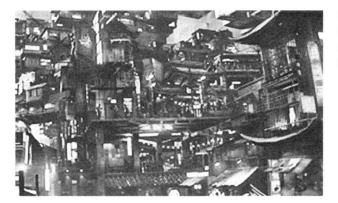

Figure 1: Wiseman's Global
South megacity: the global
creolization of architectural
forms as new habitat

twentieth-century past, is instead depicted in a new register as: an underdeveloped region; an amalgamation of the Global South's futurity; a Hollywoodized Global South megacity that can be thought of in relation to Miraftab and Kudva's apt words on real Global South cities; or, a set of "physical collections of built form specific to a context and global movement, or a mix of cultures over time."[6] The Colony's spatial features, with its translocal cultures and "global mélange" of Chinese-Korean-Brazilian-Mexican-Egyptian signage, graffiti, and languages also provides a realism to its modular habitats.[7] This creolization of architectural forms refers back to Hong Kong's cramped and decaying Chungking Mansion, to South Africa's townships and their simple brickwork designs, and to Egypt's crusty but historically integrated Cairo districts; all these signal the further integration and the biunicity of South and North. These new spaces in *Total Recall* historically reference not only a form of Third Worldism but also send a clear view from the South.

Bursting with revolutionary potential due to its repressed citizens living in dilapidated spaces and dealing with poor working conditions, *Total Recall*'s narrative and spatial interventions come by way of identifying with the Colony's laborers who challenge the automation of jobs and geographical segregation on Wiseman's stratified Earth. The intra-Earth connection via the gravity elevator between North and South provides a further futuristic entanglement "of the South and the North in one another, and the reconfiguration of spatial relationships through the globalization" of location (wealthy megacity versus poor megacity), communication (UFB's control of global media in the South) and labor chains (exploitation of workers from the Colony).[8] In effect, my ACDDC concept presents a Global South topography that recenters the power relations and living spaces, through transnational and subaltern resistance and through social and economic misalignment, which are contingent on Global South urbanization (real and cinematic) reimagined by Hollywood.

Keith B. Wagner is assistant professor of Global Media and Culture in the Centre for Multidisci-plinary and Intercultural Inquiry at University College London. He is the coeditor of *Neoliberal-ism and Global Cinema: Capital, Culture and Marxist Critique* (2011) and *China's iGeneration: Cinema and Moving Image Culture for the Twenty First Century* (2014). His monographic study entitled *Living with Uncertainty: Precarious Work in Global Cinema* is under contract with a major US academic press and will be published in 2019.

Notes

1. Dirlik, "Global South: Predicament and Promise," 15.
2. Miraftab and Kudva, *Cities of the Global South Reader*, 3.
3. Andersson and Webb, "Introduction: Decentring the Cinematic City," 6.
4. Esteves and Assunção, "South-South cooperation and the international development battlefield."
5. See, for example: Wagner, "Globalizing Discourses"; Traverso, *Southern Screens*.
6. Miraftab and Kudva, 3.
7. Pieterse, *Globalization and Culture*.
8. Miraftab and Kudva, 3.

References

Andersson, Johan, and Lawrence Webb. 2016. "Introduction: Decentring the Cinematic City: Film and Media in the Digital Age." In *Global Cinematic Cities: New Landscapes of Film and Media*, edited by Andersson and Webb. New York: Columbia University Press.

Dirlik, Arif. 2007. "Global South: Predicament and Promise." *The Global South* 1, no. 1.

Esteves, Paulo, and Manaìra Assunção. 2014. "South-South cooperation and the international development battlefield: between the OCED and the UN." *Third World Quarterly* 35, no. 10.

Miraftab, Faranak, and Neema Kudva, eds. 2015. *Cities of the Global South Reader*. London: Routledge.

Pieterse, Jan Nederveen. 2009. *Globalization and Culture: Global Mélange*. Lanham, MD: Rowman and Littlefield.

Traverso, Antonio, ed. 2017. *Southern Screens: Cinema, Culture and the Global South*. London: Routledge.

Wagner, Keith B. 2015. "Globalizing Discourses: Literature and Film in the Age of Google." *Globalizations* 12, no. 2.

Changing Paths and Histories

Mapping Precolonial Connections in Africa

Aharon de Grassi

Often invisible in their ubiquity, rural paths are perhaps the most frequently used transport infrastructure for rural people, yet also some of the most taken for granted and neglected by academics, policy makers, and cartographers. This article presents and analyzes one of the—if not the—first detailed single maps of paths in (mostly) precolonial Africa as a way to comprehend geohistories of connection in the Global South.

The new map overcomes limits of existing ones that neglect indigenous shaping of landscapes and instead emphasize political kingdoms, migration, railroads (as European-built drainage channels to the coast), rivers (as unchanging natural features), or blank spaces. The stark map presented here helps make the imaginative jump from logically understanding that people created and used paths to sufficiently appreciating the extent and significance of landscapes of precolonial connection.[1] With examples from Angola, I first give background on the original and new maps, and then I address their uses and limits, raise some related issues, and conclude with implications for pressing matters of political economy and social change.

The map is derived from the 1:2,000,000-scale series of sixty-two maps finished by 1890 by the French colonial military cartographer Richard de Régnauld de Lannoy de Bissy. To compose the map, freely available digital images of the maps were used from France's National Library website, and then the routes in the maps traced with a digitizer pen and touchscreen using open-source Quantum Geographic Information System software. Any presumption of precision however quickly meets messy

Radical History Review

Issue 131 (May 2018)   DOI 10.1215/01636545-4355305

© 2018 by MARHO: The Radical Historians' Organization, Inc.

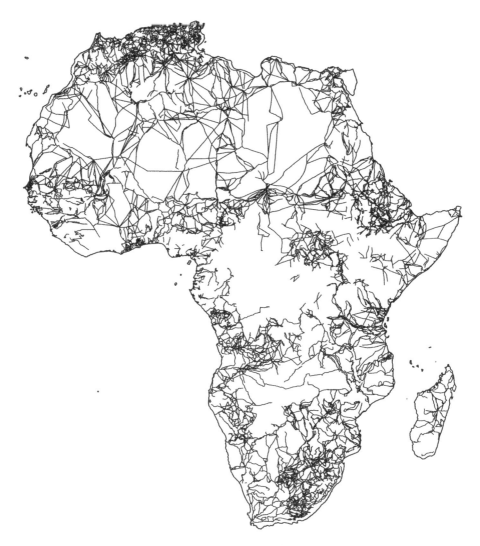

**Figure 1: Paths and Itineraries Before c. 1882–1891 in Lannoy de Bissy's Map.
Map created by author.**

reality. These maps were produced using information from—and to facilitate—
imperial conquest and colonial administration.[2] What the overview map here shows
as hundreds of thousands of kilometers of "paths" groups together what the original
map legend distinguishes as *chemins* (paths), *sentiers* (trails or tracks), and *itinerai-
res* (itineraries), which were identified by Lannoy de Bissy on the basis of maps and
reports that drew on roughly six hundred explorers making 1,800 journeys.[3] These
include coastal areas in North and South Africa where there was already some colonial influence (distinctions between colonial presence, conquest, tribute, occupation, and so on merit discussion elsewhere), which appear to shape both the extent
of paths there and the level of detail in mapping those paths.

Such dynamic and recursive aspects of paths, labor, mapping, and power are evident in Angola's history over the centuries and recent decades. From the early seventeenth century, hundreds of "vassals" indirectly ruled by the Portuguese were required to provide laborers to maintain paths. The first detailed map of routes for Angola in 1863 drew on an earlier 1790 map of much of contemporary Angola, which emerged through an "imperial-scale circulation of geographical and historiographical knowledge" between Portugal, Brazil, and Angola since "it was the slave trade itself that needed a policy of territorialization."[4] Emphases on road work increased from the mid-nineteenth century under colonial modernizers and postabolition shifts to trade in commodities rather than "self-transporting" slaves. Yet much of this road work by Angolans is read out of de Blissy's map. For example, the map sheet for western Angola designates the centuries-old routes between the outposts of Ambaca, Cambambe, and Pungo Andongo (routes which appear on an earlier 1863 map) only as the 1877–1880 itinerary of the Portuguese explorers R. Capelo and H. Ivens, who were sent by the Geographical Society of Lisbon to consolidate colonial claims and rule (and who corresponded with Lannoy de Bissy). Such maps in turn fostered further construction of paths and roads: when the Capelo later became Angola's governor, he emphasized road work, which then entailed further mapping. Subsequent decades saw inventories, studies, contracts, regulations, maintenance initiatives, and rail plans.

The labor of building paths and roads in Angola only increased in the twentieth century, with profound effects that continue to have relevance today. Beginning with Angola's modernizing Governor Norton de Matos in 1912 drivable roads were built through compulsion, villages were resettled, and taxes proliferated. District administrators were responsible for marshalling unpaid labor to build and maintain roads, trails, and paths, which by the early 1960s amounted to well over 100,000 km. That total was strikingly more than the only several thousand kilometers of paved roads in Angola at that time that are sometimes cited as evidence of Portugal's inattention to Angola's non-cash-crop countryside, and as evidence of Africa's purported lack of infrastructure. After this forced labor regime prompted nationalist revolts in 1961, the Portuguese responded with counter-insurgency reliant on attenuating labor compulsion in military and developmental projects by mechanizing road construction and agriculture. These roads then became pivotal to the postcolonial armed conflict 1975–2002. However, the late-colonial emphasis on labor-saving mechanized construction of roads has been revived during postwar reconstruction, buoyed by oil revenues used to contract Chinese, Brazilian, and Portuguese road construction reportedly to the tune of $26 billion for some 12,000 km.

Given such histories of recursive and dynamic relations, the significance of the summary version here of Lannoy de Blissy's map should be approached with caution. Interpreting the map requires "reading beneath the lines" in the sense that many routes labeled as itineraries of explorers were likely already existing paths produced by African knowledge and labor. So, while the map presents a spatial chronicle of Western explorers' masculine agency in swashbuckling across Africa, there are good grounds (literally) for a subversive, generative reading based in African contributions. Often the paths that the map portrays only as explorer itineraries actually connect villages that were already almost certainly linked by paths. Indeed, village food supplies and resting points were often logistical prerequisites for exploration (and slave and commodity trade). The map also tends to show more paths in areas of French interest because Lannoy de Bissy used internal French documentation of paths (and some internal documentation from others), while for other areas he relied on and emphasized explorers' itineraries more.

We can also "read around the lines" for blank spaces—the Congo basin, Kalahari and Sahara Deserts, and Liberia and Ivory Coast—that did have paths.[5] Lannoy de Bissy lacked information for some areas, while in others rivers were key for transport. The map hints at diverse roles and relevance of transport and paths. Cartographically erasing and appropriating Africans' paths was part of colonial attempts to appropriate and regulate space.

For these reasons, to even assess if precision is possible by checking its sources would be a massive undertaking (hundreds of thousands of pages) unlikely to be worthwhile. The new map here is useful not for precise route coordinates: it should not be used for statistical regressions about the roots of contemporary development in past conditions, and it contradicts such approaches (see below). Rather, the map's visual ensemble of routes suggests new understandings and questions.

Research might be more fruitful if focused on paths in specific areas and transformations over time, using oral history, archaeology, and other methods to examine the sociopolitical dynamics of paths beyond the economics of "trade routes" or centralized polities's road regulations, construction, and maintenance (e.g., Dahomey, Asante, and Buganda). Whether a given path would be used (and maintained), by who, how, for which purposes, and whether it would be neglected or even blocked depended on conjunctures of cultural, economic, political, social, and biophysical processes. Beyond indirect maintenance by the footsteps of porters and everyday users, path labor included brush burning, bridge work, repairs, detours, grading, clearing obstacles, edge trimming, sign-posting/demarcation, blocking, and facilitating supporting camps. People built on and facilitated animals' use and creation of paths and worked on social relations of information sharing about routes, terrain, porters, social infrastructure, and transit conditions (material and political). Paths changed in relation to extractive economies of slave trade, ivory, rubber, wax, and other goods.

Connected with such detailed research are broader questions of how rethinking paths can recast relations of cartography, colonialism, and capitalism. Rather than cartography being an imposed Western "logic," the development and use of paths in the slave trade, precolonial exploration, and extractive economies recursively stimulated the global networks developing cartography.[6] Examining paths can enrich studies of the origins and dynamics of capitalism, because sizeable values of slave labor went beyond direct commodity production and included labor for transport and construction of infrastructure.[7] Non-Western infrastructure was more than a "spatial fix" to internal contradictions of Western capitalism. In addition, such histories of paths shaped indirect rule—extensive paths were both objects of and essential to the colonial administrative practices of hundreds of thousands of native authorities and other indigenous frontline state functionaries.

Recognizing paths also helps situate late colonialism in Africa amidst worldwide competitive shifts from rails to roads, which prompted administrators to attend to spatial logistics to recoup rail construction expenses. Administrators emphasized roads in order to use automobiles to break the bargaining leverage of porters and enable state revenue from bulky and low value-to-weight primary exports produced by labor "freed" from porterage. Some paths were the "ground work" upon which roads were built. But other winding riverside paths were replaced by new roads elsewhere that were more straight, flat, ridge-top, standardized, and governable, and built by decades of brutal compulsion of numerous men and women. These paths remain important even though they are ignored by most statistics.

Such "regrounding" of the political economy of African states helps overcome conventional pathologizing comparisons with an ideal-type Western territorial state in which democracy emerged from direct taxation of citizens. A purported intrinsic African "indifference to a permanent attachment to a particular place" coupled with the expense and rarity of rails and roads is seen to have left countries with "narrow, export-oriented infrastructure" and "gatekeeper states" unable to "broadcast power," prompting people to pursue not national development but rather "strategies of extraversion" focused on trade rents, customs revenues, and looting state assets.[8] With these assumptions and a battery of regressions, today's "mouse pad" economists and political scientists recall Victorian armchair anthropologists in claims to esoteric expertise and implications of trusteeship: Africans are unable to develop because they cannot free themselves from domestic "path-dependent" extractive institutions.[9]

In contrast, studying infrastructural transformations can elucidate paths as processes, simultaneously social and environmental, always in flux, requiring continual maintenance to be reproduced. This can help destabilize seductive metaphors of "path dependency" that resuscitate determinism in the guise of a familiar spatial day-to-day referent.[10] Invoking "path-dependency" is a political move that highlights the agency of some, hides that of others, and works to convince potential actors to divert their political efforts or not bother at all.

In various ways, historicizing how people produce paths and roads can reveal political possibilities and alliances, not least by recasting patronage as amenable to change (because investment in social relations is geohistorically produced rather than innate), by expanding redistributive claims based in infrastructure labor as part of shared histories of state engagement, and by highlighting novel contemporary socio-spatial connections. Firstly, paths as processes reveal how—in contrast to the "fiscal fetish" of conventional tax-state approaches—colonial conquest, production, commerce, revenue, and rule were only made possible by the fixed capital of infrastructure that is a product of past labor performed as tax in kind. Secondly, roads and paths as sedimentations of forced labor are still remembered as both grievances and vectors for anticolonial and nationalist mobilization and consequently can be used to help legitimize rural claims to national wealth and to unlink conflations of nationalist development with expensive modernist mechanized road paving. Lastly, perceiving paths as shifting constellations of social relations can help foster alliances by drawing attention to histories of interconnection (including the often gendered social and mental labor involved in knowledge of paths)—a much needed contrast to militarizing binary notions of capitalist enclaves versus blank ungoverned spaces. Material and social connections made through old and new paths—and hence possible alliances—are also now being reconfigured as mobility expands significantly, and in gendered ways, with the proliferation of millions upon millions of mass-produced (mostly Chinese and Indian) motorcycles of unprecedented affordability. Amidst contemporary infrastructural transformations and social changes, what remain key are these diverse, often complex, and indirect spatial and temporal connections between rural, infrastructural, and urban dynamics.

Aharon de Grassi works on issues of political economy, geography, and rural development in Africa. His interdisciplinary and multimethod research focuses on infrastructure and agrarian change in Angola, combining archival, ethnographic, and field research.

Notes

1. Rockel, *Carriers of Culture.*
2. Bassett, "Cartography and Empire Building."
3. Ibid., 317; Loiseaux, "Régnauld de Lannoy de Bissy's Nineteenth Century Map of Africa."
4. Madeira Santos, "To round out this immense country," 156, 159.
5. Vansina, *Paths in the Rainforests.*
6. MacArthur, *Cartography and the Political Imagination.*
7. Beckert and Rockman, *Slavery's Capitalism*; Simone, "People as Infrastructure."
8. Kopytoff, *The African Frontier*; Cooper, *Africa*; Herbst, *States and Power in Africa*; Bayart, *L'État en Afrique.*
9. Austin, "African Economic History in Africa."
10. Moors, *On Trails.*

References

Austin, Gareth. 2015. "African Economic History in Africa." *Economic History of Developing Regions* 30, no. 1: 79–94.

Bassett, Thomas. 1994. "Cartography and Empire Building in Nineteenth Century West Africa." *Geographical Review* 84, no. 3: 316–35.

Bayart, Jean-François. 1989. *L'État en Afrique.* Paris: Fayard.

Beckert, Sven, and Seth Rockman, eds. 2016. *Slavery's Capitalism.* Philadelphia: University of Pennsylvania Press.

Cooper, Frederick. 2002. *Africa: The Past of the Present.* Cambridge: Cambridge University Press.

Herbst, Jeffrey. 1989. *States and Power in Africa.* Princeton, NJ: Princeton University Press.

Kopytoff, Igor, ed. 1987. *The African Frontier.* Bloomington: Indiana University Press.

Loiseaux, Olivier. 2016. "Régnauld de Lannoy de Bissy's Nineteenth Century Map of Africa at a Scale of 1:2,000,000." *The Cartographic Journal* 53, no. 3: 282–93.

MacArthur, Julie. 2016. *Cartography and the Political Imagination.* Athens: Ohio University Press.

Madeira Santos, Catarina. 2014. "'To round out this immense country': The circulation of cartographic and historiographic knowledge between Brazil and Angola in the Eighteenth Century." In *Negotiating Knowledge in Early Modern Empires*, edited by L. Kontler, A. Romano, S. Sebastiani and B.Z. Török. New York: Palgrave MacMillan.

Moors, Robert. 2016. *On Trails.* New York: Simon & Schuster.

Rockel, Stephen. 2006. *Carriers of Culture.* Portsmouth, NH: Heinemann.

Simone, AbdouMaliq. 2004. "People as Infrastructure." *Public Culture* 16, no. 3: 407–29.

Vansina, Jan. 1990. *Paths in the Rainforests.* Madison: University of Wisconsin Press.

Manifesto

Networks of Decolonization in Asia and Africa

Afro-Asian Networks Research Collective

If the Third World was a project to which millions contributed, then historians have yet to unravel the many threads by which they did so and to approach its history with the spirit with which it was originally imagined: one that sought communication and solidarity across difference.[1] The gathering of political elites at the 1955 Afro-Asian Conference in Bandung has garnered a great deal of scholarly attention as the key event heralding a new era of solidarity in the decades of Asian and African decolonization.[2] With the exception of Laura Bier's chapter in Christopher Lee's *Making a World After Empire* on the connections between Egyptian and Indonesian women's movements in the Bandung era, little has been written on the way in which nonstate actors throughout the Global South interacted and conversed with each other.[3] The 1950s and 1960s were not just an era of postcolonial diplomacy, but a period of intensive social and cultural interaction across the decolonizing world. African and Asian women, socialists, communists, trade unionists, intellectuals, activists, and revolutionaries conversed across national, linguistic, and ideological borders. Artists, poets, and performers travelled and experimented with new ideas and techniques for intellectual and cultural expression to create new visions for the nation and for the world. They engaged critically with communist, socialist, and democratic ideas in circulation, constantly reevaluated their political loyalties, and built up networks of intellectual and radical sociability. Outside the key sites of international diplomacy, we know much less about the way in which actors across the South conversed with each other in the early Cold War era. At the same time, the methods of our

Radical History Review

Issue 131 (May 2018)   DOI 10.1215/01636545-4355317

© 2018 by MARHO: The Radical Historians' Organization, Inc.

historical discipline and the institutional structures that govern research continue to devalue scholarship outside the Western academy and to underrepresent the voices of women and people of color. In other words, researchers need to ask new questions together and encourage practices that do not reinforce the hierarchies that the decolonizing world has sought to overcome.

This Manifesto is a call to acknowledge the larger Afro-Asian environment in which the "Bandung moment" took place. A more inclusive history of this period requires a research agenda that takes the focus away from the interstate relations found in official records and moves it onto networks created and maintained by actors that are harder to identify in the archive. Rather than view this era through the lens of diplomatic relations or particular nation-states, we outline a research agenda that privileges transnational networks of affinity across Asia and Africa, while also inviting research that expands these networks to other geographies across the South. This is a call to discover the different types of mobility and horizontal connection that characterized South-South relations and to see vectors of solidarity alongside the competitive, hierarchical, and familial nature of new South-South relationships of the postcolonial generation. But this Manifesto is also a call to recognize the need for collaborative history in approaching decolonization from the point of view of the Global South. This requires radical changes in academic historical practice. As scholars based at Euro-American universities, we are implicated in the privileges of the current system even as we look to readjust its inequalities and limitations. In order to fully understand the dynamics of South-South connections, we need to orient our vision to one that traces these networks, subverts the boundaries of Area Studies, and abandons the "lone-scholar" model in the writing of a truly global history of decolonization.

Modes of Internationalism

The era of Afro-Asian solidarity in the mid-twentieth century was composed of multiple modes of internationalism. In shifting our view from interstate diplomacy, we see new internationalisms that intersected and overlapped with each other and transnational actors who belonged to multiple, sometimes competing international organizations. As the lead image from *Spotlight on Africa*'s 1955 issue on the Bandung conference (Figure 1) shows, it is, above all, individuals and people who comprised the Afro-Asian world, and we place them at the heart of our analyses. We seek to uncover the worlds of intermediaries who navigated multiple internationalisms and placed them at the heart of postcolonial nation-building: Asian socialists who moved in and out of the realms of power; writers, artists, and athletes both celebrated and vilified by states; Caribbean, and African American trade unionists who travelled both Africa and Asia. In this era, people moved between nationalism and internationalism in a manner that defies scholarly obsession with this supposed dichotomy. Instead, we want to unearth the principles and ideas that guided them.

Figure 1: "Review of the Asian-African Conference," May 1955. *Spotlight on Africa* 14, no. 5.

This changes our understanding of the nature of global society itself. The claims to globalism of internationalist organizations based in New York, London, Brussels, or Moscow were wholly dependent on interactions with multilingual actors in Asia and Africa who contested Western frameworks and channeled their own forms of internationalism through these expanding networks.

This era of competing internationalisms puts the Afro-Asian moment *in* the Cold War, but does not make it *of* the Cold War. Asian and African actors navigated, ignored, and subverted the power dynamics of the Cold War. The highly mobile activists, writers, scientists, and artists of the Afro-Asian moment encountered visa regimes, boycotts, censorship, and other obstacles to the free movement of people and ideas. A certain amount of navigation was therefore necessary. Mobility was a key feature of this era; air travel enabled these actors to meet and erase distances. But the cost of this travel put up new barriers, as patronage from competing powers—Western, Soviet, and Chinese—as well as home-grown capitalists often decided who could move across newly constructed borders.

This was an era defined by imagined as well as actual movement. Indeed, Afro-Asianism at a popular, public level almost cheerfully ignored the imagined geographies of the Cold War. Central Asia, for instance, was very much part of Afro-Asian initiatives, as seen with the Afro-Asian Writers Conference in Tashkent as well as the presence of Uzbek and Tajik intellectuals and Bukharan dancers in other Afro-Asian gatherings. Indeed, internationalism was not just the domain of a burgeoning, multilingual civil society and creative class. It intimately tied distant worlds and worldviews into the lived experiences of actors in small landlocked towns. Consider the 1954 marches for Afro-Asian peace in northern Indian cities like Gwalior and Patiala, or the call for Afro-Asian solidarity in women's groups across the Indonesian archipelago. This is a level of international engagement well below that of the highbrow ideological commitment to global governance, and it is indicative of a much more pervasive mentality of internationalism than is currently accounted for in historiography.

What is also clear is that approaching "Bandung" as a network of affinity and awareness forces us to ask more questions about the temporal frames we use to define this era. The presentation of Bandung as a "break" from the past sought to address a number of issues, including conceptions of freedom and liberation, of history and civilization, and of methods of communication across difference. Yet it is possible to view people moving within different temporal frames depending on the questions they are seeking to address. The 1966 Tricontinental Conference came to widen this frame to include Latin America, and as a recent conference in Coimbra on its legacies showed, the individuals, organizations and networks involved at Bandung, Cairo, Havana, Algiers, and beyond often grew out of and in relation to each other. Similar questions about how imperialism functioned, what freedom and liberation actually looked like, and how to achieve these goals animated these networks across the temporality of "Bandung" or the "Tricontinental." Is there a moment at which one ends and the other begins? Research into the individuals and organizations that connected these movements can help us to better understand how their ideas shifted over time and blur the boundaries implied by Afro-Asianism as well as imperial and Cold War frameworks.

New methodologies

This research agenda requires collaboration in a way that is not common practice in the academy. The global reach and local impact of these networks cannot be seen fully unless a sizeable group of regional experts can view this "moment" from multiple archives, languages, and perspectives. This requires working across the regional boundaries created by Area Studies—regional divisions with their own political roots, from the invention of the "Middle East" and "Southeast Asia" to the academic "erasure" of Central Asia. Importantly, this type of collaborative history also forces us to think past the single-authored articles lauded by our institutions. We call for an attitudinal shift where research is not "owned" or "discovered," but enabled and shared. While collaborative research is essential to truly global, multicentered historical research, it goes unrecognized by promotion criteria and national research assessments. We propose that continuous, "real-time" collaboration—from project conception to group archival research, source-sharing, and online collaborative spaces—both enriches individual research and provides the diversity of viewpoints essential to understanding the networked history of early Cold War Afro-Asia in all its complexity.

It was precisely this *collaborative* approach to the archive that formed the foundation for our network. Over the course of one week, twelve of us worked together in the reading room of the International Institute of Social History (IISH), the world's most important collection of materials on social and emancipatory movements. We delved into a range of sources, from pamphlets of the Afro-Asian People's Solidarity Organization in Cairo to the newsletters of the Anti-Colonial Bureau in Rangoon. Several researchers worked on the archive of the International Confederation of Free Trade Unions. The opportunity for researchers with different regional specialisms to collaborate in real time allowed us to track commonalities, linkages, and cleavages between African, Asian, and Western activists committed to building a new postcolonial world. This yielded new insights on the modes of internationalism that may have taken years for a single scholar to piece together on their own. It is impossible to achieve a full picture of the internationalism of this era by working in a single archive—it depends instead on the ability of scholars operating within different regional contexts and distinct historiographies to pull together multiple archival threads. Alongside the archives of the IISH, we depend on our own familiarity with the regional contexts in which Asian and African actors interacted with new international bodies, drawing on state archives in Asia and Africa, newspapers, associational literature, memoirs, artistic production, and oral history interviews. Collaborative research enriches the very practice of history itself; moreover, it is essential in uncovering the rich, world-spanning experiences of the international Left, particularly in Asia and Africa. Out of this collaborative research, we are preparing a special collection on the way in which trade union networks crystallized many of the solidarities and cleavages that characterized the transnational left in the early ages of the Cold War, as well as an additional collection on wider movements undertaken by artists, intellectuals, athletes, and activists across the Global South.

We recognize that we now live in a world undergoing a frenzy of digitization. This has obvious benefits in allowing archives to make sources available to those unable to travel and collaborate and has helped to stimulate new appetites for transnational history. But these opportunities come at the risk of decontextualization, which, as Lara Putnam has pointed out in the *American Historical Review* last year, is a worrying feature of working digitally and may even help perpetuate knowledge hegemonies of the global North.[4] We maintain that there are still virtues to place-based research and to digesting archives in their fully material context. This is especially so for Asian and African archives, which are so often unevenly digitized, as well as for the "grey literature" of international institutions—the reams of memos, reports, paper machinery of organizations and institutions, and substrata of bureaucratic documentation—impossible to digitize in their magnitude, but out of which truly subaltern histories of internationalism can be woven. Here, dialogues between archivists and historians may help create more support for collaborative enterprise.

The "digital" has become one of the most important sites of knowledge production in the twenty-first century, and while we welcome its potential, we also hope to encourage critical postcolonial engagement with its geopolitics.[5] On the one hand, we seek to prevent the digital humanities from unwittingly reproducing the inequalities of global knowledge production that embedded systemic Eurocentrism in the Western academy.[6] On the other, we seek ways to bridge digital humanities ecosystems that are rarely in dialogue with each other, often because they are unable or unwilling to speak past national and linguistic barriers. Our research has begun to show that Afro-Asianism was a transnational and translingual project, as well as one that sought to assert the subjecthood of Global South actors. If this is to be fully represented in digital space, we need to reconfigure our methods as much as the disciplinary and cartographic divides that have arisen out of area studies models and nation-making paradigms.[7] It is for this reason that, against the grain of present structures of academic incentive, we believe in scholarship that expands rather than territorializes knowledge. We have begun to envision digital components to our project that embody these convictions. Our blog, medium. com/afro-asian-visions, was built with openness in mind and has already begun to expand our research network, widen our perspectives, and reach out to others working on similar themes. We have also produced a dynamic visualization that charts the lesser-known conferences and gatherings in which Afro-Asian networks converged, as well as biographies of those who traversed the Afro-Asian world. This comes as a product of our collaborative research, built on a database infrastructure designed to be as open as possible to contributors from academic institutions as well as nonacademic participants across the world—including and especially from the Global South.

In short, we seek to resurrect the Bandung spirit in our academic collaborations, repurposed for the digital age. We invite you to join us.

The **Afro-Asian Networks Research Collective** is a continuously expanding international network of scholars working on Afro-Asianism in the early Cold War. It began as a project funded by the Arts and Humanities Research Council (AHRC) directed by Su Lin Lewis (Bristol University) and Carolien Stolte (Leiden University). The project maintains a static website (http://afroasian networks.com/) as well as a blog (https://medium.com/afro-asian-visions). Co-led by Rachel Leow (Cambridge University), they are producing a moving historical map of events and individuals uncovered through their collective research.

Notes

This manifesto is a product of conversations among members of the Afro-Asian Networks Research Collective. It was written jointly by Reem Abou-El-Fadl, Leslie James, Rachel Leow, Su Lin Lewis, Gerard McCann, and Carolien Stolte.

1. Prashad, *The Darker Nations.*
2. Tan and Acharya, *Bandung Revisited*; Lee, *Making a World After Empire*; Miscovic, Fisher-Tine, and Boskovska, *The Non-Aligned Movement and the Cold War*; Finnane, *Bandung 1955*; Shimazu, "Diplomacy as Theatre;" Menon, "Bandung is Back."
3. Bier, "Feminism, Solidarity, and Identity."
4. Putnam, "The Transnational and the Text-Searchable."
5. Lothian and Phillips, "Can Digital Humanities Mean Transformative Critique?" See also the *Decolonizing the Digital / Digital Decolonization* project at the Center for Global Studies and the Humanities at Duke University https://globalstudies.trinity.duke.edu /volume-31–decolonizing-the-digitaldigital-decolonization.
6. McPherson, "Why are the Digital Humanities So White?" See also the work of Mark Graham, e.g., "Inequitable Distributions in Internet Geographies."
7. Digital humanities projects and initiatives that have already begun to do this, including the Mellon Global South Initiative http://ihgc.as.virginia.edu/mellon-global-south-initiative and the Cornell Global South Project http://www.globalsouthproject.cornell.edu/.

References

Bier, Laura. 2010. "Feminism, Solidarity, and Identity in the Age of Bandung." In *Making a World After Empire: The Bandung Moment and its Political Afterlives,* edited by Christopher Lee, 143–72. Columbus: Ohio State University Press.

Finnane, Antonia. 2010. *Bandung 1955: Little Histories.* Caulfield, Australia: Monash University Press.

Graham, Mark. 2014. "Inequitable Distributions in Internet Geographies: The Global South is Gaining Access but Lags in Local Content." *Innovations* 9, no. 3–4: 17–34.

Lee, Christopher, ed. 2010. *Making a World After Empire: The Bandung Moment and its Political Afterlives.* Columbus: Ohio State University Press.

Lothian, Alexis and Amanda Phillips. 2013. "Can Digital Humanities Mean Transformative Critique?" *Journal of e-Media Studies* 3, no. 1 http://journals.dartmouth.edu/cgi-bin /WebObjects/Journals.woa/xmlpage/4/article/425.

McPherson, Tara. 2012. "Why are the Digital Humanities So White? Or, Thinking the Histories of Race and Computation." In *Debates in the Digital Humanities.* Print edition Minneapolis: University of Minnesota Press, online edition http://dhdebates.gc.cuny .edu/debates/text/29.

Menon, Dilip. 2014. "Bandung is Back: Afro-Asian Affinities." *Radical History Review,* 119: 241–245.

Miscovic, Natasa, Harald Fisher-Tine, and Nada Boskovska, eds. 2014. *The Non-Aligned Movement and the Cold War: Delhi, Bandung, Belgrade.* New York: Routledge.

Prashad, Vijay. 2008. *The Darker Nations: A People's History of the Third World.* New York: The New Press.

Putnam, Laura. 2016. "The Transnational and the Text-Searchable: Digitized Sources and the Shadows They Cast." *American Historical Review* 121: 377–402.

Shimazu, Naoko. 2014. "Diplomacy as Theatre: Staging the Bandung Conference of 1955." *Modern Asian Studies* 48, no. 1: 225–52.

Tan, Seng, and Amitav Acharya, eds. 2008. *Bandung Revisited: The Legacy of the 1955 Asian-African Conference for International Order.* Singapore: National University of Singapore Press.

Coffee, Cash, and Consumption

Rethinking Commodity Production in the Global South

Jelmer Vos

Edwardo Bedi became a teacher for the Baptist Missionary Society in northern Angola in the late 1930s. Like fellow church members, Bedi was also a bit of an entrepreneur and skillfully used his own education at the mission for different trades, thus working his way up in colonial society. When coffee cultivation spread all over northern Angola after World War II, Bedi developed a small farm to grow *robusta* beans, which North Americans especially were consuming in ever-larger quantities. By 1960, the investment was paying off so well that he could buy himself a scooter for £75 and sustain his son's reputedly sluggish lifestyle in the Angolan capital, Luanda.[1] While agricultural production in colonial Angola is usually associated with low wages and forced labor, the example of Edwardo Bedi and others like him shows that for some Africans coffee created economic opportunities. In fact, missionary and business records on the coffee trade in Angola highlight a dimension of global commerce often ignored in the study of commodity production in Africa and the Global South generally, namely the role that commercial farmers played as consumers of imported goods.

Angola had been a leading coffee producer on the African continent since the nineteenth century, thanks in no small part to the entrepreneurship of peasant cultivators who added coffee as a cash-crop to their subsistence economy. Angola was also the African region supplying the most human captives to the Americas

Radical History Review

Issue 131 (May 2018)   DOI 10.1215/01636545-4355329

© 2018 by MARHO: The Radical Historians' Organization, Inc.

during the transatlantic slave trade. Because coffee became the country's most successful export crop after the suppression of the slave trade in the 1860s, coffee cultivation in Angola goes to the heart of the historical study of transitions from the slave trade to commodity production in Africa.[2] Although European merchandise began to flood the Angolan market during this crucial period in the history of western Africa, it is important to recognize that Europe has not always been Angola's main overseas trading partner. Since the opening of oceanic trade in the late fifteenth century, Angola has drawn valuable imports from different sources, not in the least from places in the Global South. In the era of the Atlantic slave trade, Indian textiles dominated imports; many of these textiles were shipped to Angola via Brazil, which also supplied large quantities of locally produced *aguardente* (rum). In the nineteenth century, cheap Manchester cloth undermined the popularity of Asian fabrics in Angola and elsewhere, while Portugal used differential tariffs to promote its domestic textile industry in Angola, making Portuguese products economically attractive to African buyers. But now that the centers of global textile manufacturing and many other consumer goods industries have moved backed to the Global South, Angola has strengthened its commercial ties with countries like China, South Korea, South Africa, and again Brazil. In the long term, therefore, the dominance of European manufactures in the Angolan trade was only temporary.

Since the rise of "legitimate" commerce and throughout much of the colonial period, however, Dutch trading companies were dominant on the coast of Angola. The first was the Afrikaansche Handelsvereniging, which began trading in Angola and the Congo in the 1850s. This Rotterdam firm shipped a range of local products, including coffee, to the Netherlands, although its Angolan branch was shut down when a three-decade-long boom in wild rubber production ended in the 1910s. Then, around 1920, the Zuid-Afrikaansch Handelshuis (Zuid), based in Amsterdam, started operations in Angola, fully focused on the coffee trade. The result of Dutch ascendency in Angola's postabolition economy was not only that the Netherlands became a prime destination for Angolan robusta exports, but also that Dutch manufacturers found new markets for their products in West Central Africa.[3] Indeed, analyzing extant records of Zuid, it becomes clear that coffee cultivation connected Angolan farmers to the global economy in more than one way.

Around 1930, Zuid had agencies in Luanda and Ambriz (a former slave port on Angola's northern coast) which bought up coffee and provided imported goods on credit to small-scale traders in the interior. One employee claimed the company was "the largest coffee exporter [in Angola] before the war."[4] After World War II, Zuid apparently stopped exporting coffee on its own account and concentrated more on diversifying its import business. It seems that, except for a series of annual reports, the archives of Zuid have not survived the firm's merger with the Curaçao Trading Company (later known as Ceteco) in 1968.[5] Significantly, however, the annual reports continually describe Angolan farmers not as producers, but rather as consumers whose "purchasing power" depended on annual coffee harvests and the prices their robusta beans reaped in the global market.[6]

This should not be surprising. Anyone studying the operations of trading companies in colonial Africa will recognize the emphasis they placed on domestic consumption.[7] In the case of Angola, however, the historiography has been so concerned with labor coercion and land expropriation under Portuguese rule (which were both very real) that independent African production and trade has been almost totally ignored. But right up to independence, in 1975, agricultural production remained largely in the hands of African peasants, who made Angola practically self-sufficient in food crops and a net exporter of maize. In northern Angola, coffee also long remained predominantly a peasant crop.

To understand how Angolans became cash crop producers in the nineteenth and twentieth centuries, histories of consumption must be tied into those of production. While tax imperatives and state coercion can explain to some degree why Africans labored in the colonial economy, "there was always also, and indeed primarily, a demand for goods."[8] Acknowledging the role imported commodities played in the development of colonial economies also means that the expanding literature on consumer cultures in Africa must take a slight "economic turn" and relate more to questions about labor and production.[9]

Secondly, the preponderance of cotton textiles in the import ledgers from Ambriz points to a remarkable continuity in consumer demand in the coastal hinterland from the era of the slave trade to the 1890s and onward.[10] What generally changed because of the nineteenth-century cash crop revolution in Africa was that more people gained access to imported luxury items. How did consumer tastes change over time? It seems that for a long time, Angolan coffee farmers invested their money mainly in traditional goods like textiles and livestock. In 1942, for instance, an Anglican missionary in Uíge observed, "Coffee paid a good price and many benefited by it so much that they bought better wearing apparel and others bought livestock. . . . The men had dressed their wives better too this last dry season."[11] Nonetheless, around 1960, Unilever agents reported on Angola that their soap and butter products began to "reach the bush" via wholesale traders like Robert Hudson, another longtime player in the Angolan coffee market.[12] Around the same time, farmers used the proceeds of their coffee harvest to buy bicycles and scooters. Textiles were still the main fashion, but after WWII, Angolan consumer tastes increasingly resembled those of the industrialized world.

Finally, although the growth of Angolan coffee production coincided with an expansion of Portuguese imperial ambitions in that corner of the world, the networks that connected farmers in Angola to consumers and manufacturers elsewhere in the world were global rather than colonial. Portuguese shopkeepers dominated the retail business in Angola, and much of the country's overseas trade passed through Lisbon because of Portugal's protectionist tax regime. But ultimately, most Angolan coffee was roasted in the United States and the Netherlands, and the merchandise retailers exchanged for coffee was manufactured in countries like England, Germany, Japan, and the United States.[13] More importantly, Angolan farmers had been connected to global manufacturing centers since the mid-nineteenth century, before the advent of colonial rule, or much earlier still if we include the era of the slave trade. Colonialism probably accelerated Angolans' exposure to modern consumer goods, but Angolans were not dependent on European rule to become global consumers.

Some of the most exciting work on African consumption approaches the subject from a global perspective. For instance, Jeremy Prestholdt has analyzed how East African demand for specific foreign textiles influenced the development of cotton manufacturing in cities like Salem and Bombay.[14] Similar connections between African consumers and European industries can be observed in the archives of textile manufacturers in the Netherlands, with whom Zuid placed orders for their Angolan clients. When Zuid started in Angola, the firm immediately approached different manufacturers to produce the fabrics they needed to compete in this market. Around 1920, for instance, Van Heek & Co. in Enschede were asked to produce cotton blankets on behalf of Zuid's agent in Luanda, while in the 1930s, the Luanda office mainly demanded khaki sateen. Some requests were not fulfilled. When Zuid's agent in Luanda brought up the possibility of producing table cloth and cheap khaki drills for the Angolan market, Van Heek replied that such products "did not fit" their production line, meaning Zuid had to look elsewhere.[15] Indeed, different manufacturers produced different kinds of cloth. In the 1920s, the Koninklijke Stoomweverij (royal steam weaving mills) at Nijverdal, for instance, supplied Casa Zuid with white shirtings, but not much else.[16] Although research on Dutch textile production for the African market has mainly concentrated on the famous and colorful wax prints, this and other evidence suggests that before the war cotton blankets, khaki, and white drills were very much the standard in northern Angola.[17]

In short, recent advances in the study of global commodity chains, focusing on the links between producers, middlemen, and world markets, have taken the history of commodity production in the Global South beyond the national framework of colonial history.[18] This essay suggests that a fuller understanding of Africa's integration in the world economy in the nineteenth and twentieth centuries can be obtained by viewing Africans not just as producers, but also as consumers of goods. If it is impossible to understand the Atlantic slave trade without considering the role that imported goods, especially textiles, played in African societies, then the same could be argued for African production and trade in the postabolition era.

Jelmer Vos is an associate professor of history at Old Dominion University. He is the author of *Kongo in the Age of Empire* (2015). His work on slavery, the Atlantic slave trade, and the history of labor in Angola has been published in the *Journal of Family History*, *African Economic History*, and *History in Africa*, among other places.

Notes

This essay was first presented at the African Studies Association Annual Meeting in 2015 and, more recently, at the Instituto de História Contemporânea, Universidade Nova de Lisboa. I would like to thank Marissa Moorman for her thoughtful comments on the final draft.

1. David Grenfell, Annual report to former workers. 1960. Regent's Park College, Angus Library (henceforth AL), BMS, A/44/8b.
2. Law, *From Slave Trade to "Legitimate" Commerce*.
3. Nationaal Archief, NAHV (2.18.10.09), 72/167, Annual Report 1880.
4. Van der Graaf, "My Years in Angola."
5. The Ceteco archives are housed at the Stadsarchief Amsterdam.
6. International Institute of Social History, IISG ZK 59663, Zuid-Afrikaansch Handelshuis, Annual Reports.
7. For instance, see chapters 3 and 4 of Burke, *Lifebuoy Men*.
8. Ross, et al., "Introduction," 5.
9. For instance, see chapter 6 of Martin, *Leisure and Society*; chapter 2 of Fair, *Pastime and Politics*; and chapter 2 of Ivaska, *Cultured States*.
10. Portugal, *Relatório do Ministro*, 180–203, 246–51.
11. Cooper to Patterson, Uíge, December 31, 1942. North Angola Mission archives (private collection, henceforth NAM).
12. E. W. Pera, "Visit to Angola." November 1963. Unilever Archives, UNI/RM/OC/2/2/2/2.
13. Portugal, Repartição Central da Estatística, *Colónia de Angola*.
14. Prestholdt, *Domesticating the World*.
15. Historisch Centrum Overijssel, Firma Van Heek & Co te Enschede, 166/1520, August 1938.
16. Ibid., Koninklijke Stoomweverij te Nijverdal, 167.4.1/24 and 167.4.1/810.
17. W. D. Grenfell, San Salvador Station, January 1939. AL, BMS, A/44/8(1); "God's Enabling." February 1936. Letter from Joy Peters, Uíge, November 19, 1935 (NAM). The journal *Textielhistorische Bijdragen* contains several contributions on Dutch wax prints.
18. Topik and Clarence-Smith, "Introduction."

References

Burke, Timothy. 1996. *Lifebuoy Men, Lux Women: Commodification, Consumption, and Cleanliness in Modern Zimbabwe*. Durham, NC: Duke University Press.

Fair, Laura. 2001. *Pastimes and Politics: Culture, Community, and Identity in Post-Abolition Urban Zanzibar, 1890–1945*. Athens: Ohio University Press.

Ivaska, Andrew. 2011. *Cultured States: Youth, Gender, and Modern Style in 1960s Dar es Salaam*. Durham, NC: Duke University Press.

Law, Robin, ed. 1995. *From Slave Trade to "Legitimate" Commerce: The Commercial Transition in Nineteenth-Century West Africa*. Cambridge: Cambridge University Press.

Martin, Phyllis M. 1995. *Leisure and Society in Colonial Brazzaville*. Cambridge: Cambridge University Press.

Portugal. 1898. *Relatório do Ministro e secretário d'Estado dos negócios da marinha e ultramar*. Lisboa: Imprensa Nacional.

Portugal, Repartição Central da Estatística. 1938. *Colónia de Angola*. Luanda: Imprensa Nacional de Angola.

Prestholdt, Jeremy. 2008. *Domesticating the World: African Consumerism and the Genealogies of Globalization*. Berkeley: University of California Press.

Ross, Robert, Marja Hinfelaar, and Iva Peša. 2013. "Introduction: Material Culture and

Consumption Patterns. A Southern African Revolution." In *The Objects of Life in Central Africa: The History of Consumption and Social Change*, edited by Ross, Hinfelaar, and Peša, 1–13. Leiden, Netherlands: Brill.

Topik, Steven, and William Gervase Clarence-Smith. 2003. "Introduction: Coffee and Global Development." In *The Global Coffee Economy in Africa, Asia, and Latin America, 1500–1989*, edited by Clarence-Smith and Topik, 1–17. New York: Cambridge University Press.

Van der Graaf, Andries. 2012. "My Years in Angola, 1950–1970." http://www.asclibrary.nl/docs /341/217/341217840.pdf (accessed July 31, 2015).

Toward Thick Solidarity

Theorizing Empathy in Social Justice Movements

Roseann Liu and Savannah Shange

My brother and I call each other that day to commiserate about an email from our mom asking us to "Pls support Peter Liang"—the Chinese American police officer indicted for killing Akai Gurley, an unarmed Black man. "What did you do with it?" I ask him. "I deleted it," he replies, sounding resigned. "What did you do?" he asks me. "I was gonna write back . . . but I didn't know what to say." A week later, we are walking through the plaza near the Brooklyn courthouse. My mom points to a grassy patch and proudly tells us that was where she, along with ten thousand others, protested in support of Peter Liang. They were joined by thousands of Asian Americans across the country, marking the greatest show of political engagement from the Asian American community in decades.

My mom, like many others who were there that day, was angry that Liang was a scapegoat for the legions of white officers who have escaped indictment for their murders of Black and Latinx people. They also expressed what some refer to as empathy. In an article interviewing supporters of Peter Liang, one woman said in Cantonese that she was "heartbroken that an innocent man has died and a young cop's career has been cut short. 'I feel very sad. It's bad for both sides.'"[1] The crux of this sentiment was advertised on protest signs at the Brooklyn courthouse that read: "One tragedy, two victims." The slogan asserts *both* Gurley *and* Liang were victims of an unjust system. It is emblematic of broader attempts to forge toward Black-Asian solidarity that rely problematically on an erasure of the specificities of anti-Blackness and anti-Asianness. Though supporters of Liang argued that there

Radical History Review

Issue 131 (May 2018)   DOI 10.1215/01636545-4355341

© 2018 by MARHO: The Radical Historians' Organization, Inc.

was "one tragedy, two victims," only one of those victims was actually killed. Solidarity based on notions of shared suffering often creates a false equivalence between different experiences of racialized violence. Our position is that this leads to a kind of empathy that is genuine, but "thin." We're interested instead in forging toward notions of what we conceptualize as *thick solidarity*—that is, a kind of solidarity that mobilizes empathy in ways that do not gloss over difference, but rather pushes into the specificity, irreducibility, and incommensurability of racialized experiences.[2]

Thick solidarity is based on a radical belief in the inherent value of each other's lives despite never being able to fully understand or fully share in the experience of those lives. Exploring the role that empathy plays in forming solidarities is an attempt to understand the "personal and affective dimension to . . . political commitments."[3] In this article, we practice thick solidarity as we flow back and forth between the personal dimensions of one author's family (Liu), and our collaborative musings on their implications for political and scholarly commitments (Liu and Shange). We built this piece in response to one set of historical and ethnographic events, but it is the product of several years of working alongside one another. After meeting while taking coursework together at the University of Pennsylvania, we deepened our relationship by thinking in tandem about the dilemmas of multiracial coalition revealed by our respective fieldwork sites. As we write together from our embodied experiences as Asian American (Liu) and Black (Shange), we understand more fully the specificity and irreducibility of these racialized experiences, and yet our relationship as friends and colleagues induces us to care and empathize despite incommensurability. Our practice of thick solidarity makes our theorizing more incisive. Though the issue of Black-Asian solidarity that we explore in this piece is situated in US racial politics, by introducing the concept of thick solidarity we offer an affective approach toward thinking about the challenges and potentials of cultivating global south solidarities more broadly.

African Slavery and Indentured Chinese Labor as "the Same"

Many months after our jaunt through Brooklyn my mom and I are at a wedding together. I've been wanting to address her support of Peter Liang. I say to her, "Mommy, do you know how a lot of Black people in this country got here?" "No," she says, looking quizzical. I tell her about the Transatlantic slave trade, its brutality, and its severance of kinship ties. This is the first time she's ever heard of this. I tell her how slaves were treated "not like humans, but like dogs," appealing to a phrase I've heard her say in Cantonese when she is indignant about the mistreatment of people. She seems to know what I am getting at. She says something like, "Well that's not right. . . . But a lot of time has passed and they need to work hard to improve their lives." My mom summons the well-worn Horatio Alger bootstrap ideology that denies the afterlife of slavery. I attempt to rebuff her by explaining Jim

Crow laws, redlining, and racially restrictive covenants, but I cannot figure out how to say all that in Cantonese.

Weeks later I visit my family in New York. My mom brings up the conversation we had at the wedding and says to me, "You know, you said that Black people were treated badly—well they did the same thing to Chinese people." "They," in this case, were white Americans, British, and Spanish colonialists, and "the same thing" referenced indentured Chinese laborers who, through subterfuge and kidnapping, were sent to work on plantations in the nineteenth century. "You and your brother only care about helping Black people," she finishes. Caught off guard, I retort, "Well if they did the same thing to Chinese people shouldn't you care more? I mean, that was bad, but it's not the same."

There are obvious connections between the Transatlantic slave trade and the coolie trade, since the abolition of the slave trade by Britain and the United States in 1807 and Spain's abolition of slavery in 1811 prompted the need for Asian labor. To prop up the highly profitable plantation economies of the United States, the Caribbean, and other parts of the New World, slave masters looked to the East to replace chattel slaves, creating similar conditions on ships and on plantations leading to high mortality rates among Asian laborers. This has led some scholars to question whether Asian indenture was a form of slavery closely associated with Black chattel slavery.[4] It also led Wong Chin Foo, a late nineteenth century Chinese American writer and activist, to "mobilize the deep figurative associations between coolie-ism and chattel slavery for political effect."[5] Imitating the style of slave narratives, Wong wrote a short story of a "'fugitive coolie'"[6] to draw attention to the struggles of Asian indentured laborers. While refusing to "assert equivalence between the New World slave and coolie . . . [Wong] directs readers toward a political critique of Asian indenture by way of its structural likeness to enslaved labor."[7] Likewise, politicians who sought to abolish indentured labor drew on a comparison with the slave trade and drew on highly publicized instances of ship rebellions to show the involuntary nature of the coolie trade.[8]

Thus, my mother's association of Asian indenture with Black chattel slavery has historical antecedents. However, unlike Wong who refused to "assert equivalence" between the slave and the coolie, my mother counts them as "the same," leading her to not only draw attention to the injustices perpetrated against indentured Chinese but to also decenter the position of Black chattel slavery in race-making projects.[9] Instead of viewing slavery as pivotal and as the raison d'être for national and transnational projects of race-making from which other racial formations would follow,[10] it is simply viewed as one among many forms of racial domination. Yet for all the historical connections and "structural likeness" between slavery and indentured labor, asserting that they are "the same" simply erases basic facts about the scale and scope of these events.[11] About half a million indentured Chinese

were transported from the ports of British Amoy and Portuguese Macau (inciden
tally where my mother was born and raised) to Cuba, Peru, and the United States
south during the nineteenth century,[12] while the Transatlantic slave trade thrived
from the sixteenth century to the nineteenth century and transported twelve million enslaved Africans from such a large number of ports that dotted West Africa
that it was commonly referred to as the "Slave Coast."[13]

Moreover, my mother's readiness to count indentured Chinese labor as "the
same" as the African slave trade lays bare the insufficiencies of drawing on shared
histories of oppression to evoke empathy. Although my mom asserts that "they did
the same thing to Chinese people," she fails to use this as a point for standing in solidarity with ongoing Black struggles. In fact, the point of the statement is to highlight
the position of Chinese victimhood by showing that we were treated just as badly
as African slaves. She attempts to create parity between these histories as a way of
getting my brother and me to care more about Chinese victimhood because, as she
perceives it, we "only care about Black people." Here, my mother downplays and
even completely ignores different forms of exploitation to the extent that indentured
Chinese labor and chattel slavery are seen as "the same." Yet as Jared Sexton points
out, it is both curious and telling that the experience of racial injustice is only conveyed most potently when Blackness is used as "the grounding metaphor of social
misery."[14] This was the case with politicians who sought to abolish the coolie trade,
and it was the case with Wong Chin Foo even though he refused to create equivalence between the coolie and the slave. In both instances, increasing public empathy
toward indentured laborers was effective by associating the coolie trade *with the
slave trade*. Curiously, the reverse is not true. Even though "they did the same thing
to Chinese people"—an appeal to our shared history of oppression—this failed to
mobilize my mom's empathy for Blacks. This is made apparent in the exasperated
tone in which I question my mom, "if they did the same thing to Chinese people
shouldn't you *care* more?" The answer, apparently, is "no."

Creating Parity between Michael Brown and Vincent Chin

In 2014, *Time* magazine published an article by Jack Linshi entitled "Why Ferguson Should Matter to Asian Americans."[15] The article took on an apologist's tone,
attempting to convince Asian American readers to stand in solidarity with those
fighting against systemic racism and violence toward Blacks. To rally Asian Americans, Linshi drew parallels between the deaths of Michael Brown and Vincent Chin,
a Chinese American Detroit man who was beaten to death in 1982 by disgruntled
white autoworkers. He wrote that in the cases of Michael Brown and Vincent Chin,
their attackers were "both white, both uncharged in a racially-motivated murder;
[and both] unified [their] communit[ies] to demand protection under the law."[16]
According to Linshi:

The Asian-American experience was once a story of racially motivated legal exclusion, disenfranchisement and horrific violence—commonalities with the African-American experience that became rallying points in demanding racial equality. That division between racial minorities also erased a history of Afro-Asian solidarity born by the shared experience of sociopolitical marginalization.[17]

He provided further examples, focusing on Asian Americans fatally shot at the hands of the police. These included the 1997 death of Kuanchang Kao, a Chinese American man who police said were threatened by his "martial arts moves";[18] Câu Bich Trần, a Vietnamese American killed in 2003 because police misidentified the vegetable peeler she was holding as a cleaver; and Fong Lee, a Hmong American shot dead in 2006 by police who thought he was carrying a gun. Linshi marshaled these examples to make shared experiences of police violence a point of solidarity between Black and Asian American communities.

In an effort to promote multiracial unity, Linshi referenced the "history of Afro-Asian solidarity" and went on to name key figures like Yuri Kochiyama and Grace Lee Boggs, who are emblematic of third world solidarity.[19] That history, though, begins before 1965 when Kochiyama knelt alongside Malcolm X's dying body in the Audubon Ballroom, and even before Boggs' decades-long collaboration with CLR James beginning in 1951.[20] The Council on African Affairs (CAA), founded in 1937, was committed to international anticolonialism and linked the struggles of Black Americans to colonized people worldwide, including Asians living in Asia and in the diaspora. For instance, the CAA, which counted W. E. B. Dubois and Mary McLeod Bethune among its membership, formed an alliance with the government of India to protest the mistreatment of Indians in South Africa.[21] On a transnational scale, the 1955 Bandung conference was a germinal event for the development of Afro-Asian solidarities. The gathering brought together hundreds of nonwhite political leaders and intellectuals from twenty-nine nations. Bandung attendee and Black American novelist Richard Wright remarked that "the agenda and subject matter had been written for centuries in the blood and bones of the participants."[22] Grace Lee Boggs herself helped coordinate the event in which Malcolm X delivered his "Message to the Grassroots" speech, in which he affirms the need for unity between Asian and African diasporas as they fight their common enemy: white supremacy.[23] The internationalist commitments to diaspora reached a peak with vocal opposition to the Vietnam War echoing across the Black political sphere, with the Student Nonviolent Coordinating Committee (SNCC), Congress of Racial Equality (CORE), and of course Martin Luther King, Jr. each linking systemic racism at home to military aggression abroad.[24]

Bandung's bloodstained agenda was taken up a generation later by organizations like the Bay Area's Third World Liberation Front that formed in 1969 to mobilize Black, Chicano, Asian American, and Filipino students, as well as by Asian led organizations that were deeply allied with the Black Panthers, like Los Angeles's Asian American Political Alliance and the Yellow Brotherhood. The latter was particularly resonant with the Panthers because the Brotherhood organized young, working-class Asian Americans, some of whom were affiliated with gangs and street economies.[25] On the East Coast, I Wor Kuen was a radical Chinese American formation that pursued leftist organizing and alliances with Black and Puerto Rican movements in New York's Chinatown in the 1970s. More recent nodes of Black-Asian solidarity include the Bus Riders Union, which uses public transit as a site of anti-imperialist, antiracist organizing of Black, Asian American, and Latinx bus riders in Los Angeles, and the national strategy think tank Race Forward, based in Dallas.[26]

By highlighting Asian American deaths at the hands of police and by referencing a few threads of this intricate tapestry of Afro-Asian alliance, Linshi attempted to recuperate the understanding that, despite the model minority discourse that sought to divide and conquer, Asian Americans shared a *similar history* and experience of oppression with African Americans. He attempted to mobilize those shared histories and experiences as a way of summoning empathy among his Asian American readership and to serve as the basis for uniting Blacks and Asians.

But not all social suffering is created equal. Sexton refers to this refusal to parse out the historical, social, subjective, and embodied differences among racial minorities as *people-of-color blindness*.[27] While colorblindness denotes the refusal to acknowledge a system of privileges and marginalization based on race, people-of-color blindness refuses to acknowledge the systematic privileges and oppression that exist among different people of color (POC). There's no doubt that non-Black POC also experience forms of structural violence. But, according to Sexton, "it is the specific genealogy that links slavery to Jim Crow to the ghetto to the prison that warrants my claim about the singularity of racial domination of blacks."[28] Other racial minorities in America come out of "profoundly different historical processes and trajectories."[29] These profound differences make it difficult to cultivate solidarity based on empathy that is conjured up through an appeal to our shared oppression. So, where else can we start? What strategies can communities and scholars draw on to build a just and sustainable multiracial solidarity?

Toward Thick Solidarity

Though Linshi insists on empathy for Black suffering and my mother resists it, it is significant that both employ a framework of parity for thinking across race. Vincent Chin *is* Michael Brown, and like my mom said, "they did the *same thing* to Chinese people." In contrast to this racial equivalence, Asian American and Asian Canadian organizers are developing other models of solidarity that do not rely on people-of-color blindness. The Letters for Black Lives project centers their work on the very differences that Sexton brings up. The crowdsourced project, started by Christina Xu in New York, is a set of letters translated into more than twenty-three languages that initially targeted the Asian community. Since then it has been adapted by Latinx, African immigrants, and other communities of color to try to address anti-Blackness across generations. The Letters project states:

It's true that we face discrimination for being Asian in this country. Sometimes people are rude to us about our accents, or withhold promotions because they don't think of us as "leadership material." Some of us are told we're terrorists. But for the most part, nobody thinks "dangerous criminal" when we are walking down the street. The police do not gun down our children and parents for simply existing.[30]

Here, the Letters project highlights the differential distribution of life chances under white supremacy and draws a bold red line connecting the dots between criminalization, police, and Black death. In other words, the Letters project acknowledges the "singularity of racial domination of blacks."[31]

While Letters for Black Lives refuses to conflate anti-Blackness with anti-Asianness, it nevertheless hinges on empathy as the engine for action. The authors ask their elders to "try to empathize with the anger and grief of the fathers, mothers, and children who have lost their loved ones to police violence." Yet this is an empathy paired with responsibility, because it accounts for differential histories and political economies of state violence. Moreover, they assert, "the American Dream cannot exist for only your children. We are all in this together, and we cannot feel safe until *ALL* our friends, loved ones, and neighbors are safe" (emphasis original). Ultimately, the project is one geared toward an empathy that is inclusive *and* intersectional—an empathy that acknowledges our interconnectedness *and* our interstices.[32] This is the dance I was trying to begin with my mother, one that highlights the missteps of the "one tragedy, two victims" logic while moving us toward responsible and consequential empathy.

Similar to Letters for Black Lives is Asians for Black Lives, a collective started in the Bay Area. Inheriting the legacy of I Wor Kuen and the Yellow Brotherhood, which mobilized four decades ago alongside the Black liberation movement, both the Letters for Black Lives and Asians for Black Lives campaigns acknowledge the centrality of fighting anti-Blackness in their organizing work. The title of one of the Asians for Black Lives guiding protocols is "Embrace Frontline Leadership, Center Blackness"—an unequivocal rejection of the "one tragedy, two victims" parity frame. They go on to say, "We understand that the path to liberation for all communities travels through the liberation of Black communities in America, and when Black people have justice and liberation, we all move one big step closer to real freedom." The clarity of the Asians for Black Lives platform is an antidote to people-of-color blindness. This was made concrete in December 2015, when members of the collective organized a series of actions to call attention to the disproportionate state violence faced by the Black community. These included shutting down the Oakland Police Department for 4 hours and 28 minutes, the same amount of time that Mike Brown's dead body languished in the street in Ferguson.

In lieu of the widespread practice of thin notions of solidarity, both the Letters for Black Lives project and the Asians for Black Lives collective offer a robust, polyvalent approach to crossracial coalition building—what we might think of as a thick solidarity. Thick solidarity layers interpersonal empathy *with* historical analysis, political acumen, and a willingness to be led by those most directly impacted. It is a thickness that can withstand the tension of critique, the pulling back and forth between that which we owe and that which we share. We offer this concept as a way of thinking more broadly about the kinds of activism and solidarities that can be forged among those in the Global South. Indeed, as ethnographers of multiracial communities, we work towards thick solidarity as a research methodology, one that we begin to practice in this paper as we think and write together across race and toward justice. Activists on the front lines have already laid out the stakes of this work—it is up to us as scholars to take them up on it, even if our mothers think we only care about Black people.

Roseann Liu is visiting assistant professor in educational studies at Swarthmore College. Her research focuses on the anthropology of youth, race and migration, and urban spaces.

Savannah Shange is assistant professor in anthropology at the University of California, Santa Cruz, and a postdoctoral fellow at the Rutgers Center for Historical Analysis. Her research focuses on Blackness, anti-Blackness, and the anthropology of the state.

Notes

1. Wang, "Awoken."
2. Liu, *Intimate Differences.*
3. Lee, *Frantz Fanon,* 29.
4. Hu-DeHart, "Chinese Coolie Labor in Cuba"; Hu-DeHart, "'La Trata Amarilla'"; Jung, *Coolies and Cane.*
5. Wong, "Storytelling," 110.
6. Ibid.
7. Ibid., 112.
8. Ibid., 114.
9. Ibid., 110.
10. Settler colonialism and the concomitant dispossession and genocide of indigenous people is also pivotal to understanding the "triad structure of settler-native-slave" (Tuck and Yang 2012), but it is beyond the scope of this article.
11. Wong, "Storytelling," 112.
12. Meagher, *The Coolie Trade.*
13. Hartman, *Lose Your Mother.*
14. Sexton, "People-of-Color Blindness," 47.

15. Linshi, "Why Ferguson Should Matter to Asian Americans."
16. Ibid.
17. Ibid.
18. Ibid.
19. Ibid.
20. Ward, *In Love and Struggle.*
21. Von Eschen, *Race Against Empire.*
22. Wright, *The Color Curtain,* 14.
23. Marable and Felber, *The Portable Malcolm X Reader.*
24. Lucks, *Selma to Saigon.*
25. Ogbar, "Yellow Power."
26. Mann, "Building the Anti-Racist, Anti-Imperialist, United Front."
27. Sexton, "People-of-Color Blindness."
28. Ibid., 54.
29. Ibid., 54.
30. We acknowledge the problematic way in which different experiences among Asian Americans becomes flattened in an attempt to build a broad-based Asian American coalition to support the Black Lives Matter movement. Specifically, the observation that "nobody thinks 'dangerous criminal'" is simply not true for Muslim Asian Americans and Southeast Asian groups.
31. Sexton, "People-of-Color Blindness," 54.
32. Lee, *Frantz Fanon.* Our conceptualization of empathy includes elements of what Christopher Lee refers to as "radical empathy." An area of contrast is the way in which difference is treated. While we advocate for a kind of empathy that recognizes the different sets of experiences created by processes of racialization, Lee's notion of radical empathy articulates a "transcendence of identity" (Lee, *Frantz Fanon: Toward a Revolutionary Humanism,* 32) and difference. His de-emphasis of difference is an attempt to avoid reifying colonial distinctions and constructions of social hierarchy. However, both conceptualizations of empathy acknowledge a productive dialectical tension between recognition of, and moving beyond difference.

References

CAAAV (Committee Against Anti-Asian Violence). 2001. "Police Brutality in the New Chinatown." In *Zero Tolerance: Quality of Life and the New Police Brutality in New York City,* edited by Andrea Mcardle and Tanya Erzen, 221–42. New York: New York University Press.

Hartman, Saidiya. 2006. *Lose Your Mother: A Journey Along the Atlantic Slave Route.* New York: Farrar, Straus, and Giroux.

Hu-DeHart, Evelyn. 1993. "Chinese Coolie Labour in Cuba in the Nineteenth Century: Free Labour or Neo-slavery?" *Slavery and Abolition* 14, no. 1: 67–86.

Hu-DeHart, Evelyn. 2007. "'La Trata Amarilla': The 'Yellow Trade' and the Middle Passage, 1847–1884." In *Many Middle Passages: Forced Migration and the Making of the Modern World,* edited by Emma Christopher, Cassandra Pybus, and Marcus Rediker, 166–83. Berkeley: University of California Press.

Jung, Moon-Ho. 2006. *Coolies and Cane: Race, Labor, and Sugar in the Age of Emancipation.* Baltimore: Johns Hopkins University Press.

Lee, Christopher J. 2015. *Frantz Fanon: Toward a Revolutionary Humanism.* Ohio Short Stories of Africa. Athens: Ohio University Press.

Linshi, Jack. 2014. "Why Ferguson Should Matter to Asian-Americans." *Time*, November 26.

Liu, Roseann. 2016. "Intimate Differences: Cultivating Recognition and Multiracial Solidarity in a Philadelphia School." PhD diss., University of Pennsylvania.

Lucks, Daniel S. 2014. *Selma to Saigon: The Civil Rights Movement and the Vietnam War.* Lexington: University of Kentucky Press.

Mann, Eric. 2001. "Building the Antiracist, Anti-Imperialist, United Front: Theory and Practice from the LA Strategy Center and the Bus Riders Union." *Souls* 3: 87–102.

Marable, Manning, and Garrett Felber, eds. 2013. *The Portable Malcolm X Reader: A Man Who Stands for Nothing Will Fall for Anything.* New York: Penguin Classics.

Meagher, Arnold J. *The Coolie Trade: The Traffic in Chinese Laborers to Latin America 1847–1874.* Xlibris.

Ogbar, Jeffrey O. G. 2001. "Yellow Power: The Formation of Asian-American Nationalism in the Age of Black Power, 1966–1975." *Souls* 3: 29–38.

Sexton, Jared. 2010. "People-of-Color-Blindness: Notes on the Afterlife of Slavery." *Social Text* 28, no. 2 (103): 31–56.

Tuck, Eve, and K. Wayne Yang. 2012. "Decolonization is Not a Metaphor." *Decolonization: Indigeneity, Education & Society* 1, no. 1: 1–40.

Von Eschen, Penny M. 2014. *Race Against Empire: Black Americans and Anticolonialism, 1937–1957.* Ithaca, NY: Cornell University Press.

Wang, Hansi Lo. 2016. *"Awoken" By N.Y. Cop Shooting, Asian-American Activists Chart Way Forward: Code Switch: NPR.* Accessed January 26.

Ward, Stephen M. 2016. *In Love and Struggle: The Revolutionary Lives of James and Grace Lee Boggs.* Chapel Hill: University of North Carolina Press.

Wong, E. 2015. "Storytelling and the Comparative Study of Atlantic Slavery and Freedom." *Social Text* 33, no. 4 :109–30.

Wright, Richard. 1956. *The Color Curtain: A Report on the Bandung Conference.* Jackson: University of Mississippi Press.

"Get Used to Me"

Muhammad Ali and the Paradoxes of Third World Solidarity

Sean Jacobs

This article focuses on Muhammad Ali's internationalism, particularly in relation to the African continent. It highlights the tensions and energies that defined Ali's political engagements outside the United States: The takeaway is that Ali's actions were at times principled and progressive, at other times naïve, opportunistic, and/or conservative. The larger point is to show how Ali's actions personified the paradoxes and complications of Third World solidarity, racial nationalism, and postcolonial politics. In this essay, I revisit, in quick order, five particular moments in this history: first, Ali's 1964 visit to three African countries (Ghana, Nigeria, and Egypt); second, the legendary "Rumble in the Jungle" fight between Ali and George Foreman in Zaire (now the Democratic Republic of the Congo) in 1974; third, Ali, on two separate occasions, seriously contemplating participating in boxing matches in South Africa (including one against a policeman convicted of intimidating witnesses and who had shot a Black protester); fourth, Ali's Cold War diplomacy on behalf of the United States government; and, finally, Ali's visit to a newly freed Nelson Mandela in South Africa.

Though it would be easy to condemn Ali for his inconsistent and often reactionary political choices, in writing this, I was reminded of what political scientist Adolph Reed Jr. cautioned about idealizing political figures: Reed's case was that Malcolm X

Radical History Review
Issue 131 (May 2018)   DOI 10.1215/01636545-4355353
© 2018 by MARHO: The Radical Historians' Organization, Inc.

was just like the rest of us—a regular person saddled with imperfect
knowledge, human frailties, and conflicting imperatives, but nonetheless trying
to make sense of his very specific history, trying unsuccessfully to transcend it,
and struggling to push it in a humane direction.[1]

What I am guarding against is to reduce Ali to a one-dimensional figure or to use
him to settle political scores in the present. Basically, I want to treat Ali as a figure
of his time.

After Muhammad Ali died on June 3, 2016, tributes poured out from all
corners of the globe and from across the political spectrum. But many people also
indignantly denounced would-be eulogists whose beliefs and politics the boxer
would have abhorred. On Twitter, young Black people, employing the lexicon of
their own era, rejected the notion that Ali was racially "transcendent," arguing white
commentators and public figures were trying to coopt his legacy.[2] A common retort
was "He was black and proud and not part of your liberal project."[3]

At the same time, others suggested that the fact that even reactionaries felt
compelled to claim Ali's legacy was the ultimate sign of his triumph. For example, Indian Prime Minister Narendra Modi—implicated in fomenting communal
violence and advancing a frightening Hindu nationalism agenda in government—
tweeted that Ali "demonstrated the power of human spirit & determination."[4]

Those people resisting attempts to make Ali transcendent were of course
entitled to be angry. They were celebrating the Ali who in 1966 announced that he
would reject the military draft, claim conscientious objector status, and not fight for
the United States in Vietnam. That act would turn out to be Ali's most selfless contribution: at the height of his powers, he chose his political principles over his boxing
career, thus facing jail time, the loss of his title, and a ban from boxing that lasted at
least four years. The events of 1966 also had other consequences: Most importantly,
Ali's actions inspired a tradition of American athletes taking public political stances.

Not surprisingly, most appraisals of Ali's political life thus end with that
brave, principled opposition to the Vietnam War. Look at any recent documentary
film or most book length accounts of his life.[5] The problem with this framing is
that it obscures the complexity of his political life, which was being shaped already
before 1966 and that would be subject to a range of contending forces, including the
Cold War, Black radicalism, African nationalism and Black Muslim ideologies.

What is often forgotten about Ali is that he was thrust onto the global stage
and became the subject of rhetorical struggles over US foreign policy and US racism while still a teenager: he won a gold medal at the Rome Olympics in 1960 when
he was only 18. Foreign, especially Soviet media, treated him as a representative of
American ideals. At the medals ceremony, a reporter from the Soviet Union asked
Cassius Clay how it felt to represent a country in which racial segregation was toler-
ated. Ali responded: "Tell your readers we've got qualified people working on that

problem, and I'm not worried about the outcome. To me, the USA is still the best country in the world, counting yours. It may be hard to eat sometimes, but anyhow I ain't fighting alligators and living in a mud hut."[6] This mix of US propaganda and racist stereotypes of Black Africans, even among African Americans, were not unusual public opinion in the United States at the time, so Ali's response did not come as a surprise to many. But Ali soon grew disillusioned with American apartheid, segregation, and racial violence in the early 1960s. This led him to seek out the Nation of Islam, a homegrown Muslim social movement that combined a regimented lifestyle with a radical critique of American racism, a rejection of America's political system, and bizarre beliefs about white people's origins. This new association would shape Ali's political choices over the next decade or so.

Shortly after Clay won his first heavyweight title and changed his name to Muhammad Ali, he undertook a trip to three African nations. He visited Ghana, Nigeria, and Egypt. Overall, the trip was a success for Ali. In Ghana, where Ali stayed for three weeks, he was greeted by expectant crowds who feted him as a Black hero and he met with President Kwame Nkrumah.[7] His Nigeria stop was much shorter: He stayed for just three days before he traveled on to Egypt. The decision to shorten his visit to Nigeria angered his hosts as well as the US government. His Nigerian hosts felt insulted, while the US government worried his decision would affect perceptions of the United States in Nigeria, despite the fact that they knew well that Ali wasn't on an official State Department cultural tour and had no obligations to the US government.[8]

Ali's decision to cut his trip short ultimately reflected his ideological commitments to the Nation of Islam, whose leader Elijah Muhammad revered Egypt, which he saw as the origin of the so-called "Asiatic black man" and singled out Egypt as the most powerful Black Muslim nation on earth.[9] Muhammad had traveled to Africa in 1959 and came away with a very negative view of newly independent, sub-Saharan African nations.[10] Muhammad thus viewed a visit to Egypt as good public relations and made sure to send his son, Herbert, along as Ali's adviser.

It would be on the same trip, where Muhammad Ali's commitment to the Nation's racial nationalism would trip up his more radical instincts. In this case, it was displayed in Ali's public rejection of Malcolm X when their paths crossed in Ghana in 1964. When Ali first joined the Nation, it was Malcolm X, then its national spokesperson, who had a profound influence on Ali's politics. It was Malcolm X's teachings, sermons, and media appearances which Ali drew upon for his declaration:

I am America. I am the part you won't recognize. But get used to me. Black, confident, cocky; my name, not yours; my religion, not yours; my goals, my own; get used to me.[11]

Ali and Malcolm X's encounter in Ghana coincided with the time that Malcolm X parted ways with the Nation over Elijah Muhammad's hypocritical behavior and what Malcolm X deemed the limits of the Nation's political ideology.[12] By this time, Malcolm X had begun to espouse mainstream leftist positions on the United States' wars in Southeast Asia, apartheid in South Africa, and Israel's treatment of Palestinians. Malcolm X also threatened to bring the United States before the United Nations because of what he perceived as its political and economic wars on poor and Black Americans.[13]

When the two men crossed paths in the Ghanaian capital, Ali, influenced by the Nation's propaganda, turned his back on Malcolm X, who he blamed for abandoning Elijah Muhammad.[14] However, Ali never had the chance to reconcile with him before Malcolm X was assassinated in New York City a year later. Although the Nation of Islam blamed the American government, the men charged with Malcolm X's murder were active members of the Nation. Ali, in his 2004 autobiography *The Soul of a Butterfly*, expressed regret over his public shunning of Malcolm X, after leaving the Nation himself.[15]

Assessments of Muhammed Ali's early political career often read back his actions retroactively and project all kinds of politics onto it. For some, his decision to reject the military draft and refuse to serve in the US war in and occupation of Vietnam is prima facie evidence of his rejection of militarism, empire, or neocolonialism. This might be how Ali would later view his own actions in hindsight, but at the time, Ali objected to the draft primarily on religious grounds. For Ali, America's occupation of Vietnam was a "Christian war."[16] Similarly, his visits to Ghana, Nigeria, and Egypt, were subject to tensions between Third World solidarity politics as well as being caught up in the ferment of African political independence on the one hand and the propaganda aims of the Nation of Islam on the other.

Mobutu's Africanism

Some of the most indelible images of Muhammad Ali come from his 1974 trip to the Congo. He was there for "Rumble in the Jungle," his title bout with the champion George Foreman. The fight itself displayed Ali's boxing smarts. It was there that he perfected his "rope-a-dope" strategy, in defeating Foreman in eight rounds to become world champion for a second time.[17] More importantly, during the trip, Ali was the celebrated guest of Congolese dictator Mobutu Sese Seko, who had renamed the Congo as Zaire in 1971.

Ali framed "Zaire '74" as a demonstration of Black pride: An African government hosted the fight and paid for it, Black pilots flew him there, and his trip amounted to a kind of homecoming for a descendant of African slaves.[18] But the "Rumble in the Jungle" was far from the harmonious picture of Black advancement Ali and his media acolytes painted. Instead, the fight highlighted—even more than his 1964 African trip—the contradictions of postcolonial politics and racial nationalism.

Mobutu was far from a progressive Third World leader. For one thing, he was accused of working with Western powers to murder Patrice Lumumba—the first prime minister of the newly independent Congo—in 1961.[19] The United States, Britain, and Congo's former colonizer Belgium, along with their local allies, opposed Lumumba's agenda for genuine independence, which included nationalizing the country's natural resources to implement large-scale development and infrastructure projects. Mobutu, who had been Lumumba's right-hand man, seized power in 1965. By the time Ali arrived in the country nearly a decade later, Mobutu had turned the state treasury and the country's natural resources into his private property and imprisoned or killed off most dissenters.[20] While Mobutu hosted and bankrolled the fight, President William Tolbert—who also ran a one-party dictatorship in the West African country of Liberia—paid for a "cultural festival" to accompany the fight.[21]

That Ali said nothing about Mobutu (or even Tolbert's) despotism may have surprised many, but it was consistent with racial and Cold War politics at the time. African American support for movements that espoused Africanist-centered politics was very high during the late 1960s and into the 1970s.[22] Mobutu mastered this rhetoric.

Mobutu's government promoted what he called *authenticité*: This meant banning Western aesthetics and culture and instead promoting African music, dress, names, and hairstyles.[23] This was echoed in some African American cultural practices, especially those associated with Afrocentric movements, and parallelism became its own politics.[24]

North American activists working or identifying with African revolutionaries found these developments frustrating. The civil war that broke out in neighboring Angola just months after the Ali-Foreman fight was a case in point. Angola had recently attained its independence from Portugal. Western powers, especially the United States and their surrogates in the region like apartheid South Africa and Mobutu's Zaire, were not happy when the left-wing People's Movement for the Liberation of Angola (MPLA) came to power. The rival National Union for the Total Independence of Angola (UNITA) movement of Jonas Savimbi—supposedly anti-communist and funded variously by the United States and South Africa—presented itself as more Africanist than MPLA, which had some white and creole leaders. Thus, many African Americans supported UNITA over the MPLA. This led historian and activist Walter Rodney, in a 1976 speech at Howard University, to remind his mostly Black audience, "We must of course admit that to declare blackness is a very easy thing to do."[25] In Zaire, Ali made a similar move in his admiration of Mobutu: unwilling or unable to look beyond the pageantry of racial nationalism, he embraced a narrow politics that avoided that bigger questions raised in fora like the Pan-African Conferences of the mid-twentieth century or Bandung.

Separate, but Equal

Perhaps more surprising was Ali's agreement to fight in South Africa, then governed by an oppressive, white minority regime. In 1972, after Ali had defeated former world champion Floyd Patterson in a rematch at Madison Square Garden in New York City, he signed a contract to fight in Johannesburg, South Africa, against another Black American fighter, Al Jones. The contract stated that the crowd for the fight would be segregated: that "separate, but equal" seating would be allowed.[26] Curiously, the South Africans promised Ali's and Jones's entourages that they would be given what amounted to "honorary white" status—they would be exempted from discriminatory laws and allowed to stay in "whites only" hotels and to access other amenities. In the end, the fight was cancelled after the South African promoters failed to produce the necessary financial letters of credit.[27] But as Thomas Hauser, Ali's biographer, points out, "The fact remains that, at the time, Ali was willing to fight in South Africa."[28] Herbert Muhammad, who accompanied Ali on his first trip to three African states, now advised Ali and negotiated the contract. He explained the decision to agree to a fight in South Africa:

The position of the Nation of Islam is that Ali was a fighter, and that as champion of the world, he should be able to fight anywhere on earth. We didn't get into that thing about South Africa. My father didn't look no different at South Africa than he did at the United States; he believed both were run by devils. And to say don't fight in South Africa because they're doing wrong; well, some of the same crimes are done in the United States against black people. So, my father didn't have the attitude that you could fight in the United States but not in South Africa.[29]

A few years later in 1978, Ali was again seriously considering the possibility of boxing in South Africa. This time, significantly, he would fight against a white South African boxer, Kallie Knoetze, in Johannesburg. The choice of Knoetze as an opponent was an odd choice. Knoetze was a former policeman who had been convicted in South Africa for trying to coerce two witnesses to withhold their testimonies against a fellow policeman and had shot a 15-year-old Black youth in both legs during a protest in a Black township outside the South African capital in 1977.[30] In a 1978 *Rolling Stone* magazine interview with the writer Hunter S. Thompson, which included questions about the proposed Knoetze fight, Ali said he would not travel to South Africa if "other African nations and Moslem countries" or the "masses of the country" were opposed to the fight. Ali would only go to South Africa if "the world" said "well, this case is special, they've given the people justice. His going is helping the freedom." He wondered aloud, however:

What worries me is getting whupped by a white man in South Africa. . . . I don't think it would be wise for me to fight him in South Africa. If I beat him too bad and then leave the country, they might beat up some of the brothers. Or if he whup me too bad then there may be riots.

Figure 1: President Jimmy Carter greets Muhammad Ali at a White House dinner celebrating the signing of the Panama Canal Treaty, Washington, DC. To the left is Ali's wife, Veronica Porsche Ali.

Then he added, aware of his own power: "It'd be good if I don't go to nothing like that. It's too touchy—it's more than a sport when I get involved."[31]

What is remarkable is how much Ali's own political responses reflected the ideological and strategic crisis of post-Civil Rights Black politics in the mid-1970s. There were unconfirmed rumors that Ali was convinced by Black South African sports activists and their US allies to refuse the Knoetze fight. All the same, it was clear that his politics was evolving and not at all fully formed.

Ali, the Failed Diplomat

In 1979, the United States announced it would boycott the 1980 Olympics in Moscow over the Soviet Union's invasion of Afghanistan.[32] The Carter administration set off on a lobbying campaign to gain support for its stance and dispatched Ali on an "African diplomatic tour" to lobby leaders to support the boycott.[33] For Carter, Ali was an ideal candidate because of his fame and popularity in Africa, but also because Ali would show "we have black Americans who have been successful with a diversity of religious commitments."[34] Ali visited Tanzania, Kenya, Liberia, Nigeria, and Senegal.

The trip reflected Ali's political naïveté as well as his lack of familiarity with Cold War politics—at one point, Ali compared the Soviet Union to an errant child who nicked cookies out of a cookie jar who had had to be taught a lesson. But, more significantly, the trip illustrated how Ali publicly wrestled with accusations that he was a mere puppet of the US government.

In Kenya and Liberia, Ali was granted audiences with the countries' presidents and his messages were well received. These meetings aimed to solidify US Cold War alliances. The Kenyan and Liberian leaders used the meetings to press for more aid. In Senegal, Ali met Leopold Senghor. They read poetry together, but Senghor reiterated Senegal's position that sports could not interfere with politics and that Senegal would be sending its athletes to Moscow.[35] But it was the reaction he received in Tanzania and Nigeria which made Ali stall, publicly doubt his intentions, and question whether he was in over his head.

Tanzania was his first stop on the trip. There the president, Julius Nyerere, refused to see him, and the local media accused Ali of being an American puppet and of shilling for American power.[36] His hosts also reminded Ali of the US double standards: that when African nations boycotted the Montreal Olympics in 1976 in opposition to South African apartheid, the United States refused to support them and were slow to implement trade and other sanctions against South Africa.[37] His interlocutors informed him that the Soviet Union supported Southern African liberation movements, then still considered terrorists by the United States. Ali reacted strongly: "Nobody made me come here and I'm nobody's Uncle Tom."[38] He was surprised to learn about the Montreal boycott, about the extent of US government support for apartheid South Africa, and that the Soviets supported southern African liberation movements, while the United States considered these to be terrorist movements.[39] Ali returned to the United States disillusioned by his reception in Tanzania and Nigeria, and for a while he was less committed to the idea of himself as an "unofficial ambassador."[40]

In the recently published *We Are An African People: Independent Education, Black Power and the Radical Imagination*, the historian Russell Rickford tells the story of 1960s and early 1970s Pan-Africanists in the United States, who in reaction to American racism and inequalities in the public school system founded and funded their own schools.[41] Rickford traces this group's often contradictory journeys from racial Pan-Africanism wedded to principles of racial fundamentalism, cultural nationalism, and the politics of Black unity to forms of Left Pan-Africanism rooted in a fundamentally anti-imperialist, anticapitalist, and "Third Worldist" outlook.[42] Rickford explained that these activist-intellectuals eventually left the United States to "travel throughout Africa and the Diaspora, and were thus forced to confront some of the political and social complexities of societies and governments that they had previously viewed through a very simplistic lens."[43] At best, these African Americans rethought the basis of their connection to Africans, moving away from racial mysticism and thoroughly Western essentialism and "moving toward solidarity based on common circumstances and political perspectives/objectives."[44] In his later years, Muhammad Ali appeared to have undergone a similar, though not linear, journey.

Going Home

Muhammad Ali later became a vocal supporter of the Palestinian people and visited refugee camps in Lebanon, and he also lent his celebrity to protest marches in American cities against Israel's occupation of Palestinian land.[45] Finally, reflecting the strength of the boycott movement by the mid-1980s, Ali became a strong supporter of the anti-apartheid movement. It was therefore fitting that Ali put off visiting South Africa until April 1993—three years after Nelson Mandela was released, the main opposition movements were legalized, and the African National Congress (ANC) began negotiating a new constitution with its former jailers and torturers.

When they met finally met, Mandela told Ali he was his inspiration in prison: "I thought of his courage and his commitment to his sport."[46] Ali also visited Soweto, posing with local boxers and play-sparring with locals. But most significantly, Ali's trip coincided with the murder of Chris Hani, a charismatic ANC and Black communist leader, at the hands of white racists. Hani was known for his independence even within the ANC, even risking death, and since 1990 he had demanded that the ANC be held accountable for the piecemeal and narrow basis of South Africa's economic and political transition after apartheid.[47] When he was alive, Hani was the most popular ANC leader after Mandela, especially among ordinary members and supporters. At his funeral, Mandela called him "one of the greatest revolutionary leaders the country has ever seen."[48]

Ali insisted on attending Hani's funeral. He went with little fanfare or media attention and comforted Hani's children.[49] As his lawyer told the Associated Press later, "it had a deep emotional impact on the mourners [Chris Hani's family] and the country that Muhammad happened to be there at that moment. It gave them, I think, a level of comfort."[50]

This is a beautiful ending to a complicated and winding story of political evolution that is far more interesting and instructive than a simple tale of ideological heroism. The best way to celebrate Ali's life is to mourn the ways his politics failed so that we can reimagine what a progressive politics of the Global South might look like. As the sports sociologist Ben Carrington cautions: "We need to more dispassionately map the constitutive contradictions [that sport contains] . . . and more precisely locate when and where such interventions may produce progressive political outcomes that are genuinely disruptive to the dominant heteropatriarchal capitalist racial order and of course, when they are not."[51]

Sean Jacobs is an associate professor of international affairs at The New School in New York City. He founded and is editor of *Africa is a Country*. He has held fellowships at Harvard, The New School, and New York University. His writing and research focus on the intersection of politics and popular culture, including sport. Jacobs was born and grew up in Cape Town, South Africa.

Notes

This essay was first presented as a paper at the "Black Matters: The Future of Black Scholarship and Activism" Conference at the University of Texas, Austin in September 2016. I am grateful for the comments made at the gathering as well as to Jessica Blatt and Aubrey Bloomfield.

1. Reed, "The Allure of Malcolm X and the Changing Character of Black Politics," 232.
2. Jay Davo-O, "Once they no longer feel threatened . . . "
3. Chigumadzi, "Not today. You will not co-opt our Greatest . . . "
4. Modi, "RIP Muhammad Ali."
5. Renmick, *King of the World*; Marqusee, *Redemption Song*. The same goes for the films *The Trials of Muhammad Ali* (2013), *Ali's Greatest Fight* (2013) and *I am Ali* (2014)
6. Remnick, "American Hunger."
7. Marqusee, *Redemption Song*, 125, 127.
8. Hauser, *Muhammad Ali: His Life and Times*, 109.
9. Marqusee, *Redemption Song*, 130.
10. Remnick, *King of the World*, 213–17.
11. Obama, "Muhammad Ali shook up the world."
12. Remnick, *King of the World*.
13. Marable, *Malcolm X*, 12, 367.
14. Remnick, *King of the World*, 215.
15. Ali with Ali, *The Soul of a Butterfly*.
16. Tischler, *Muhammad Ali: A Man of Many Voices*, 128.
17. Hauser, *Muhammad Ali: His Life and Times*, 259–79.
18. Ibid.
19. Ntzongola-Ntalaja, *Lumumba*; De Witte, *The Assassination of Lumumba*.
20. Ntzongola-Ntalaja, *The Congo*.
21. Malaquais, "Rumble in the Jungle," 232.
22. Rickford, *We Are an African People*. Thanks to Dan Magaziner for pointing me to Rickford's work. See also Magaziner's interview with Rickford, "Racial nationalism and the political imagination," *Africa is a Country*, 24 May 2016.
23. Campbell, *Middle Passages*, 393.
24. Rickford, *We are African People*.
25. Jordan, "The 1970s: Expanding Networks" 140.
26. Hauser, *Muhammad Ali: His Life and Times*, 249.
27. Ibid.
28. Ibid., 250.
29. Ibid.
30. Breslin, "Jesse KOs boxer with a jawbone." Knoetze was later denied a visa by the United States on grounds of "moral turpitude" and obstruction of justice. See Katz, "U.S. Revokes Knoetze's Visa," A19.
31. Thompson, "Last Tango in Vegas."
32. Goldblatt, *The Games*, 293.
33. Sarantakes, *Dropping the Torch*, 157.
34. Hauser, *Muhammad Ali: His Life and Times*, 396.

35. Sarantakes, *Dropping the Torch*, 117.
36. Ibid., 116.
37. Hauser, *Muhammad Ali: His Life and Times.*
38. Sarantakes, *Dropping the Torch*, 116.
39. Hauser, *Muhammad Ali: His Life and Times.*
40. Ibid. Ali was deemed an ambassador for "dissident America" from 1964–1975 and later as an "official ambassador (and apologist) for the White House, the State Department and the Pentagon" after 1975.
41. Rickford, *We Are an African People.*
42. Magaziner, "Racial nationalism and the political imagination."
43. Rickford quoted in Magaziner, 2016.
44. Ibid.
45. Abulhawa, "The Greatest was a black man who supported Palestinians."
46. Staufenberg, "Muhammed Ali dead."
47. Smith and Tromp, *Hani.*
48. *The Vancouver Sun*, "Millions shun work to honor slain leader as death toll mounts."
49. Associated Press, "Boxing great Muhammad Ali pays tribute to Mandela."
50. Ibid.
51. Carrington, "Raced Bodies and Black Cultural Politics," 136.

References

Abulhawa, Susan. 2016. "The Greatest was a black man who supported Palestinians," *Al Jazeera.* June 13. http://www.aljazeera.com/indepth/opinion/2016/06/greatest-black-man -supported-palestinians-muhammad-ali-160612050518697.html.

Ali, Muhammed, with Hana Yasmeen Ali. 2004. *The Soul of a Butterfly: Reflections on Life's Journey.* New York: Simon & Schuster.

Associated Press, 2013. "Boxing great Muhammad Ali pays tribute to Mandela." December 5. http://www.usatoday.com/story/sports/boxing/2013/12/05/muhammad-ali-pays-tribute -nelson-mandela/3885287/.

Breslin, Jimmy. 2017. "Jesse KOs boxer with a jawbone," *Chicago Tribune*, January 14.

Campbell, James T. 2006. *Middle Passages: African American Journeys to Africa, 1787–2005.* New York: The Penguin Press.

Carrington, Ben. 2017. "Raced Bodies and Black Cultural Politics." In *Routledge Handbook of Physical Cultural Studies*, edited by Michael L. Silk, David L. Andrews, and Holly Thorpe. Abingdon, UK: Routledge.

Chigumadzi, Panashe. [panashechig]. June 4, 2016. "Not today. You will not co-opt our Greatest. Not today. He was Black and Proud and not part of your liberal project." [Tweet.] Retrieved from https://twitter.com/panashechig/status/739154261603430400.

De Witte, Ludo. 2003. *The Assassination of Lumumba.* New York: Verso.

Goldblatt, David. 2016. *The Games: A Global History of the Olympics.* New York: W. W. Norton.

Hauser, Thomas. 1992. *Muhammad Ali: His Life and Times.* New York: Simon & Schuster.

Jay Davo-O. [ChocnessMonsta]. July 16, 2016. "Once they no longer feel threatened (King's death. Ali's deterioration), then they become 'beloved'/'transcendent.'" [Tweet.] https:// twitter.com/ChocnessMonsta/status/754999273973018624.

Jordan, Joseph F. 2007. "The 1970s: Expanding Networks." In *No Easy Victories: African Liberation and American Activists Over a Half Century, 1950–2000*, edited by William Minter, Gail Hovey, and Charles Cobb Jr. Trenton, NJ: African World Press, Inc.

Katz, Michael. 1979. "U.S. Revokes Knoetze's Visa; He is out of Miami 10–Rounder," *The New York Times*, January 10, A19.

Malaquais, Dominique. 2012. "Rumble in the Jungle." In *Afropolitics*, edited by Kerstin Pinther, et al. Johannesburg: Jacana.

Marable, Manning. 2011. *Malcolm X: A Life of Reinvention*. New York: Penguin Books.

Marqusee, Mike. 2005. *Redemption Song: Muhammad Ali and the Spirit of the Sixties*. New York: Verso.

Modi, Narendi. June 4, 2016. "RIP Muhammad Ali. You were an exemplary sportsperson & source of inspiration who demonstrated the power of human spirit & determination." [Tweet.] https://twitter.com/narendramodi/status/739032017904369664.

Ntzongola-Ntalaja, Georges. 2014. *Lumumba*. Athens: Ohio University Press

Ntzongola-Ntalaja, 2002. *The Congo: From Leopold to Kabila: A People's History*. New York: Zed Books.

Obama, Barack. 2016. "Obama: Muhammad Ali shook up the world. And the world is better for it." *Los Angeles Times*, June 5. http://www.latimes.com/la-remembering-muhammed-ali -world-react-obama-muhammad-ali-shook-up-the-1465047001–htmlstory.html.

Reed Jr., Adolph. 1992. "The Allure of Malcolm X and the Changing Character of Black Politics." In *Malcolm X: In Our Own Image*, edited by Joe Woods. New York: St Martin Press.

Renmick, David. 2005. *King of the World: Muhammad Ali and the Rise of an American Hero*. New York: Vintage Books.

Remnick, David. 1999. "American Hunger." *The New Yorker*, October 12.

Rickford, Russell. 2016. *We Are an African People: Independent Education, Black Power, and the Radical Imagination*. New York: Oxford University Press.

Sarantakes, Nicholas Evan. 2011. *Dropping the Torch: Jimmy Carter, the Olympic Boycott, and the Cold War*. New York: Cambridge University Press, 2011.

Smith, Smith, and Beauregard Tromp. 2010. *Hani: A Life Too Short*. Johannesburg: Jonathan Ball Publishers.

Staufenberg, Jess. 2016. "Muhammed Ali dead: From George Foreman to Nelson Mandela—what others said about 'The Greatest.'" *The Independent*, June 4. https://www .independent.co.uk/news/people/muhammad-ali-dead-what-others-said-about-the -greatest-a7065176.html.

Thompson, Hunter S. 1978. "Last Tango in Vegas: Fear and Loathing in the Far Room, Part II." *Rolling Stone*, no. 265, May 18.

Tischler, Barbara L. 2016. *Muhammad Ali: A Man of Many Voices*. New York: Routledge.

Vancouver Sun. 1993. "Millions shun work to honor slain leader as death toll mounts." April 20.

Between Two Clarities

Vijay Prashad

Isn't our life a tunnel between two clarities?
—Pablo Neruda, *Libros de las preguntas*

In his final press conference as Secretary-General of the United Nations in December 2016, Ban Ki-moon turned his attention to climate change. "The Paris Agreement on climate change is a precious achievement that we must support and nurture," he said. "There is no turning back."

Secretary Ban's comment—*there is no turning back*—was pointed. It comes in the context of the rise to political office of a number of "climate sceptics," political leaders who believe either that global climate change is not occurring or who believe that there is little that humans can do to reverse these changes. Such political leaders—people like Donald Trump of the United States—would like to set aside the 2016 Paris Agreement on climate change. Erik Solheim, the head of the UN Environmental Programme, indicated his concern that "some elite American politicians deny science. You will be in the Middle Ages if you deny science."

Denial of climate science is only the symptom of a much deeper problem that confronts the planet. It is the endemic crisis-ridden capitalism that lashes about like an injured dragon, breathing fire here and whipping its tail over there. Fatally wounded, capitalism seeks regeneration through any means—whether by the seizure of precious natural resources or the cannibalization of human labor. Whether it is talk of "sustainable development" or "carbon-based development," the common factor here is to increase growth rates by greater exploitation of nature and human-

Radical History Review
Issue 131 (May 2018) DOI 10.1215/01636545-4355365
From *Will the Flower Slip Through the Asphalt.*
Copyright © 2017 by Vijay Prashad. Used by permission of LeftWord Books.

ity. The various reports of the United Nations' Intergovernmental Panel on Climate Change show that human life cannot be sustained if the growth trajectory continues along the path set by capitalism. There is a powerful contradiction between the needs of a parasitic capitalism and its natural and human host. Both cannot survive. One will have to vanquish the other.

The idea that capitalism has no respect for nature and the habitat of our planet has been clear for generations. In a moving letter to her friend Sophie Liebknecht, Rosa Luxemburg wrote on May 2, 1917:

Yesterday I was reading about the reasons for the disappearance of songbirds in Germany. The spread of scientific forestry, horticulture, and agriculture, have cut them off from their nesting places and their food supply. More and more, with modern methods, we are doing away with hollow trees, wastelands, brushwood, fallen leaves. I felt sore at heart. I was not thinking so much about the loss of pleasure for human beings, but I was so much distressed at the idea of the stealthy and inexorable destruction of these defenceless little creatures, that the tears came into my eyes. I was reminded of a book I read in Zurich, in which Professor Sieber describes the dying-out of the Redskins in North America. Just like the birds, they have been gradually driven from their hunting grounds by civilised men.

The Russian Revolution had broken out a few months previously. Tensions in Germany had alerted Luxemburg and her comrades to the possibility of an uprising in the heart of Europe. Luxemburg was in prison when she wrote this letter. Why was this revolutionary—steeped in the ethos of revolutionary change at the time of great anticipation—writing about songbirds? Not because, she told her friend, "like so many spiritually bankrupt politicians, I seek refuge and find repose in nature. Far from it, in nature at every turn I see so much cruelty that I suffer greatly." The intimate linkage between capitalism's disdain for the natural world and its scorn for the working class seemed apparent to Luxemburg. Her ethic was not to bemoan the demise of nature because it would hinder human consumption of the natural world. She was upset by the death of the songbirds because of the necessary linkage in capitalist history between the eradication of nature and the genocide of humans. This was not *human nature* at work, but the system of capitalism that required nature and humans as resources for the ceaseless profit motive.

Luxemburg's assessment of capitalism—*The Accumulation of Capital* (1913)—had made the case for capital's relentless search for new investment opportunities, vanquishing all barriers, devouring all resources. Her letter to Liebknecht should be read in light of Luxemburg's colonize argument about how capitalism seeks to colonize the noncapitalist environment, and how without this terrain it would collapse onto itself. This is what Marx meant when he wrote in *Capital, vol. 3*, that the "limit of capital is capital itself." Without this permanent ravaging of natural and human resources, capital cannot function. When human misery, social inequality, or climate change become limits, they have to be set aside. The attack on basic liberal concern for the poor (demonstrated through welfare payments and humanitarian aid) and the attack on climate science are of a piece—they are essentially attempts to conduct ideological war on the cultural barriers to untrammeled capitalism as preparation for the destruction of natural and human habitats. Capitalism developed, Marx wrote in *Capital*, out of the "discovery of gold and silver in America, the extirpation, enslavement entombment in mines of the aboriginal population, the beginning of the conquest and looting of the East Indies, the turning of Africa into a warren for the commercial looting of black-skins." This is what Marx called originary accumulation (*ursprüngliche akkumulation*). It would reappear each time capitalism ran into a crisis—the eternal return of brutal accumulation. Marx and Luxemburg produced thunderous prose to denounce the destruction of nature and the humans who had been othered. This was their jeremiad against "civilization."

A generation later, in 1950, Joseph Schumpeter—an Austrian Finance Minister in 1919 and Harvard University Professor—looked carefully at the dynamic of capitalism and worried that it would collapse because its own "creative success" had pushed it to its limits. Competition between firms leads to the production of massive amounts of goods (overproduction), which cannot be purchased by workers whose wages either decline or remain flat (underconsumption). Firms go out of business and capitalism enters a phase of stagnation. It is only technological breakthroughs of one kind or another that enable capitalism to reemerge with great dynamism. Schumpeter called this "creative destruction," annotating what Marx had noted in his *Grundrisse*, that capitalism contains an "endless and limitless drive to go beyond its limiting barrier. Every limit appears as a barrier to be overcome." Schumpeter did not share the tone of denunciation that was common to Marx and Luxemburg. His was a bloodless prose, hopeful in the capacity of civilization to prevail over its worst instincts. In this, Schumpeter was wrong. Technological change, for Schumpeter, would save capitalism from its inherent problems. Talk of "green capitalism" is along this grain. It is not that new technologies—wind turbines, solar panels—will not be valuable, it is that capitalism as a social system will be unable to transform itself from the needs of profit to the needs of society. For example, the massive investment needed to change the energy systems from fossil fuels to green energy would hamper profit and encroach on private property rights and private investments. Without a direct challenge to capitalist profit and the idea of ceaseless growth, no such major and essential transformation is possible. Instead, what we find is that nuclear energy—highly profitable thanks to massive subsidies—and "clean coal" are smuggled in as "green energy."

Naomi Klein's *This Changes Everything* (2014) has a subtitle that puts the point bluntly and quite perfectly: *Capitalism vs. The Climate*. Either capitalism is allowed to continue its devastating dynamic, or the climate, namely the natural and human habitat, will be able to survive. There are, Klein argues, no capitalist solutions to the climate problem. Nor are there capitalist solutions to the problem of human inequality and underdevelopment. In 1979, Raúl Prebsich, the first secretary general of the UN Conference on Trade and Development (UNCTAD), remarked that "we thought that an acceleration of the rate of growth would solve all problems. This was our great mistake." Only the demographically insignificant "privileged consumption society," he said, benefits from the growth. Development plans that were authorized by the Global North resisted "changes in the social structure," Prebisch said mournfully, while what was truly need was a "complete social transformation." Klein emphatically says that for the climate to be saved, capitalism must be overcome:

Our economy is at war with many forms of life on earth, including human life. What the climate needs to avoid collapse is a contraction in humanity's use of resources; what our economic model demands to avoid collapse is unfettered expansion. Only one of these sets of rules can be changed, and it's not the laws of nature.

There are two clarities—that of capitalism and that of climate. They produce different realities, says Naomi Klein: one malevolent and the other benevolent. The choice is stark, which is why she poses it as a question. There is no nuance here. Nuance will not help the people of the South Pacific. They are drowning in capitalism's surge.

Canaries in the South Pacific

Sitting in the United Nations General Assembly chamber to listen to the president of Kiribati at the opening of the UN session is always a sobering experience. The presidents—Teburoro Tito, Anote Tong, and Taneti Mamau—have been spokespersons for the islands and island cultures that totter on the edge of extinction as a result of climate change. "Already we have whole villages being washed away," Tong said in 2012. "There's no running away from that reality." Over a decade before he made these comments, the islands of Abanuea and Tebua Tarawa vanished under the waters. The island of Tepuka Savilivili lost its coconut trees due to salination. Kiribati, located in the center of the Pacific Ocean, takes its name for a certain pronunciation of the last name of Captain Thomas Gilbert. On the way to China after having dropped off a boatload of convicts at Botany Bay in 1788, Gilbert chanced on these islands. They took his name. One of them had an earlier name, Abanuea, which means *the beach which is long lasting.* It lasted a long time, but could not withstand the rising ocean in 1999. That is when it went under. The Gilbertese lost two islands that year. Others have since followed. Five of the Solomon Islands (Kale, Rapita, Rehana, Kakatina, and Zollies) vanished in the past decades. They are all climate victims.

The Fate of the Small Island is to Disappear

Abanuea, the island with beaches that were fated to last forever, was the canary. No wonder President Tong lived with his nightmares. "For some time I did not sleep because I didn't have a solution to a problem that there wasn't a solution to. What happens to us in the future? Do we disappear as a culture?"

In May 2012, at the UN's Economic and Social Commission of Asia and the Pacific (ESCAP), Pacific Island nations came to talk about climate change and their cruel fate. Kiribati's Finance and Economic Development Minister Tom Murdoch announced that his small island state had established the largest marine protected area in the Ocean—the Phoenix Islands Protected Area, which is more than 400,000 sq. km, or 11 percent of Kiribati's Exclusive Economic Zone. "The Ocean is fundamental to our cultural identity," Murdoch said: "Our green economy is very *blue*. It has been said that we are not a small island developing country but rather a large ocean developing economy. We are trying to do our part in the sustainable management of our ocean and marine environment." The language of sustainable development whipped around the ESCAP discussion. No one had the courage to say that the system was fundamentally committed to detrimental climate change, and that only a transformation of the system would save the small islands. The voters rejected Murdoch in 2015. People want something more powerful than the idea of "sustainable development." It is empty of content. They want a new compact, a new way to live and to organize our social and natural wealth.

Tuvalu's Minister of Trade, Lotoala Metia, told his fellow officials that his country is trying to move away from fossil fuels, on which the island is totally dependent, to renewable energy by 2020. There is something obscene about these pledges coming from countries that barely contribute to the climatic shifts. Out of the 186 countries that reported figures for greenhouse gas emissions, Kiribati came in at 185. The three biggest emitters are the United States, European Union, and China. It is worth recollecting that at the 2011 Durban meeting, the major environmental NGOs wrote to US Secretary of State Hillary Clinton pointing out that the United States was the "major obstacle" to any progress in global talks. Even the European Union openly criticized the United States for "overlooking the facts" of climate disturbances. This was when US liberalism was in charge. Now Donald Trump is the president. He rejects the idea of climate mitigation. Will his Secretary of State—the oil magnate Rex Tillerson—be worse than Clinton? Will he want to sign a climate treaty with a drilling bit instead of a pen?

Behind the scenes of that Durban meeting, as one of the Wikileaks tranches demonstrates, the United States colluded with the Europeans to scuttle any attempt by the United Nations and by the BASIC (Brazil, South Africa, India, and China) countries to create an effective climate treaty. Despite the public declarations on behalf of climate legislation by President Barack Obama, his administration used every dirty trick, including withholding aid, to secure votes against effective climate legislation at Copenhagen and Durban. Michael Froman, US deputy national security advisor, wanted to deny the BASIC states a victory not only for climate negotiations but also to break their political momentum. "It is remarkable how closely co-ordinated the BASIC group has become in international fora," Froman wrote from Brussels, "taking turns to impede US/EU initiatives and playing the US and EU off against each other. BASIC countries have widely differing interests, but have subordinated these to their common short-term goals. The US and EU need to learn from this co-ordination and work much more closely and effectively together ourselves, to better handle third country obstructionism and avoid future train wrecks on climate, Doha or financial regulatory reform."

The newly confident Global South did not roll over. The largest states, the BASIC countries, stood by their own view that any cut back on carbon would have to come with technological transfers and financial assistance to facilitate "leap frogging" over a carbon modernity towards a noncarbon civilization. Even this is a tepid program. The BASIC countries are reliant upon carbon development, pillaging the planet in the name of poverty eradication but actually benefitting very small minorities of the über rich. But even this limited demand by the BASIC countries could not be accepted by the North. It would rather try to use its minuscule foreign aid program to break the coalitions of the Global South. In 2010, the Danish Ambassador to Bolivia told the US chargé in La Paz, "Danish Prime Minister Rasmussen spent an unpleasant 30 minutes with Morales, during which Morales thanked him for [$30 million a year in] bilateral aid, but refused to engage on climate change issues. The Danes said they are 'fed up' with Bolivia and the ALBA [Bolivarian Alliance for the Peoples of Our America] countries, who continue to mount legal and propaganda arguments against the Copenhagen Accord, but that they will continue to consult with their European Union partners on ways to influence the [Bolivian Government's] position." No such luck. Morales remained obdurate. The North must cut its high per-capita fossil fuel emissions and provide a fund for the South to move to renewable energy. In terms of energy use per capita, the top five users are the United States, Russia, France, Germany, and Japan. Energy use per capita in the countries of the Global South is a fraction of what one sees in the North. Morales picked the sore that the Northern bureaucrats wanted to keep covered over.

Unfortunately, the imperatives of rapid economic growth had dented Morales own commitment to people-centered, noncarbon development. Pablo Solón, Bolivia's former ambassador to the United Nations and the coordinator of the World People's Conference on Climate Change and The Rights of Mother Earth, resigned his positions and wrote an open letter to Morales in 2011 protesting the road being built through the Indigenous Territory and National Park of Isibore Secure: "One cannot speak of defending Mother Earth and at the same time promoting the construction of a road that will harm Mother Earth, doesn't respect indigenous rights and violates human rights in an unforgiveable way."

Dr. Kosi Latu, a leader of the small island states, complains about the direction of the climate debate and joined President Tong in his despondency: "For us in the Pacific, it's more than [poverty reduction and green technology]. I'm talking about the survival of our peoples in the sense that due to climate change impacts, we stand to lose our land, our histories and cultures, our nationalities." Writing this down in my notebook, I wondered in the margin whether there would be anyone paying attention to this aspect of the demise of the small islands—the death of cultures that have been developed over thousands of years. When the island vanishes, the material basis of the culture of its people will also go. Those who survive will become "climate refugees," a term that the United Nations is trying to establish. They will move to New Zealand or even Zambia (whose late president welcomed the I-Kiribati)—although New Zealand has fought tooth and nail to refuse to allow Ioane Teitiota to become the first "climate change refugee" (he was deported to Kiribati in 2016). Since most "climate change refugees" are already "othered," living—as Naomi Klein put it—in "fossil fuel sacrificial zones," who cares about the Nigerian coastal communities or the Mi'kmaq island communities?

Lives will be altered. The basis of the I-Kiribati will shift. There is nothing wrong with that in essence. Culture is not eternal—social forms from elsewhere transact into our lives, and if these enrich our cultural world in some way, they stick. But what is to take place to the I-Kiribatis and their fellows is not the essence of normal cultural interchange—after all, the I-Kiribatis take their own name from Thomas Gilbert and are not averse to cultural transactions (former President Tong's family came to the island from China after World War II). What is at issue is the forewarned but cataclysmic annihilation of the social basis of I-Kiribati cultural life—an annihilation that is comparable to the cultural genocide visited upon the Native Americans by the Colombian crossing.

Is there a future of the "sea of islands"? Not if the carbon civilization continues its pace onward. "The rising seas will reclaim our ground," sings the I-Kiribati poet Jane Resture in 1999, "as Abanuea sinks under the sea":

While far away they pour their fumes into the clear blue sky

not knowing and never caring why
the world is beginning to die.

In 2003, the literary critic Fredric Jameson wrote, "Someone once said that it is easier to imagine the end of the world than to imagine the end of capitalism" (Jameson was most likely channeling the novelist J. G. Ballard). In our time, this is perfectly true. Novels and films, television shows, and memes are more likely to acknowledge the destruction of the planet through climate change than to portray a future world free of the system of capitalism. Our task as writers is to help people imagine the end of capitalism before the end of the planet. It should be an easy choice.

Vijay Prashad is the Executive Director of Tricontinental: Institute for Social Research (thetri-continental.org) and the Chief Editor of LeftWord Books (leftword.com). This essay is extracted from his introduction to *Will the Flower Slip Through the Asphalt. Writers Respond to Climate Change* (2017), which collected the essays of Naomi Klein, John Bellamy Foster, Ghassan Hage, Rafia Zakaria, Masturah Alatas, Shalini Singh, and Amitav Ghosh.

Keep up to date on new scholarship

Issue alerts are a great way to stay current on all the cutting-edge scholarship from your favorite Duke University Press journals. This free service delivers tables of contents directly to your inbox, informing you of the latest groundbreaking work as soon as it is published.

To sign up for issue alerts:

1. Visit **dukeu.press/register** and register for an account. You do not need to provide a customer number.

2. After registering, visit **dukeu.press/alerts**.

3. Go to "Latest Issue Alerts" and click on "Add Alerts."

4. Select as many publications as you would like from the pop-up window and click "Add Alerts."

read.dukeupress.edu/journals

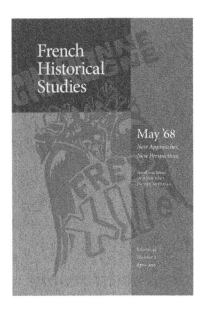

Printed and bound by CPI Group (UK) Ltd, Croydon, CR0 4YY

13/04/2025

14656483-0004